D0824269

HERE'S WHAT PEOPLE WHO KNOW ~~~ ABOUT BOB DOLE . . .

"Always waits to see 'which way the political wind is blowing.' "
>—Nancy Kassebaum, Kansas Senator

"The self-appointed tax collector of the welfare state."
>—Newt Gingrich, Speaker of the House

"A 'maddening figure,' a 'self-destructive' personality."
>—*The New York Times,* Editorial, June 1994

"If Dole is elected president, I'd leave the country."
>—Elliot Kaplan, former lawyer to convicted Dole aide, David Owen

"Almost Jekyll-Hyde."
>—Joseph Rauh, Washington civil rights lobbyist

"So unpopular among his peers that he 'couldn't sell beer on a troop ship.' "
>—Senator William Saxbe, former Ohio Senator

"Still doesn't know if he's a liberal or a conservative, as he didn't know in 1950."
>—John Woelk, Russell County attorney who recruited Dole to run for the legislature in 1950

SENATOR
FOR
$ALE

AN UNAUTHORIZED BIOGRAPHY OF
SENATOR BOB DOLE

STANLEY G. HILTON

St. Martin's Paperbacks

TO L.G.
FOR ALWAYS TRYING

SENATOR FOR SALE

Copyright © 1995 by Stanley G. Hilton.

Illustration on p. 265 by Rick Geary.

Cover photograph courtesy AP World Wide.

Library of Congress Catalog Card Number: 95-24220

ISBN: 0-312-95925-7

Printed in the United States of America

St. Martin's Press hardcover edition published 1995
St. Martin's Paperbacks edition/March 1996

10 9 8 7 6 5 4 3 2 1

When special interests contribute money,
they want something in return other than good
  government.

—BOB DOLE

AUTHOR'S NOTE

I would like to thank my research assistants and word processors, Raquel E. Villalba, Jaci S. Murray, Lisa Olbrantz, Tony Vrondissis, Gene De Forrest and James Chaffee for their indefatigable help in preparing this book. I would also like to thank the staffs of the Federal Election Commission, the Citizens' Research Foundation of the University of Southern California, and the Center for Responsive Politics for their cooperation and assistance in providing campaign finance and fund-raising records that have been used throughout this book. I am grateful, as well, to the staffs of the Kansas Legislature, the Kansas State Library, and the University of California at Berkeley for their help. Finally, special appreciation goes to John F. Rothmann, a peerless scholar of the Republican Party, who provided invaluable insights and documents and whose immense personal library of fifteen thousand volumes on politics and history was a great resource.

I would also like to extend special appreciation to Tom Dunne, my editor at St. Martin's Press, and to his assistant, Neal Bascomb, and production editor Robert Cloud for their unflagging and priceless assistance and support of this work.

I regret that Bob Dole's office refused to cooperate and spurned my request for an interview with the senator. I had wished to offer him the opportunity to give his side of the story on the many controversial issues I raise. His staff said curtly he was "too busy" to be interviewed.

CONTENTS

INTRODUCTION

I worked for Bob Dole as his Senate counsel and aide
back in 1979 and 1980, when the Republican Party was
still in the minority and he was just a small player on the
national scene.

The years since then have seen a dramatic surge in the
fortunes of the Republican Party and in the career of Bob
Dole, who is now the Senate majority leader. The historic
party realignment that began with Ronald Reagan's election in 1980 and culminated in the Republican sweep of
both houses of Congress in 1994 can be explained largely
as the result of special interest money buying elections, in
a symbiotic relationship with conservative Republicans,
while exploiting popular disgust with the status quo.

Who is the real Bob Dole? Answering that question is
my purpose in writing this book. After many years of
following the senator's career, I have come to believe
that he lacks any real commitment to the conservative
agenda of his own party or to *any* other agenda, and that
he is largely a special interest slot machine, a human
pendulum dancing to the tune of the highest contributors.

As Dole's counsel and aide, I had contact with him
virtually every day. I worked on many of the issues
still at the forefront of his agenda today, such as the
constitutional amendment requiring a balanced budget,
revising the federal criminal code, slashing government
social programs, and doling out corporate welfare. Daily

contact enabled me to take a hard look at the kind of man Bob Dole is. I was repeatedly struck by the banality and superficiality of his character and personality. He liked to communicate with staff via one-page memos and one-liners. He had little interest in details. He didn't like to read. His only real concern seemed to be raising money. He had contempt for common voters. And he believed in nothing.

I bear no antipathy to Dole as a person. We parted on good terms, for I chose to return to my native California to take a job with higher pay.

In his letter of recommendation for me, Dole wrote:

> Stanley G. Hilton has . . . contributed substantially to my work in areas as diverse as the strategic petroleum reserve, a mandated balanced budget, and anti-trust legislation. He has demonstrated a sure and growing knowledge of the energy field, and is more than conversant with economic and political trends.
>
> In addition, Stanley has worked closely with my staff, bringing to his work not only intellectual ability, but also personal enthusiasm and highly impressive judgment. He is an idea person who has talent for getting along with others—and in Washington. That's a potent, if somewhat rare, combination. He has tried to expand on his assigned duties and initiate new political and legislative ideas which has been quite useful.
>
> Stanley has done excellent work for me, and I am convinced he would do the same for anyone else who seeks someone with Washington experience for either a legislative or political campaign capacity.

While I liked Bob Dole as a person and was amused by his superb sense of humor, I was appalled by his utter lack of commitment to any ideals or beliefs. Working in his office was like being aboard a ship piloted by an aloof and mysterious sea captain, who navigated without a clear or consistent sense of direction.

Today, Senator Bob Dole bestrides Washington like a Colossus, a towering figure who has endured longer than any politician since Richard Nixon. He has been in Congress for thirty-five years. The epitome of the establishment politician, and the most powerful political boss since Huey Long, he is the nation's top elected Republican official, U.S. Senate majority leader, and, according to the polls, the front-runner for the 1996 Republican presidential nomination. He has set an all-time record for the largest number of appearances on the Sunday morning talk shows on all the major networks and is in high demand as a speaker throughout the country. His public approval ratings are above 60 percent. Yet behind the mask of Mr. Republican, I believe he remains a hollow man.

To liberals, his favorite target, he is a dark, menacing tyrant, a right-winger with a destructive mean streak, a gunslinger out for blood. To true conservatives, he is a nebulous moderate whom Newt Gingrich has called "the self-appointed tax collector of the welfare state." *The New York Times,* in a June 1994 editorial, called him a "maddening figure" with a "self-destructive" personality that goes for the jugular, yet it also praised his legislative prowess. Without question, there is something mysterious and sinister about Senator Dole that fascinates the American people. And indeed, Bob Dole's Dr. Jekyll and Mr. Hyde personality—unpredictable, disturbing, yet invariably exciting—has long intrigued me as well.

As the title of this book suggests, Senator Bob Dole may indeed be for sale in the world of Washington politics. Despite the intention of our founding fathers that the American political system present true equality and "one man, one vote," the stark reality is that we currently have a system of "one dollar, one vote." The intersection of money and politics makes for an unholy witches' brew of greed, fraud, and exploitation—all to the detriment of the American people, who have been duped by Dole and his party into believing that "liberals" alone have caused all their problems.

In 1995, Bob Dole raises over $500,000 every *week* via his main political money machine, Campaign America, and his presidential campaign committee attracts more money in two days than he earns in a whole year as a senator (and this figure represents only contributions made before his presidential bid has hit high gear). During the 1993–94 campaign cycle, Campaign America raised $8.6 million. On one night alone, his gala produced half a million dollars. The other arms of his money machine raise comparable sums from his corporate clientele. He has amassed a substantial personal fortune and is a multimillionaire. In addition, he stands to collect a federal pension worth an estimated $4 million, if and when he retires. The senator has created a political-financial empire best called Dole, Inc.

An examination of Bob Dole and Big Money sheds light on the symbiotic relationship between Senate power and the ability to raise money on command. Throughout his career, Dole has shown few qualms about using his Senate office and staff for de facto campaign and fund-raising purposes. For years, his chief liaison with lobbyists has been Jo-Anne Coe, his top Senate secretary for nearly three decades and now the official head of Campaign America. When lobbyists came to see Dole in his Senate office and solicited his support for their pet bills or asked him to lobby federal agencies and bureaucrats on their behalf, Coe would sometimes take them aside and ask them to raise campaign contributions and/or to promise to host a large fund-raising event for Dole before she allowed them to see the senator on official business or legislation. Promises to raise up to $50,000 to $100,000 were not uncommon.

Because of her years of experience in Dole's Senate office, Coe quickly slipped into the official role of his chief fund-raiser when she finally became the head of

Campaign America and turned it into the mightiest political money machine this country has ever seen.

Being a Senate staffer is excellent preparation for being a fund-raiser. Everyone understands how the "Dance of Legislation" is performed—and who calls the tune.

Throughout his career, Dole has accepted campaign contributions from business lobbying groups that have a vested financial interest in legislation he proposes and supports in the Senate.

An example can be seen in Dole's long record of pushing "regulatory relief" legislation in the Senate, to scale back federal environmental, health, safety, and other regulations, usually to the detriment of consumers and workers but in the interests of corporations wanting to cut corners and be free of the burden of "red tape." He has had a long record of sponsoring such legislation, dating back to the days when I worked for him during his first presidential campaign, and elevated to a new frenzy in 1995, during his current bid.

Although Dole claims that his zeal for "regulatory relief" bills derives from a philosophical belief that the federal government's red tape should be curtailed because it inhibits businesses and thus "costs jobs," there is another side of the coin that should be examined. When I worked for him, I was struck by his obsession to please "the Contributors," as he referred to lobbyists, in hopes of attracting campaign contributions from those lobbyists demanding regulatory "reform" and "relief" via legislation then being considered by the Senate Judiciary Committee.

Things don't seem to have changed much. According to the *Congressional Quarterly* and Federal Election Commission reports, many businesses, trade associations, and law firms with vested interests in reducing federal regulations have showered money on Dole's campaign committees. It is these entities that have been most heavily involved in the lobbying game, in favor of reducing federal regulations.

During the first three months of 1995, these entities

contributed at least $20,000 to Dole's presidential campaign, and Dole raised a total of $113,900 from PACs during this time. His contributors are affiliated with the two major business coalitions now lobbying Congress for regulatory relief: Project Relief and the Alliance for Reasonable Regulation.

How has Dole fared as the new Senate majority leader in 1995?

As he did during his previous reign in that post ten years ago, Dole in early 1995 has shown a determination to disregard the nation's fiscal and political needs in order to pander to the right wing of the Republican Party. Dole has allowed the presidential politics of 1996 to poison the atmosphere of the Senate in 1995, as he seeks to outflank his more extreme right-wing competitors for the presidential nomination—men like Senator Phil Gramm (R-TX) and Congressman Bob Dornan (R-CA).

Because Dole believes that courting the extreme right is essential to winning his party's presidential nomination, he has supported mindless tax cuts that will make the deficit burgeon, and he has supported a "regulatory reform" bill that would allow restrictions on federal regulations to be applied retroactively to long-standing environmental, safety, and health rules across the country. He also called for a ban to all affirmative action programs and for a repeal of the assault gun ban enacted by Congress in 1994. These right-wing extremist proposals are likely to engender more gridlock, as Senate Democrats have vowed to mount "the mother of all filibusters" against them, and as Clinton has threatened to veto them.

To please his corporate clientele, in May 1995 he introduced an amendment to the sweeping tort reform bill that would limit punitive damages in all civil lawsuits in the country and that would strip the states of power they have had over such suits for more than two hundred years, by federalizing all tort law in the country—an outrageous proposal that would strip ordinary citizens of any meaningful power to challenge corporate wrongdoing by suing companies for damages.

This shows the Dolean Double Standard, whereby Dole is willing to increase federal power and the role of the federal government when that suits his corporate clientele's interests, while paying lip service to the Republican slogans calling for "devolution" of federal power and turning over more power to the states.

Why is there a need for a biography of Senator Dole by someone who once worked for him and knew him personally? Because the public cannot seriously expect to get a true and accurate impression of what a candidate is really like in fifteen-second cliché-ridden sound bites on television. I have tried to meticulously research Bob Dole's career and have interviewed hundreds of people who have known him in Kansas, Washington, and around the country, for the purpose of assessing Dole as he now enters the climax of his career. I have also drawn on my own recollections to piece together the Dole Puzzle.

I am writing this book to assess what type of president Dole would be. After more than thirty-four years in Congress, can he take credit for a single significant piece of legislation bearing his name and bettering people's lives? Or can he point only to a multitude of obscure, made-to-order laws that benefit his real constituents—big business and the very rich? Such corporate welfare legislation has only ballooned the federal deficit, of which he is a principal architect.

Of course, the senator denies that he is ever influenced by the money he raises from special interest groups. But the record speaks for itself: Why would people contribute money to a politician unless they wanted something in return? And why would Bob Dole so consistently go to bat for his benefactors? It is, therefore, altogether fitting that we place Senator Dole under a microscope and examine his fitness for the presidency.

Bob Dole has come a long way from the sunbaked streets of Russell, Kansas, where he grew up tasting hard times in the dust bowl during the Great Depression. Far from being a "prairie populist," he has come to symbolize an entire political system that seems to be for sale to the highest bidder, a system in which real decisions are influenced by dollars behind closed doors, a system in which words ring hollow, money talks, and idealism balks. And this applies to both Democrats and Republicans, for the most part, be they right, left, or center.

In early 1995, as Dole prepares to mount his third campaign for the presidency, he shows disturbing signs of remaining a senator for sale. In March 1995, he abandoned decades of support for affirmative action, stating that he would propose legislation to ban it in the future. In quest of campaign contributions from the National Rifle Association, he announced an effort to repeal the ban on assault rifles, which had passed Congress in 1994.

These flip-flops reveal a lack of inner-core consistency and a propensity to sacrifice principle for expediency. Indeed, Bob Dole's career symbolizes much of what is wrong with American politics: the shameless selling of office and legislation to the highest bidder, demonizing the opposition, scapegoating the poor, mudslinging, vindictiveness, a lust for power as an end in itself, and the lack of any true ideology. The closest thing to ideology that Dole has is a contempt for the needy and a concern for the greedy.

His career can be summarized as a symbiotic relationship with moneyed special interests. It vividly illustrates that American politics in the late twentieth century has largely become a Tale of Two Congresses: the First Congress, designed for public consumption and operating via seemingly free elections on the principle of "one person, one vote"; and the Second Congress, which operates largely behind closed doors on the principle of "one dollar, one vote."

Although they do not realize it, the vast majority of the American people are disenfranchised from the Second Congress because they cannot afford to pay thousands of dollars to politicians to get their needs serviced. Since the money exchanged in the Second Congress largely determines which candidates win election to the First Congress, as money buys mass media advertising time, an argument can be made that, as this century draws to a close, the vast majority of Americans have in fact lost the power of their votes.

The genius of Dole and his "conservative" Republican Party over the past fifteen years has been to obscure the workings of the Second Congress and to convince the middle class that its interests lie in supporting anything requested by moneyed special interests because such legislation will lead to "jobs," "tax cuts," and "less government." This chimera, promoted by simplistic sloganeering, and aggravated by a media obsessed with reporting election trivia, has largely concealed the workings of the more real and more powerful Second Congress from the American people. As a result of decisions made in this Congress, the American Dream has been slowly dying for millions of people as they experience a decline in the standard of living and real wages; chronic, massive federal deficits generating a mountain of debt for our children; massive poverty among children; a decline in the quality of life; a de-industrializing economy rapidly replacing real jobs with low-paying, menial, temporary "McJobs"; and a widespread malaise and pessimism in the land. America, once the land of opportunity and until 1980 the biggest creditor nation in the world, has now become the world's biggest debtor state and is plagued with social unrest, crime, and a growing underclass. In this dire state, corporate welfare has flourished under laws crafted by Dole and his party, while human welfare has been slashed and condemned.

This book seeks to shed some light on the more powerful, real Second Congress that has produced the society we live in now, and that Dole aspires to lead as our next president.

I

DOLE, THE MAN:
DR. JEKYLL OR MR. HYDE?

No party can command respect which supports this year what it opposed last.

—Abraham Lincoln

The evil side of my nature, to which I had now transferred the stamping efficacy, was less robust and less developed than the good which I had just deposed. . . . Even as good shone upon the countenance of the one, evil was written broadly and plainly on the face of the other. Evil besides (which I must still believe to be the lethal side of man) had left on that body an imprint of deformity and decay. And yet when I looked upon that ugly idol in the glass, I was conscious of no repugnance, rather of a leap of welcome. This, too, was myself.

—Robert Louis Stevenson,
Dr. Jekyll and Mr. Hyde
(statement of Dr. Henry Jekyll)

1

"SENATOR SARDONICUS": CAPITOL KING OF COMEDY

B ob Dole is probably the most talented comedian ever to hold a seat in the United States Senate, so talented that he was invited to host NBC's "Saturday Night Live." Dole's humor reflects his personality: raw, biting, cynical, terse, and sardonic.

In 1961, a B-grade horror movie, *Mr. Sardonicus*, chilled audiences across the country. The star (who coincidentally bears a remarkable physical likeness to Dole) sported a mouth perpetually frozen in a ghastly, mocking grimace that had been caused by his experiencing a horrific event. Deformed and embarrassed, Mr. Sardonicus camouflaged his feelings, then unleashed them in violent, unreasonable outbursts of rage.

Dole uses humor as a weapon. Freud commented that at the heart of all humor is a desire to destroy, and that the best comedians are destructive personalities. The senator's personality is reflected in his humor, and his talent as a natural stand-up comic is unparalleled. His specialty is black comedy of the one-liner variety and carefully aimed barbs. Dole once said that if he had not gone into politics, he would have loved to become a stand-up comedian or a "Tonight Show" host.

"People tend to listen to you closer if you can make them laugh," he has commented. "The key to humor comes in preparation." For some annual events and special occasions, such as the Gridiron Dinner in Washington, Dole turns to professional joke-writers for help. For example, *The New York Times* named Dole "one of the funniest speakers" after he had hired Landon Parvis, Reagan's former joke-writer, to provide material for his speeches. But most of Dole's jokes are his own work or that of his staffers. "You've got to get up and read the morning papers," he has explained. "The joke has to be current to keep people interested."

Dole's humor is often self-directed. When he began his career in the 1950s he explained that he had "suffered some head injury in the war and then had gone into politics." After losing the 1976 vice-presidential election, he said, "I went for the jugular—my own." But generally he aims elsewhere, usually at a Democrat's hide. He described Democratic presidential candidate George McGovern as a "left-leaning marshmallow" in 1972, then called Jimmy Carter a "chicken-fried McGovern" in 1976. After winning his bid for a second term in the United States Senate in 1974 by defeating Dr. Bill Roy, Dole made fun of the fact that Roy was both a doctor and a lawyer. "Before the election, they said Roy was one in a million," Dole cracked. "Well, now he's one in ten million—he's unemployed."

At the celebrated Senator Strom Thurmond's ninetieth birthday party in 1993 he called for "Dr. Kevorkian," the notorious suicide doctor. Then he said, "Tell Dr. Kevorkian to call back in ten years."

Ethnic and racial jokes aren't off-limits either, as evidenced by comments about Michael Dukakis and Howard Baker. "Dukakis?" asked Dole mockingly. "Never had it." When the diminutive Howard Baker dropped out of the 1980 presidential campaign, Dole said, "Howard can now open a tall men's shop in Japan."

His clever banter also reflects Dole's lighter side. When his wife was nominated to be Secretary of Transportation in 1983, he told the Senate committee, "I regret that I have but one wife to give for my country's infrastructure." And when asked if he saw any "conflict of interest" in Liddy's nomination, he replied, "No conflict, but plenty of interest." On the "Tonight Show" in 1993, Dole said, "A lot of people think I'm grumpy. But you have to remember, my wife's president of the Red Cross. I never know how much blood I gave during the night." Indeed, the senator has a whole repertoire of Bob and Liddy jokes, which he recites at dinners and speeches. Asked if he felt jealous about his wife's role as a potential presidential candidate, he quipped, "At least there will be one Dole in the White House."

He is perhaps at his funniest and most appealing when he ridicules himself. When it was revealed that Nixon had secretly recorded all conversations in the Oval Office in the 1970s, he said, "Thank God I only nodded when I was in there." After the Watergate burglary made front-page news in 1972, Dole commented, "At least we got the burglar vote." When it was mentioned that he was the Republican National Committee Chairman at the time of the burglary, he quipped, "Thank God it was my night off."

In 1984, when he became Senate majority leader, Dole was presented with a new dog by his wife and daughter, and it was named Leader. Dole then remarked, "They say that dogs often take on the characteristics of their owners, and I must admit Leader and I have quite a few similarities. We both call press conferences, we are both intensely loyal, and we both bark at liberals from time to time."

When Dole was branded as "Senator Gridlock" in 1993, he responded, upon receiving an honorary degree at Colby College in Maine, by quipping, "From now on you'll have to call me 'Dr. Gridlock.' " After losing the 1976 vice-presidential election as Ford's running mate, Dole claimed to be "untroubled" and "unbothered by the defeat." He told reporters that after losing the election he had gone home and slept like a baby: "Every two hours I woke up and cried." In his 1980 presidential campaign, Dole mocked himself for failure to attract money: "My opponent, John Connally, sweeps through town with a vacuum cleaner; I come along later with a whisk broom.''

Bob Dole has even ridiculed fellow Republican conservatives. In 1982, when he began to snipe at supply-side Reaganomics, he would say, "There is good news and bad news. The good news is that a busload of supply-side economists went over a cliff and everybody was killed. The bad news is that two seats were empty."

And he has roasted rivals. He dubbed Dan Quayle "Mr. Potato Head" after the vice president misspelled "potato" as "potatoe" in a widely publicized gaffe, and he acidly remarked that Jack Kemp, who sports a blow-dried coiffure, "wants a business [tax] deduction for hair-spray."

In 1988, White House Chief of Staff John Sununu, the former governor of New Hampshire, had been instrumental in bringing about Dole's defeat in the New Hampshire primary.* When news reports in 1991 blasted Sununu for flying to New Hampshire on a military jet for barber and dentist appointments, Dole taunted him at a meeting before the National Association of Manufacturers. "I don't know whether Sununu flies too much, but I understand he won't start a cabinet meeting until the seats and tables are in their full upright positions," he said. "The last time Sununu came to my office for a meeting, he asked for a window seat." Dole later referred to Sununu as the "Chief of Chaff," and to Presidents Ford, Carter, and Nixon, as "See No Evil, Hear No Evil, and Evil."

In 1994, at an evening forum with representatives of the Health Insurance Association of America (HIAA), Dole recited a "poem" that ridiculed the Clinton health plan. The poem ends with a reference to Harry and Louise, the fictitious couple who were featured in HIAA's television commercials criticizing the plan as ill-conceived and restrictive.

---

*The New Hampshire primary was so crucial to Bush's winning the 1988 presidency that Bush made Sununu his chief of staff as a political reward for defeating Dole. Dole never forgot or forgave Sununu, who was eventually pressured into resigning.

There once was a President named Bill
Who thought health care was ill
So, from the White House
He and his spouse
Sent a plan to Capitol Hill

The plan was a policy wonk's dream
Over a thousand pages, it seemed
If you read it straight through
You will surely turn blue
When you see their financing scheme

At first it looked like a joke
Their numbers were mirror and smoke
Taxes would increase
And small business would cease
Under paperwork that would make them choke

I've now reached the end of my tale
As you're starting to look quite pale
So, I'll end with a prayer
I know we all share,
"Lord, let Harry and Louise prevail"

When Clinton was running for president in 1992, Dole joked that "the only foreign policy experience he has had is playing the 'Vienna Waltz' on his saxophone."

Dole loves joking about President Clinton, and in early 1993 he christened the presidential jet "Hair Force One" after Clinton tied up air traffic at Los Angeles International Airport to get a $200 haircut.

Dole is less tolerant when he is the target. During the Academy Awards in March 1994, comic Whoopi Goldberg told a national TV audience that her favorite fantasy was for "Bob Dole to meet Lorena Bobbitt." Dole sent a nasty letter to Goldberg, taking it personally because he thought she was ridiculing his prostate cancer surgery of 1991.

Following Dole's successful filibuster of Clinton's $16 billion economic job stimulus package in April 1993,

Clinton told a White House dinner that "Senator Dole and all his Republicans said, 'You just don't understand, this thing's full of pork. It's a dad-gum scandal.' I was appalled. Then I read yesterday in *The Wall Street Journal* about a senator from Kansas who asked for $23 million to convert a senior-citizens' center into a boathouse in Kansas. And he was right after all. I apologize to Senator Dole." Dole was outraged. In fact, the boathouse was an $850,000 project financed with private donations. Dole fired off angry press releases with a huge headline reading WHITE HOUSE'S $23 MILLION LIE and Clinton ended up eating crow and apologizing to Dole.

Dole was furious as well when Jack Kemp joked in 1985 that "in a recent fire, Bob Dole's library burned down. Both books were lost. And he hadn't even finished coloring one of them yet." Yet Dole was much more genial when introduced as "the Darth Vader of American politics," on the "Tonight Show" in June 1993. Jay Leno suddenly stopped his "Tonight Show" monologue and complained that his jokes about President Clinton had become "awful mean" lately. "Oh, look, it's Dole who's writing them," Leno quipped, grinning. As he spoke, the camera panned to the audience, and there stood Bob Dole actually holding up a big white cue card, wearing his trademark sardonic smile.

When Dole appeared as a guest, Leno deadpanned, "We put some raw meat and a scratching post in the Green Room for Dole to get warmed up on." As the senator sat side by side with Leno, trading one-liners, Dole joked, "I like Bill Clinton. And he likes me. We've agreed on that."

In early 1993, during Clinton's first one hundred days in office, Jay Leno joked that "Clinton said we'd all be tested in the next one hundred days. The president would be tested for leadership, Congress would be tested on the economy, and Bob Dole would be tested for rabies. Right before Clinton's press conference, Bob Dole held a news conference to announce that he's going to disagree with everything Clinton's probably going to say."

"When Dole met Ross Perot," Leno told a national TV audience, "I thought they were Dr. Frankenstein with his sidekick, Igor." In Christmas of 1993, Leno cracked, "You can really tell the holiday season has started down there in Washington, D.C. Last night, Bob Dole turned his garden hose on his first group of carolers."

"He's a great subject for jokes," Leno has said. "He laughs at himself and he's sort of a proven entity. He seems like a decent man, I like him, and he is very well-respected. So any jokes that jab at him are just that, just jokes."

In a November 1993 episode on the TV show "Murphy Brown" Dole played himself. He appeared in Murphy Brown's nightmare as a right-wing Senate hatchet man, out to get her for her liberal views. Later, after the episode had aired on TV, Dole recounted how he and his wife had once shared a table at the White House with Murphy Brown (actress Candice Bergen). He said that when they got up to dance, Bergen wolfed down all their sherbet. "She denied it, of course, but it was shameless considering how orange her tongue was," Dole said.

Dole has also been invited to host "Saturday Night Live," whose comedy skits have routinely portrayed him as vitriolic, self-pitying, disabled, and vicious. One famous skit in 1993 showed Dole chasing a shrewish Hillary Clinton around a desk, arm raised to strike her, and advising her husband Bill, "I'll show you how to deal with her." In another, comic Dan Aykroyd played Dole as a nasty, dour, self-pitying presidential candidate. Asked what he thought of the performance, Dole said, "I liked it. But he's put on a lot of weight. I think he's going to have to get on a Slim-Fast diet."

Elena Newport of the Capitol Steps, a Washington-based comedy troupe, has recommended that to further improve his comedy stock, Dole should "go swimming naked in the tidal basin. It would help." The Capitol Steps have regaled audiences with the Dole-inspired song, "50 Ways to Peeve Your Leader."

Mark Sheehan, of the Center for Media and Public Affairs, which tracks political humor on television, said that "it is interesting that media comedians have generally ridiculed Dole for his mean streak and obstructionism. I think it's this thing that many people remember, because it's pointed out that it's humorous."

Ridicule of Dole's mean streak and dour persona has not been confined to the television screen. In a cartoon in *The New Yorker* magazine, two overstuffed businessmen at a men's club whine, "Just when everything looks bleakest, along comes a fellow like Dole."

Cartoonist Mike Keefe has caricatured Dole as an executioner, walking into Attorney General Janet Reno's office with a hood on his head and an ax in his arms, proclaiming: "I hear you might be looking for a Special Prosecutor [in the Whitewater scandal]."

Political cartoonists have had a field day with Dole's negative image, threatening physical appearance, disability, and outlandish tactics. They have generally depicted him as a beetle-browed, dark, five-o'clock-shadowed sinister figure muttering some ridiculous or menacing phrase. He has been drawn as an executioner, a killer bee, a malevolent cult leader, a vampire, and a sour old man.

In July 1993, his Senate obstructionism led a group of disgruntled entrepreneurs at shops throughout Washington to print and sell a T-shirt showing Dole as "Senator Gridlock," along with the message, "Dole, Sit Down and Shut Up." The anti-Dole T-shirts sold briskly.

Lincoln was an accomplished humorist who often joked about his physical ugliness and height. Franklin D. Roosevelt used a devastating wit to lambaste his opponents. But Dole's humor is far more revealing. Perhaps its essence was best captured in March 1988, when in an eerily self-destructive mood, he posed for a photo at Universal Studios in Florida. Flanking him on one side was Charlie Chaplin, and on the other, Frankenstein. Dole smiled sardonically between the comic and the monster, holding his thumb up as his presidential campaign was crashing down all around him. Somehow, those two characters symbolize the senator's dual nature. He can be a "good sport," and he can be very funny, but in a real sense, he is at least part clown and part monster.

Dr. Jekyll, meet Mr. Dole.

2

VIPER BOB AND HIS ENEMIES LIST

As volatile as Kansas weather, Bob Dole can be all sunshine one minute and a violent tornado the next. His reputation as the Darth Vader of American politics is richly deserved. Of all the impressions that I recall from having worked for him, the most memorable is how truly vindictive the man can be. Because Dole is utterly intolerant of opposition and because he regards, in particular, any financial contribution to a Democrat as a personal affront and threat to his livelihood, Dole routinely reviews campaign contribution disclosure documents and notes the names of all contributors to any Democratic candidates he has opposed. To Dole this is the ultimate political sin and merits punishment.

In interviewing people across Kansas for this book, I encountered evidence over and over again of the "atmosphere of fear" pervading the Sunflower State. Many people are afraid to give money to any Democrat, particularly to a Democratic opponent of Dole. Gloria O'Dell, his opponent for the 1992 Senate race, said she had great difficulty in raising money for this reason.

O'Dell recalls that right after she made a speech on national television at the Democratic National Convention in July 1992 proclaiming her Senate candidacy, she received financial contributions from people all over the country. Many of those who watched and contributed money to her were women's groups and Jews who disliked Dole because of his critical attitude toward Israel. They quickly found themselves on his enemies list, O'Dell said. "Dole was very angry when he saw me on television," O'Dell pointed out.

I have never seen a written enemies list kept by Dole. But there has never been any doubt that Dole remembers those who have crossed him politically. He never forgives and never forgets.

Even judges fear the wrath of Dole. In 1980, a Kansas lawyer named Patrick F. Kelly from Wichita, Kansas was nominated by President Carter to be a federal judge. When his name came up in the Senate Judiciary Committee, on which I worked for Dole and which must first approve all federal judicial nominees, Dole went over a recent list of contributors to Democrats and spotted Kelly's name. The sum was only about $150, but Dole held up Kelly's nomination until Kelly personally came to Dole and made amends.*

The fear engendered by Dole's powers of retaliation extend not only to voters and potential contributors, but also to the news media. As Martin Hawver, the veteran journalist and publisher of the *Hawver's Capital Report* in Topeka, has stated, Bob Dole's tendency is to "freeze out" any reporter who writes a critical story. He will

---

*Judge Patrick F. Kelly is still on the bench. A Catholic who is strongly pro-choice on the abortion issue, Kelly became a household name in Kansas and much of the country during the summer of 1991, when he showed a tough attitude toward anti-abortion protesters in Wichita during their so-called Summer of Mercy campaign in which they picketed abortion clinics. Kelly issued orders and injunctions banning thousands of protesters from blocking entrances to local abortion clinics, called in U.S. Marshals, and had more than 2,500 arrested. Kelly called reporters to his chambers to warn that people who violated his orders "should say farewell to their family and bring their toothbrush because they are going to jail." Kelly also jailed three leaders of Operation Rescue for failure to post a $100,000 "peace bond" in a civil suit brought against them by the abortion clinics.

simply refuse interviews and withhold any press releases or advance notice of news conferences. At least some reporters are intimidated.

Hawver said, "You have got to be very careful when you report the news about Dole" because "he will just shut you out if he doesn't like what you write. He won't talk to you and won't return your calls. You will be forced to deal with a junior staffer."

Hawver recalls an incident during the Republican National Convention in August 1988, when George Bush was still trying to decide on a running mate for his 1988 presidential campaign. Senator Dole had actively lobbied for the spot for several months, and had come to New Orleans with high hopes. He actively lobbied Bush for the vice-presidency. Hawver approached Dole on the convention floor and asked, "Senator, do you feel demeaned by being here and begging like this?"

Dole's face turned beet-red and his eyes flared. " 'Demeaned'?" he repeated several times. "What do you mean, 'demeaned'?"

"He picked up on the word 'demeaned,' " says Hawver, "and went about repeating it to any other reporter he found with a sound of sarcasm." Pretty soon the national media reported on television that "Bob Dole feels demeaned by Bush's process of selecting a running mate."

The next day, Bush, clearly embarrassed by the comment, precipitously settled on forty-one-year-old Dan Quayle. Dole blamed Hawver for this.

Hawver explains that "for months after that convention, I would call Dole's office, and Dole would have me talk to Walt Riker, his press secretary. And every time I asked a question, Riker would say something sarcastic, using the word 'demeaned.' You learn the power of doing nothing."

Mark Sommer, features editor of the *Topeka Capitol Journal*, also experienced Dole's intolerance of criticism. On May 23, 1993, the banner headline read: DOLE TAINTED BY OWN CAMPAIGN FINANCES. In the article,

Sommer listed Dole's long record of taking money from special interest groups, and argued that the senator was a hypocrite in arguing against Clinton's Campaign Finance Reform Bill. "Dole hit the roof," Sommer told me.

In a letter to Peter Stauffer, publisher of the *Topeka Capitol Journal*, dated May 25, 1993, and marked "Private, not for publication," Dole wrote: "I knew the *Capitol Journal* was sliding to the left, but your irresponsible and mean-spirited attack on me really went over the edge. Poorly researched, presented without any substantiation other than recycling other base smears, purposely ignoring almost all of the input from my office, and hyping it all with a reckless headline, the 'Dole Tainted by Own Campaign Finances' story has set a new low for your newspaper." Dole blasted the "elitists at the *Journal*" and concluded, "I know negativism is an easy sell these days in many newsrooms, but I expect professionalism and balance to sometimes prevail in the glow of yellow journalism."

In addition, Dole's press aide, Walt Riker, wrote a letter to the editor of the *Topeka Capitol Journal* on May 24, 1993, blasting Sommer for a "hysterical spasm to support the Democrat Party's so-called campaign reform bill."* Riker echoed his boss in accusing Sommer of a "hatchet job, agenda-driven journalism which was nothing but a rehash of inaccurate liberal news reports. . . . The only thing that is 'tainted' by this story is the *Capitol Journal's* reputation," insisted Dole's spokesman. Riker also accused the newspaper of engaging in a "partisan pack of lies about Bob Dole."

Dole's hysterical response to the story vividly reveals his intolerance for criticism and his unwillingness to admit that he indeed receives avalanches of PAC money while at the same time publicly attacking the very system that provides it.

*Dole and his staff regularly refer to the Democratic Party as "Democrat Party," a sarcastic means of referring to the opposition that dates back to the old days of Dole's political adolescence.

It should also be noted that the *Topeka Capitol Journal*, far from being a "left-leaning" scandal sheet, as Dole stridently alleged, is a very respectable, conservative newspaper that has generally supported him throughout his political career. However, the newspaper has stood by the accuracy of its story.

Yet another journalist who has felt the sting of Dole's lash is Roger Myers, a veteran reporter for the *Topeka Capital Journal*. While based in Washington, Myers covered Dole and his 1974 Senate opponent, Congressman Bill Roy. "I was covering Roy more than Dole thought I should have," says Myers, adding that the senator "didn't like some of the critical stories I wrote on him [Dole]. So he froze me out for about six months. . . . I couldn't get him to talk to me for six months." Myers no longer covers Dole in Washington.

The practical effect of Dole's policy of "freezing out" critical reporters is to discourage journalists from writing anything critical about him, for reporters need continuous access to Dole in order to earn their livelihoods. A newspaper is likely to replace a reporter on Dole's "freeze-out list" with someone who can gain access to the senator by writing flattering stories about him.

Bob Dole's wrath is not aimed only at reporters. During the New Hampshire primary campaign in 1988, a hostile questioner asked a question about nuclear weapons. Dole shot back, "Why don't you crawl back into your cave?" He often uses such taunting phrases, and he has often remarked approvingly of Richard Nixon's pattern of deliberately baiting demonstrators. In one infamous episode in San Jose, California, during Nixon's first term, Nixon faced a hostile crowd of anti-war demonstrators, deliberately stood on the top of a car, and raised his two arms, making his trademark "V" shape with his fingers. This only provoked the demonstrators into more violence. Dole loved it.

In the 1970s, Bob Brock, who managed Dr. Roy's Senate campaign against Dole in 1974 and was also a generous Democratic contributor, says he found himself on Richard Nixon's enemies list, and he insists he was harassed by the IRS because of Nixon.

In an interview with the author in 1994, Brock, a hotel magnate, gave a chilling tale of how he had been retaliated against by the IRS. He had been a top Democratic campaign aide and campaign manager to Congressman Bill Roy and aide to Governor Bob Docking in 1972. "In 1972," said Brock, "Dole spent half his time during the campaign in Kansas, even though he was Republican National Committee Chairman, in order to help defeat these two Democrats whom he saw as his likely main rivals for his 1974 Senate reelection campaign. He kept running into me everywhere in Kansas and he was bothered by my presence." Once, on a joint appearance on a national news show with Roy, Dole referred to Brock twice and cast him "icy stares."

In 1973, when John Dean, Nixon's former White House counsel during Watergate, made shocking revelations about the existence of an enemies list in the Nixon White House during the Senate Watergate Committee hearings, Bob Brock was startled to be informed by a newspaper reporter that his name was on Nixon's list. He was asked, "Do you know why you are on the list?" Brock responded, "No." Brock was one of only two Kansans on Nixon's enemies list. He had never done anything political to antagonize Nixon, only Dole, who at the time was Republican National Committee Chairman.

What did it mean to be on the enemies list? In the early 1970s, Brock owned nine Holiday Inns in Kansas. He and his partner, Ed Linquist, owned "Topeka Inn Management, Inc.," and applied for a class A club permit from the Kansas authorities, which was necessary in order to operate cocktail lounges in their hotels. In order to get the class A license according to Kansas law, they needed a nonprofit exemption certificate, which was issued by the IRS. So they set up a nonprofit organization and got the certificate. Suddenly, at the time Brock's name appeared on Nixon's enemies list, the IRS revoked the nonprofit exemption certificate for all nine hotels in

Kansas for no apparent reason. Brock filed a lawsuit and got an injunction against the IRS for "discriminatory law enforcement," but lost much business because of this. He said the IRS told him it wanted to make a "test case" out of him. Brock insisted that there were over five hundred nonprofit exemption certificates issued by the IRS for class A licenses in Kansas but that only his nine were revoked.

Shortly after this, the IRS levied a very large personal income tax assessment against Brock based on disallowing the deductions he had made for a gift of twenty acres of land near Interstate 70 at the edge of Junction City, Kansas, which he had donated to Kansas University. Brock had had the land appraised as being worth $6,000 per acre, but the IRS claimed it was worth only $2,000 per acre and said that its "highest and best use" was for "residential" property rather than "commercial," even though it happened to be at the edge of Junction City, which is clearly a commercial area. The IRS's appraisal report contained numerous errors and failed to mention that the area was a commerical zone, and incorrectly claimed that there were no public utilities accessible to the property. The IRS demanded that Brock pay an assessment of $30,000, but Brock appealed and eventually settled for $200.

The third form of IRS harassment against Brock was a "jeopardy assessment," which the IRS suddenly imposed without explanation, denying Brock all tax deductions and exemptions, drying up his credit, and permitting the IRS to liquidate all of his assets. Jeopardy assessment is the most extreme measure imposed by the IRS and is used only if it appears that a taxpayer is about to hide or remove assets out of the country. Brock finally called the IRS director in Wichita, complained about the unfair treatment he had received and got the jeopardy assessment canceled. Brock's chilling experience with IRS harassment reveals the dangers of getting on an "enemies list."

But Dole's wrath is not reserved for critics. After his

1976 vice-presidential and his 1980 and 1988 presidential candidacy disasters, Dole lashed out and fired many staffers. "He was like a snake," recalls one. In 1988, Dole needed a scapegoat and blamed his longtime top aide, Dave Owen, for a scandal that erupted over Owen's business dealings with Liddy Dole's blind trust and his alleged relationship with a crony of Dole's who obtained a Small Business Administration minority set-aside contract. Dole claimed that the scandal wrecked his presidential bid. Owen, who had stuck his own neck on the line and devotedly worked for Dole for twenty years, was blasted publicly, forced to quit, and "cut loose."

Owen found himself hounded by Kansas Republican prosecutors for the next six years, indicted on eighteen state counts and two federal tax felony counts for fundraising for Mike Hayden, a Kansas gubernatorial candidate, whom he was helping at Dole's behest. Owen wound up in federal prison, where he was illegally denied parole. The sad Dave Owen saga exemplifies the fragility of Dole's personal relationships with even his closest aides (see chapter 27). "If you even look cross-eyed at Bob," reports a former associate, "that's enough to get you on his enemies list."

When I asked Elliot Kaplan, Owen's former lawyer, if Dole was involved in somehow persecuting Owen politically, he replied, "How could you say he wasn't?" Kaplan, who has become disgusted with politics—he calls it an "unhealthy environment"—after seeing what happened to Owen, remains worried about Dole's power and the system propping up that power. "We fought the Revolutionary War to stop these sorts of abuses under King George III," he notes. "If Dole is elected president, I'd leave the country," Kaplan said.

And Owen himself notes that "Dole always blames others for his own mistakes" and that he turns on his scapegoats with fury. "He never forgives and he never forgets," said a longtime Dole aide, speaking on condition of anonymity.

The idea of persecuting political enemies was a trademark of the Nixon White House, and because Dole is so close to Nixon in spirit, he has been nicknamed "Nixon Lite." It is altogether fitting, therefore, to examine the close connection between Dole and Nixon.

3

NIXON LITE

B ob Dole's affection for Richard Nixon is deeply rooted. Nixon was by far the most influential public official in his life, and he drank at the font of "Nixonian counsel" like a thirsty man in the desert. To appreciate the full extent of his identification with the former Watergate president, we need only examine Dole's own words and deeds.

"I believe that the second half of the twentieth century will be remembered as the Age of Nixon," declared an emotional Bob Dole in his eulogy for former president Richard M. Nixon at Nixon's televised funeral in Yorba Linda, California, on April 27, 1994.* "Richard Nixon was a man of vision, the largest figure of our time, whose influence will be timeless."

Before millions of television viewers Dole broke down and wept. "Americans love a fighter," Dole proclaimed, "and in Dick Nixon, they found a gallant one." Recounting that Nixon had at one time told his wife Pat that he woke up each day solely "to confound my enemies," Dole went on to heap maudlin praise on Nixon.

Dole told me once that he admired Nixon mostly for

---

*Nixon's family asked Dole to deliver the eulogy, and this request was conveyed via Bob Ellsworth, a Kansan who had been Nixon's NATO ambassador and a crony of Dole's for decades.

his ruthless "slashing" campaign style, and for Nixon's defiant attitude toward his "enemies," whom he saw and fought everywhere. As Dole said in his eulogy, Nixon "never gave up and he never gave in."

Virtually everyone who has known Dole, both in Kansas and Washington, has pointed out their similarities. "They're like two peas in a pod," said a Kansas politician who knows Dole and knew Nixon well. While that comparison is extreme, it is certainly appropriate to view them as brothers in spirit. For more than twenty years, Dole has lived in the infamous Watergate building in Washington, D.C. He once told me that he remained a tenant in defiance of Nixon's fate, as if to say "up yours" to Nixon's detractors.

During Dole's latest Senate reelection campaign in June 1992—twenty years from the date when five Republican campaign workers were arrested for breaking into the Democrats' office in the Watergate—Nixon accompanied Dole to a hotel in Wichita, Kansas, wrapped his arm around Dole's shoulders, patted him on the back, and endorsed him for reelection for a fifth Senate term. This was one of the last campaign speeches Nixon ever made.

It seemed as though Dole felt sorry for Nixon—whom he saw as a martyr crucified by a hostile, liberal press and pinko Democrats—and wanted to pick up where Nixon left off. The two men spoke regularly on the phone for twenty years after Watergate, with Dole regularly taking advice from the former president. At Nixon's eulogy, Dole cried out for "one more drop of Nixonian counsel." He was moved by the fact that Nixon was one of the few public figures sufficiently sensitive to Dole's crippled right arm to shake hands with *his* (Nixon's) own left hand whenever the two men embraced. The "left-handed shake" was a symbolic gesture that united the men.

This close bond was vividly apparent during Dole's first Senate term, from 1969 to 1974, when he was nicknamed "Nixon's Doberman pinscher" for his slavish devotion to the president on every issue.

Dole, like Nixon, suffers from great stress when addressing the public. Dole has great difficulty in making eye contact with people, blinks a great deal, and is insecure around strangers. He usually communicates with his own staff by memo and does not like to chitchat.

In his general political outlook, Dole shares Nixon's enormous ethical blind spot. By calling the second half of the twentieth century the "Age of Nixon" in his eulogy, Dole conveniently forgot that Nixon was the only president to leave office after a scandal that eroded people's faith in the American political system. Nixon, who resigned in disgrace, had a character defect that led him to lie repeatedly to the public, cover up crimes committed in his name, and obstruct justice. Dole was never bothered by this dark side of Nixon.

After losing the use of his right arm and a kidney in a World War II firefight, Dole was unable to "look in a mirror," according to his brother, Kenny, because he "looked like he'd just come out of Dachau concentration camp." In a bizarre interview he gave to CBS's "60 Minutes," which was broadcast on October 24, 1993, Dole said he "still can't look in a mirror except to shave," suggesting a self-loathing and denial.

Both Dole and Nixon suffered from similarly deprived, lonely childhoods in which they felt victimized by a world that did not understand them and had betrayed them. As a child, Nixon called himself "Your dog, Richard," in letters to his mother. Seldom home, Dole's father never praised him. "Not bad—not good, but not bad," was Doran Dole's standard line. And Bob Dole knew it was Saturday because that was the day he got a licking from his mother. Fundamentally loners, Nixon and Dole tended to view any form of criticism as a personal attack on their integrity, meriting full-scale warfare.

Just as Nixon self-destructed by trying to cover up the Watergate break-in and failing to destroy his secret tapes, so too Bob Dole has self-destructed in orgies of chaos and disorganization during all three of his national campaigns for high office. Self-destructiveness also has manifested itself in Dole's and Nixon's tendency to flirt with disaster, to provoke "crises" in which they can be "tested to the hilt." (Nixon even entitled his 1962 autobiography *Six Crises*.)

In 1979, Dole hired as his chief Senate Judiciary Committee counsel Pete Velde, the son of former Congressman Harold Velde, who was Nixon's soulmate and neighbor on the House Un-American Activities Committee in the late 1940s. The younger Velde, who knew and respected both Nixon and Dole, shares the author's view that Dole is Nixonian. He admires both men's political and anti-Communist witch-hunting tendencies.

If Bob Dole is "Nixon Lite," he is less vindictive and less malicious than Nixon. Dole's political antennae are probably more sensitive than Nixon's, and he tends to draw back and reverse his direction when confronted with strong opposition, rather than plunging into the abyss.

He also has more charm, certainly has a far better sense of humor, and even tends to poke jokes at himself. By contrast, Nixon was a humorless grind who was nicknamed "Gloomy Gus" when a student at Duke Law School.* But the Nixonian blind spot can be seen in Dole's pattern of disregarding federal election campaign laws in 1988 and Kansas campaign laws in 1992 (see chapters 24 and 25). Dole, like Nixon, seems to feel that he is above the law. If he ever becomes president, his administration would probably bear a strong resemblance to that of Richard Milhous Nixon.

The close bond that existed between Dole and Nixon extended to the very end of Nixon's life, and was revealed in several "Dear Bob" letters Nixon wrote to Dole between 1984 and 1994, many of them handwritten and personal.

That Nixon considered Dole his favorite candidate for president, there can be no doubt. In his "Dear Bob"

---

*Dole's admiration was such that he even liked the fact that I had attended Nixon's alma mater, Duke Law School, in 1972–75. I went there because I was inspired by Nixon, *before* Watergate.

letters, Nixon showered the Kansan with praise and gave him tips on how to win the 1996 GOP presidential nomination. These letters, which Dole proudly made public in May 1995, show the extraordinary personal bond between the two men.

Praising Dole as "the most dominant legislative, political, and policy leader of the Republican Party" he had ever seen, Nixon assured Dole that he would be in a far stronger position to seek the presidency in 1996 than Nixon had been in 1968.

With characteristic Machiavellian opportunism, Nixon advised Dole that in order to win the GOP nomination, Dole would be required to campaign "as far as you can to the right because that's where 40 percent" of Republican primary voters are. But in the general election, he would "have to run as fast as you can back to the middle because only about 4 percent of the nation's voters are on the extreme right wing."

Telling Dole that he had the "brains, heart, and guts" of an outstanding leader, Nixon warned him to put on a smiling face and conceal his dark side: "Appearing mean would play into the false caricature your critics have tagged you with. Being tough with a smile is the best posture for you."

Nixon opined that Dole would not be handicapped as a presidential candidate by his old age, noting that "after four years of Clinton and his baby boomers, age may not prove to be a liability." Moreover, said Nixon, Dole in 1996 would be six months younger than Reagan had been when he won reelection in 1984.

In recommending the septuagenarian, World War II–era Kansan as the ideal man to lead the country into the twenty-first century, Nixon compared Dole to other great, old national leaders, such as "de Gaulle, Adenauer, Yoshida, and Chou En-lai," who were "all in top form mentally in their seventies."

Nixon insisted that "everyone" recognized Dole as the undisputed leader of his party, and insisted that "after 1994, you will have no one who can defeat you."

4

"SENATOR FLIP-FLOP"

Dole's record in the Senate has earned him the nick-
names "Senator Flip-flop" and "Senator Straddle."
He began his political career as a congressman "to the
right of Genghis Khan," in the 1960s. Then he became
"Nixon's Doberman pinscher" in the Senate in the early
1970s, only to eventually ally himself with such "left-
leaning marshmallow" senators as George McGovern,
with whom he forged an alliance to liberalize food stamp
eligibility in the late 1970s. After 1985, he urged stringent
cutbacks in the food stamp program and went farther to
the right than Senator Jesse Helms.

In shifting course abruptly, Dole was following the
example set by Nixon, who was notorious for making
sudden, dramatic reversals on major foreign and domestic issues. Nixon was originally a dyed-in-the-wool anti-
Communist and red-baiter, but he shocked the world in
1972 when he made a dramatic visit to Peking and initiated steps to recognize Communist China, and when he
ushered in detente with the Soviet Union. Although he
was a "conservative," Nixon instituted wage and price
controls in 1971, approved the creation of the Environmental Protection Agency in 1970, and vastly increased
spending on welfare and other entitlement programs in
the 1970s.

Dole began his career by saying that he was an opponent of higher taxes, then single-handedly crafted a bill

in 1982 (his $98 billion TEFRA bill) that resulted in the largest single tax hike in U.S. history. He advocated a massive gasoline tax in 1989 to reduce the deficit, and supported record tax hikes of $137 billion proposed by Bush in 1990. Dole also ridiculed supply-side economic theory in the early 1980s, then claimed he was a supply-sider after all. This led Republican conservative Congressman Newt Gingrich to call Dole "the self-appointed tax collector of the welfare state." Then when he campaigned for president in 1987, Dole again switched gears and announced he was opposed to higher taxes. However, in 1988 he refused to run television commercials pledging not to raise taxes, and found himself ridiculed by Bush as "Senator Straddle" on this issue. His present motto is "Down with taxes."

One is stunned by the sheer magnitude of Dole's reversals, during his more than thirty-four years in Congress, on major policy decisions on virtually every issue, ranging from taxes to foreign and domestic policy. Dole's record has been one of opportunistic conversions. Like Nixon, he has a rather hollow political soul, which lends itself to adjusting to the political winds whichever way they blow.

In 1974, and again in 1988 and 1993, he called the federal deficit "public enemy number one." Yet it is Dole himself who has been a major architect of the deficit, which has increased by more than 6,000 percent since 1974.

As detailed later in chapters 17 and 18, Dole has pushed through the Senate numerous amendments to the Internal Revenue Code to benefit specific contributors to his campaigns. For example, in 1981 he opposed granting retroactive tax breaks to Chicago commodity traders, who had been legally avoiding income taxes for years by using paper accounting techniques to roll over indefinitely their gains via commodity futures straddling. Then, in 1984, just a few months after these traders gave Dole huge campaign contributions, he not only supported the tax breaks but helped pass a new tax bill that enabled them to continue avoiding hundreds of millions of dollars in taxes.

Similarly, Dole has drained the treasury by engineering clever "made-to-order" tax breaks, which have benefited a specific trucking company in Iowa, a dubious ethanol industry, and countless other special interest groups who continue to support his campaign war chest.

While once claiming to be a deficit crusader, Dole supported the secretive midnight vote by Congress in 1991, which increased each senator's and congressman's salary by $23,000.

Although he claimed to be an advocate for the handicapped and the disabled in the 1970s and early 1980s, Dole later urged drastic slashing of federal aid to these groups, earning himself a zero rating from the Vietnam Veterans of America and other advocate groups.

At one time saying he was "against smoking," Dole has nonetheless championed the cause of the tobacco lobby in Congress after receiving campaign contributions from tobacco companies.

Declaring himself to be pro-civil rights and helping to enact the Voting Rights Act of 1982 (against the wishes of President Reagan), Dole led a vicious filibuster that killed the 1990 Civil Rights Act.

Condemning PACs as corrupt in 1982, and saying they wanted "something in return other than good government," Dole has led filibusters against any form of campaign finance reform ever since.

Dole is no more consistent when it comes to foreign policy. From the start of his career through 1988, he was a staunch supporter of Israel, sounding more hawkish even than Menachem Begin. After many American Jews refused to donate to his 1988 campaign for president, Dole urged a 5 percent cutback in U.S. aid to Israel and blasted American Jewish lobbyists for Israel as a "selfish" pressure group who put the interests of Israel above those of America.

Examples of Senator Dole's mercurial temperament include cozying up to Iraq's leader Saddam Hussein and urging "open vein" American loans and wheat sales to Iraq before 1991, and then after the Kuwaiti invasion calling Saddam the "Butcher of Baghdad." Dole supported the invasions of Panama and Grenada, yet opposed Clinton's forays into Somalia and Haiti. He opposed the creation of a special prosecutor for Iran-Contra but on Whitewater called for one. And, in 1995, Dole flip-flopped by condemning affirmative action, after staunchly supporting it for twenty-five years.

Dole's relationship with Oliver North has gone through numerous changes. When North ran as a Republican for U.S. senator from Virginia in the spring of 1994, Dole vigorously opposed him, and said he would never support North even if he won the Republican senatorial primary. North, called a liar by Reagan and convicted of perjury for lying to the Congress during the 1987 Iran-Contra hearings, was opposed by virtually the entire Republican establishment.* Senator John Warner (R-VA) personally put his career on the line by opposing North, and said he would support an independent candidate against North. But just four days after North won the Virginia GOP Senate primary on June 4, 1994, Dole publicly endorsed North, and even gave North a $5,000 campaign contribution from his leadership PAC, Campaign America.

That same year, Dole proclaimed: "There is no health-care crisis in America." Then he admitted otherwise, but said that his own modest proposal for reform, a totally toothless voluntary system, would solve the problem.

Perhaps it is kindest to describe Senator Dole as a pragmatist. As his colleague, Kansas Senator Nancy Kassebaum, has said, he "tends to move in whichever way the political winds are blowing." Dole's policy is summarized by the famous line of Stanley Baldwin, the former British Prime Minister: "I'd rather be an opportunist and float than go to the bottom with my principles around my neck."

---

*The conviction was later reversed on appeal.

5

"THE MARRIAGE OF THE HONORABLES"

Elizabeth "Liddy" Hanford became Dole's wife in 1975, after a three-year courtship. She graduated from Duke in 1958 with a B.A. degree, twenty-one years after Nixon had come away from the university with a law degree. Liddy Hanford shared Nixon's burning ambition, but little else. Liddy was born in 1936 in Salisbury, North Carolina, just an hour from the Duke campus in Durham. Her father was a florist magnate, and she grew up with a silver spoon in her mouth.

Attractive, brunette, and gregarious, Liddy Hanford's "Southern Belle" charm concealed a gnawing dissatisfaction with life and a resentment at having been born a woman in a man's world. What distinguished the young Liddy, more than anything else, was her adamant refusal to play the roles of wife, mother, and cook, which she had seemingly been destined for from birth.

After her graduation from Duke as a Phi Beta Kappa Scholar and May Queen in 1958, Liddy journeyed north to Cambridge, Massachusetts. She enrolled in Harvard's Graduate School of Education and later attended Harvard Law School, working part-time in the library. In the summer of 1959, she studied at Oxford University in England and visited the Soviet Union. The following summer, she worked as a secretary in the Washington office of North Carolina's Democratic senator B. Everett Jordan, and then joined the campaign of Democratic vice-presidential candidate Lyndon B. Johnson on a tour of the South in 1960. Her main interest was politics.

She was one of only twenty-five females in her 550-student Harvard law class and bristled with resentment at being snubbed by chauvinist professors who called on her rarely, only on "Ladies' Days." Hanford's law school classmates included Patricia Schroeder, who became a congresswoman from Colorado, and Elizabeth Holtzman, who became a congresswoman and district attorney in Brooklyn, New York.

After graduating with a law degree and a master's degree in education, Liddy moved to Washington, practiced law on her own briefly, and then got a job in the Department of Health, Education and Welfare. In April 1968, she became an assistant to President Johnson on consumer affairs, and she was also there to help Johnson promote his social welfare proposals. She said she was a liberal Democrat and supported LBJ on everything, charming the wily Texan, who called her a "sugarcoated steel magnolia."

When Nixon replaced Johnson in the White House in 1969, Liddy said she was a conservative and changed her voter registration from Democrat to Independent. One of only a handful of White House aides to survive the changing of the guard after the 1968 election, she showed remarkable powers of adaptability and a great instinct for bureaucratic survival.

She soon ingratiated herself with "Gloomy Gus" Nixon by parroting the latter's harsh anti-consumer, pro-business rhetoric. "She's a team player," Nixon noted in justifying his decision to keep her on the payroll. Here was a woman modeled after Nixon's own heart. Besides, she was a fellow Duke graduate.

In Nixon's White House, Liddy was a workaholic, dating rarely. Pleasant and personable, she made an excellent liaison to congressional staffs on Capitol Hill, federal trade commissioners, consumer groups, and corporate spokesmen. She worked directly under Virginia Knauer, with whom she had a good working relationship.

Nixon was so impressed by Liddy's loyalty that he nominated her to become a commissioner on the Federal Trade Commission (FTC), in 1973. She ran into some rough waters during her Senate confirmation hearings because many of the liberal Democrats in charge of the Commerce Committee were skeptical that she would represent consumers' true interests at the FTC. But she won them over by promising that she would be fair.

The Federal Trade Commission, a semiautonomous entity created by Congress under Woodrow Wilson in 1913 to regulate the nation's corporations and restrain them from chiseling consumers and engaging in "unfair competition," had jurisdiction to enact rules and regulations with the force of law, and to adjudicate disputes between companies, industries and consumers. As an FTC commissioner, Liddy acted the part of a judge, hearing from both sides in a dispute and issuing long, turgid, legal opinions crammed with esoteric reasoning. The job was high-profile, semi-judicial, and powerful. She was addressed as "The Honorable" Liddy Hanford.

Before joining the FTC, Liddy had been appointed to work on Nixon's 1972 Republican platform, and to write a "plank" spelling out the party's position on consumer rights issues. That's when she first met Bob Dole, while he was still RNC chairman and just a few months after he had divorced his first wife, Phyllis. She was immediately struck by Bob's resemblance to Nixon, whom she greatly admired. And she saw in Dole the same restless ambition and gnawing dissatisfaction with life that she herself had long harbored. Hanford felt she had met her match. To Dole, Liddy seemed the perfect foil to the plain-looking Phyllis. She was as unemotional and ambitious as Bob himself and she was rich and attractive. Another thing that appealed to the superstitious Dole was that Liddy's birthday was July 29, just seven days after his own.

Liddy Hanford was attractive to Dole for another reason. She represented the American dream. "She was the most eligible woman in Washington," said John LeBoutillier, later a GOP congressman, "and everyone wanted to marry her.'' Elizabeth Hanford was, for Dole, an incarnation of success, prosperity, the upper crust of American life. She was a trophy and his passport to a part of society that had been closed to him.

Bob and Liddy, the political odd couple, dated on and off and kept in touch for three years before tying the knot. Were they in love? "Love," said Bob, "is a disease of youth." They were friends more than people in love.

In Dole, Liddy recognized a man whose opportunism and towering ambitions matched her own, which included a lifelong desire to become the first woman president of the United States.

Liddy spoke regularly with Bob during his tough 1974 Senate reelection fight and urged Bob to go for the jugular in plastering Roy. After his narrow win, Bob thanked her profusely, then proposed marriage.

Bob introduced Liddy to his Kansas coterie of pols and pals, like Dave Owen. She liked Owen and would eventually hire him as an investment adviser for her blind trust. But she would cut him off when he became an albatross around her neck and Bob's.

By early 1975, Liddy saw herself as a passionate advocate of consumer rights during the heyday of Ralph Nader.* Liddy followed the political wind by issuing a series of FTC opinions and supporting consumers against Bob's own corporate clientele. Bob, himself, changed colors and began to assume his fiancée's line.

During the yearlong engagement, Dole mimicked Liddy's consumer rights antics in the Senate, sensing the anti-business climate in the air. On February 24, 1975, Bob rose to his feet on the Senate floor and praised Virginia Knauer, who had been Elizabeth's boss in the Nixon White House, as "a lady with heart" for her role as the "top consumer advocate in the [Ford] administration." Knauer, he said, "is a woman who understands

---

*Consumer rights were so fashionable in mid-1970s Washington that even Nixon's son-in-law, Ed Cox, worked as one of "Nader's Raiders."

and deals with human problems, not statistics." Three months later, on May 7, 1975, Dole spoke in the Senate on the need for "legislation to increase consumer representation in the federal government" and discussed his work on a consumer protection bill that, he claimed, had irritated "many in private industry and government."

Finally, the "Marriage of the Honorables" occurred. Bob and Elizabeth's wedding, which prompted jokes about "antitrust" implications of a "merger," took place on Saturday, December 6, 1975, and was a private fifteen-minute service performed by Senate Chaplain Reverend Edward Elson in the austere, molded stone and wood Bethlehem Chapel of the Washington Cathedral. The best man was Assistant Defense Secretary Robert Ellsworth, Bob's longtime Kansas friend, and the matron of honor was Elizabeth's sister-in-law, Burnell "Bunny" Hanford.* About seventy relatives, friends, and cabinet officers attended the wedding breakfast at the fashionable F Street Club. Among the guests were Julie and David Eisenhower and Secretary of Agriculture Earl Butz. Richard Nixon had telephoned his congratulations to Dole and Liddy the day before and invited the newlyweds to visit him in exile at San Clemente "for a cup of tea."

Dole's parents arrived from Russell, Kansas, on Thursday, December 4, and stayed at his Watergate apartment when the couple took off for a honeymoon in the Virgin Islands. But tragedy marred the Doles' honeymoon when, only two days after the marriage, on December 7, Bob's father Doran suffered a severe heart attack in Bob's apartment. He underwent surgery and died the next day. Shaken, Dole cut short his vacation and returned to Washington. He was eerily reminded of the bullet that had crippled him two weeks before the end of the war. A large portrait of Doran, who had missed only one day of work in forty years, hung above Dole's desk in his Senate office thereafter. As late as 1993, Bob cried

---

*Ellsworth is a former Kansas congressman and became Dole's initial campaign chairman in the 1988 presidential campaign.

uncontrollably on national television when reminded of his dad's visits to the hospital in 1945.

Dole wondered if he was under some sort of "curse." His gloomy, morose, dark side became even darker.

Devastated by the loss of his father, Dole eventually recovered and took up his life with his new wife. At age thirty-nine, this was Liddy's first marriage. She continued to work as an FTC Commissioner.

The political star of Elizabeth, as indefatigable as her husband, has risen along with that of Bob in recent years. And, if the nation elects Bob Dole to the White House, it will be electing not just an individual but a team—"Dole & Dole," as the buttons at the 1984 Republican convention read. These two highly motivated and fiercely independent people have managed to keep their marriage and their careers happily intact. They seem the model dual-career couple of the 1990s. When Elizabeth, under fire for being on the campaign trail and away from the job so much, resigned her position of Secretary of Transportation to campaign full-time for Bob in late 1987, some thought she had sold out. The *Louisville Courier-Journal and Times* said Elizabeth lost touch with the spirit of the women's movement "by using a stereotype about politicians' wives as an alibi for quitting." Others criticized her for deserting a department beset by problems, particularly air safety. Elizabeth countered, saying, "This is a personal decision, and that's what we women have fought for, the right to decide what is best in our own lives. I think playing a meaningful role, a substantive role in the democratic process that leads to the selection of the leader of the free world is meaningful work." In helping Bob, Elizabeth also gained national exposure.*

Elizabeth's prominence has sometimes irked Bob, a man who cannot stand being upstaged. His anxiety is particularly aroused by the suggestion that she might

---

*Interestingly, Liddy stands as a foil to First Lady Hillary Clinton, whose brashness has earned her the enmity of many. Liddy is much more palatable than Hillary, much more mellow.

become the first woman president or the GOP vice-presidential nominee in 1996 or 2000, and he is particularly annoyed by speculation that Elizabeth might become the running mate of a despised rival. The rivalry between Bob and Elizabeth is by no means bitter, however. Instead, it seems to have an invigorating influence. "We like to see who gets home last at night," Bob has said. "We try to spend time together—Sundays."

Bob's fears are probably well grounded. A week after he had announced his 1988 presidential candidacy in his hometown, a local woman walked into the drugstore where Bob had worked in his teens and announced loudly, "I wish he would step down so that I can vote for her." And, in Savannah, Georgia, where Elizabeth was campaigning for Bob in 1987, a woman in the audience was heard to declare, "She's got my vote. I think they're running the wrong Dole."

Liddy's popularity has exceeded her husband's even among his own staff. She frequently visits his office, and because of her buoyancy and charm, Bob's Senate and campaign staffers have been known to jump ship to work for her.

Mr. and Mrs. Dole, because of their perpetually busy schedules, have never found the time to look for a house; they still live in Bob's bachelor apartment in the Watergate complex. The shared experiences and family intimacy that bring happiness to most couples—a home, children, nightly dinners—are completely lacking in the Doles' marriage, but this absence never seems to have bothered either of them.

In 1984, Dole suggested that his wife be appointed United Nations ambassador to replace Jeane Kirkpatrick. "I think she needs foreign policy experience. She likes to learn anything," he said. Nothing came out of this suggestion and Elizabeth refused to comment on it, but it was an interesting statement, for the UN ambassadorship requires full-time residence in New York, 250 miles from Washington. Apparently, Dole simply does not need a full-time wife.

In her career, Elizabeth has shown the same agile pragmatism so amply demonstrated by Bob. As circumstances required, her ideology has changed from liberal to conservative, her party affiliation from Democrat to Independent to Republican. After serving Lyndon Johnson from 1968 to 1969, she served Nixon just as devotedly from 1969 to 1973. Although, at her confirmation hearing for the Federal Trade Commission, senators questioned her commitment to consumer interests, she proved to be her own woman. Once confirmed, she surprised everyone and disappointed Nixon with her pro-consumer and anti-business decisions. By the time she left the FTC in 1979, she had written more than fourteen decisions, many ruling against big business.

She served President Reagan loyally as a special assistant in the White House from 1981 to 1983. When Reagan appointed her Secretary of Transportation in 1983—a position in which her salary was slightly higher than Senator Dole's—she had had no experience in transportation or in managing a federal bureaucracy, yet she presided over 102,000 employees in nine branches, with a total annual budget of $28 billion. Among other accomplishments, she was credited with requiring all new automobiles after 1985 to mount a third red light in their rear windows. This brake light became known, unofficially, as the "Dole Light," and was credited with reducing the frequency of accidents by giving drivers extra warning of an impending stop by the car ahead. She was criticized, however, for failing to make public the results of crash performance tests of auto bumpers and for taking too much of a laissez-faire position in general.

During her four-and-a-half-year reign, Elizabeth also came under fire for not adequately managing airline deregulation and safety issues. Under her tenure, the skies became dangerously crowded around airports and the number of plane crashes increased dramatically, passenger complaints of lost and misplaced baggage reached an all-time high, and airports witnessed record delays and canceled flights. Commercial airplane accidents reached a thirteen-year high in 1987, with a record number of near misses, and the fatal-accident rate jumped almost threefold from 1986 to 1987. When she resigned in September 1987, one insider barked, "Well, at least she can't say she quit while she was ahead." And the *Los Angeles Times* published a political cartoon depicting the sky ridiculously crowded with jets, in between which a small biplane hurled a banner reading DOLE FOR PRESIDENT. The caption read, "I want to do for my husband what I did for the FAA."

In her capacity as Transportation Secretary Elizabeth once appeared as a witness before Dole's Senate Finance Committee. The press came out in droves, not to hear debate about an obscure bill involving a trucking tax, but to record the historic occasion: the first time that a husband and wife squared off as Senator and witness in a congressional hearing. The official topic was all but forgotten as they bantered back and forth, addressing each other as Mr. Chairman and Madame Secretary. Elizabeth testified, "I hope that we can come to quick agreement on these matters that are before us in all three houses." "It looks like you may get home first tonight," Bob retorted, "so you know what to do."

The Doles say that they keep their political and private lives separate, but problems almost inevitably ensue when a husband and wife lead separate prominent careers that intertwine, and they can lead to political embarrassment. In April 1984, both Elizabeth and Bob attended a party in Orlando, Florida. The party turned out to be a Bob Dole fund-raiser, and fifty developers there contributed a total of about $60,000 to Bob's campaign committee. The same developers were seeking the construction of a certain new federal highway interchange, a project under Elizabeth's jurisdiction. After the press got hold of the story Bob offered to return all the money to the developers.

The Doles' three-room suite in the posh Sea View Hotel in Bal Harbour, Florida, has also been the subject of speculation by the press. The hotel, a co-op, is managed by a corporation headed by Dwayne O. Andreas, chairman of Archer-Daniels-Midland Corporation in Decatur, Illinois, which happens to be a major producer of ethanol (gasohol), a cause Dole has championed in the Senate for years. This subject is covered in chapter 18.

Elizabeth has contributed much to Dole's campaigns. She's traveled all over the country giving speeches and raising contributions, sometimes with her husband but usually alone, and attracting praise and admiration. Although on the road, she undoubtedly has a say in strategy.

In January 1989, Liddy Dole was chosen by President Bush to be the nation's twentieth Secretary of Labor. During her two-year stint, she worked to increase safety in the workplace, improve relations between labor and management and upgrade the skills of the American workforce. She was especially interested in insuring that "at risk youth" received the skills and education needed to get a job in the workplace.

In 1991, Liddy Dole left the Bush administration and took on the position of President of the American Red Cross, which she holds to date. She oversees 23,000 staff members and over a million volunteers who make up what she calls the "world's top humanitarian organization." In addition to its main task of recruiting blood donors and drawing and screening blood for use in hospitals, some of the major activities of the Red Cross include providing emergency communication to the U.S. armed forces, collecting, processing, and distributing over half of the nation's blood supply, responding to national disasters such as floods, hurricanes, fires, and earthquakes, and teaching more than nine million Americans safety courses, including cardiopulmonary resuscitation and how to handle medical emergencies.

On her very first day on the job at the Red Cross, Liddy Dole said that the volunteers were the "heart and soul" of the organization and announced that she too would be a volunteer and would not accept any salary during her first year. She went on to accept a salary of $200,000 per year thereafter, however.

Liddy Dole's first job was to oversee the organization's largest wartime fund-raising drive since World War II. More than $26 million was raised during Bush's Persian Gulf War campaign in 1991, the proceeds of which went to Red Cross programs that assisted the armed forces in the Persian Gulf, their families at home, refugees, and the victims of the war. She has also raised more than $180 million for disaster relief worldwide.

Noting that the Red Cross owes the American public "compete fiscal integrity, and just plain good sense, when it comes to spending each and every dime," she also initiated several steps to increase the financial accountability of the organization, including creating a new position of "senior vice president and comptroller." During her tenure at the helm of the Red Cross, Liddy has overseen the implementation of the "Service Delivery 21" program, which includes restructuring Red Cross field operations to provide more efficient and effective assistance to the American public.

In May of 1991, to accommodate the AIDS crisis and the dangers of contamination, she announced a complete transformation of the way the Red Cross collects, processes, and distributes blood. But during Liddy's tenure, the American Red Cross has come under intense criticism for failing to properly screen blood. The nation's blood supply, much of which is gathered and coordinated by the Red Cross, has been found to be shockingly contaminated. The Food and Drug Administration (FDA) has taken legal action, and has sued the Red Cross for negligence, and in May 1993 the FDA secured a consent decree in federal court in Washington to raise Red Cross standards for testing blood.

In a February 23, 1994, letter, the FDA said the Red Cross "has failed to comply with the Consent Decree, and has violated the law." Even less charitable critics accuse Liddy of failing to properly run the blood division of the Red Cross. In March 1994, after a nine-week inspection, FDA inspectors found more than two dozen systemic problems at Red Cross headquarters. The Red Cross has lost track of blood, has not properly labeled blood, and has otherwise clouded the nation's blood supply under Liddy Dole's watch. It may soon be forced out of the blood bank business. The Red Cross presidency is Liddy's first job in the private sector, after twenty-five years of work as a government political bureaucrat in Washington. When she becomes sixty-two years old in 1998, she will be entitled to a hefty pension from the federal government that, combined with Bob's, will exceed $4 million.

Though she is no longer in government, countless fawning news stories about the "power couple" proliferate. One frequently repeated story is that Bob and Elizabeth were once so busy that they were surprised to run into each other in the reception line at the same dinner party.

Stories continue to circulate that Elizabeth might herself be considered as a future Republican presidential or vice-presidential candidate. But other stories, less flattering, have depicted Elizabeth as a sexless, selfish careerist without a real emotional or physical relationship with her husband. In the early 1990s, rumors swirled that the couple had separated, but Bob and Liddy said all was well. The couple often is seen publicly these days for Sunday brunch at Washington's Hay Adams Hotel, a stone's throw from the White House. There they are often joined by Dole's forty-one-year-old daughter, Robin, who works for a real estate company in government relations.

In the world of politics, fact is often difficult to distinguish from fiction, and yet some things clearly stand out: Elizabeth continues to be the major "iron lady" behind Bob's ambition, and would like to be First Lady or President herself. Like Bob, she is a creature of the federal bureaucracy, whose entire adult life has been spent in Washington, D.C.

Some of the more unkind Dole bashers have capitalized

on Liddy's Red Cross role as the "Blood Lady" of America, and have portrayed Bob as Count Dracula. Bob himself has joked on "The Tonight Show," "I give blood during the night," and he is seemingly amused by his wife's position as Red Cross chief. At least there, she has seemed as disorganized as he has during his presidential campaigns.

For all its limitations, the Marriage of the Honorables has proven to be an enduring blessing for Bob. The Bob and Liddy Show is alive and well inside the Beltway.

II

THE CLAY THAT SHAPED DOLE

That damn army almost killed him.

>   —Bub Dawson (hometown friend of Dole)

The White Whale swam before him as the mono-maniac incarnation of all those malicious agencies which some deep men feel eating in them, till they are left living on with half a heart and half a lung.

>   —Herman Melville, *Moby Dick*

6

FROM PARADISE TO THE GARDEN OF EDEN: "TO THE STARS THROUGH DIFFICULTIES"

Thirty miles from the spot where Bob Dole was born, a sign by the road reads: YOU ARE HALFWAY BETWEEN PARADISE AND THE GARDEN OF EDEN.* This is the exact geographical center of the continental United States, the heartland of America. Here at America's epicenter, as you drive past the town of Paradise (which, believe it or not, once had a mayor named Mayor Angel) and head into a vast expanse of wheat fields dotted by occasional oil rigs and farmhouses, the miles and miles of golden grain remind you that you are in the largest wheat-producing state in the Union and the heart of rural America, where tiny towns with odd names like Paradise, Lucas, and Luray pop up on the horizon and then fade away like mirages.

In the early nineteenth century, this part of the country was called the Great American Desert, a vast, empty, treeless land with a howling wind blowing ceaselessly out of the west in an unbroken sweep from the Rocky Mountains of Colorado. But today it is a remarkably productive land, whose true soul can be discerned in the Kansas state motto: AD ASTRA PER ASPERA—"To the stars through difficulties."

---

*The town of Luray is halfway between the towns of Paradise and Lucas, where the Garden of Eden—a striking collection of concrete statues depicting biblical figures and other subjects—is located.

Not so coincidentally, this state motto has been adopted as the presidential campaign theme of Bob Dole, whose roots are deeply implanted in the state where he was born. Located 240 miles west of Kansas City, just off Interstate 70, at the intersection of U.S. Routes 40 and 281, the hometown of Bob Dole—Russell, Kansas—is clearly marked by four huge billboard signs proudly proclaiming: WELCOME TO BOB DOLE COUNTRY: RUSSELL, KANSAS. Bold and brazen in their patriotic red, white, and blue lettering, they make certain that everyone who enters knows that this is the domain of Kansas's Kingfish.

Bob Dole still maintains his legal residence in his boyhood home at 1035 North Maple Street in Russell. On his occasional visits he likes to sit on the porch, pull on the special arm exercise device his father built for him half a century ago, and reminisce about the past.

Dole loves Russell because it reminds him of the time when he was still whole and still optimistic about life.

In many ways Bob Dole is a figure frozen in the past. His entire outlook was shaped by the Great Depression-dust bowl era of the 1930s, when the people of Russell faced life with stoicism and a harsh defiance. And they remember the phoenixlike resurgence of this tall, dark hero with the handsome Humphrey Bogart face, the shattered right arm, and the indomitable spirit.

The town lives by "gritty prairie values" such as the importance of hard work and obedience. "When Bob grew up in the '20s and '30s, he was surrounded by doers, achievers here in Russell," says Dean Banker, a third-generation clothier in Russell who used to fit Bob's father with 42-32 overalls. These were men like A. E. Seeley of "the Lucky Seven," a group of local bold and competitive entrepreneurs who had taken the risk of drilling for oil in a hitherto barren land, ten miles north of town and 155 miles from the nearest producing wells. These men risked their capital and their reputations for a dream, and Bob was deeply impressed by them, as he was by numerous other wildcat drillers who sparked the Kansas oil boom.

"Competition is the lifeblood of this town," Russell natives insist. "Even our sense of humor is based on competition; the idea is to get the last word in, by trading light banter, trying to be the most clever, the fastest wit, the guy who gets the most laughs." In Russell, such humor is called "one-upmanship." Frankness to the point of being blunt is also a common characteristic among Russell's citizens. The town's unofficial motto is: "Tell it like it is."

Closely related to the love of competition was the town's work ethic. "There's no such thing as a free lunch in Russell," Bob's brother Kenny Dole has said. "You gotta make the effort, you gotta go at least halfway, and the town will then welcome you with open arms," Dean Banker said. "There's a certain charisma to this town, a vibration. People who have lived here all their lives can sense it. It never leaves them. It's in their blood."

When Bob was growing up, Russell was growing as well. The population was 1,969 in 1920, 4,819 by 1940, and reached its peak of 6,483 residents in 1950.

The most powerful example of the town's work ethic was set by his own parents. Bob Dole was born in a two-room white house near the Union Pacific railroad tracks on Russell's Maple Street. (The house, razed in 1976, was located a block away from the house at 1035 North Maple Street where Dole grew up.) His parents, Doran and Bina (pronounced "Bye-na") Dole, had been married in 1921 with a reception inside Doran's own White Front Cafe. The second of four children, Bob was born two years after his sister Gloria; his brother, Kenny, was born fourteen months later, and his second sister, Norma Jean, was born in 1925. Bob was the only one destined to go to college and to leave the Russell area.

The town itself was founded in 1871 by a group of immigrants from Ripon, Wisconsin—by coincidence the birthplace of the Republican Party. Bina's father, Joe Talbott, arrived from Rising Sun, Indiana, in 1901 and was a farmer and an itinerant butcher who went from farm to farm slaughtering hogs and other animals. He married Elva Mitchell, fathered twelve children, and lived until 1960, the year Bob Dole was first elected to Congress.

Bob's paternal grandparents also arrived shortly after the town's founding. A farmer, Robert Grant Dole lost his property during the Great Depression and wound up on welfare. Bob's father, Doran, was born in 1900, served in the Army Medical Corps in World War I, bought the White Front Cafe at 833 Main Street in 1919 at the age of nineteen, and married Bina Talbott two years later. He was a hearty, muscular man who stood almost six feet tall and had a fierce independent streak, an entrepreneurial spirit, and a low-key sense of humor that worked wonders with farmers and patrons.

"Doran always had a smile on his face," said Dean Banker. Doran was a workaholic, a perfectionist, and a strikingly consistent man. "Pop woke up at five o'clock in the morning every day," Bob's sister Gloria remembered. "And, when his feet hit the floor, everyone else's had better be, too." Doran didn't get home until late in the evening, often near midnight. "He missed only one day of work in forty years," Kenny recalled. "When he wasn't working, he was serving as a volunteer firefighter—he finally retired at the age of seventy-four—or he was out at someone's home watching a sick person all night, and when he wasn't doing that, he was out hunting or fishing." Discipline was left up to Bina, who dispensed it with a belt or switch on Saturday afternoons, according to Dole. He grew up in a disciplined family, conditioned to work until he dropped.

In the 1920s Doran started a produce and dairy product exchange business, known locally as a cream and egg station, around the corner from his cafe. There he would sit for the next fifty years, acting as middleman among Russell County farmers, local merchants, and nearby creameries. At one point called Dole's Produce, the station was a focal point for business and social contact.

Typically, farmers would bring in cream, produce, chickens, and eggs, and Doran would pay for these with cash or by barter, sometimes exchanging utensils, tools, scrip, coupons for a drawing, vouchers redeemable at Banker's department store, or IOUs. Milk would be loaded and sent by rail to the Eisenhower family creamery in Abilene.

G. B. "Bub" Dawson recalls that when he'd walk to work with his brother at seven-thirty each morning "we'd always see the light on at Doran's cream and egg station." At night, Doran's light would still be on when every other business in town had closed. "There might be someone coming down the street to do business," Doran would say, and he would wait until the last light went out.

Bob took Doran's example seriously. One morning, Doran asked Bob to pick up some medicine at the local drugstore. Bob got there well before opening time, and was terrified to go home empty-handed. When Doran went to fetch him a half hour later (at 4:00 A.M.), the druggist recalls, "there was Bob, all curled up, asleep in the doorway."

When Doran was home, he was silent. "He didn't give out praise," Gloria says of her father. "You just were expected to do your work, and that was that. You didn't get a pat on the head from Dad." According to Bob, Doran always said, "There are doers and stewers," but Kenny remarked, "I doubt that Dad said that; he wasn't home long enough to say anything like that. I think that's Bob's own saying." Bob also tells the following story of "Silent Doran," the parsimonious praise-giver. "Kenny and I trimmed all the grass in our yard, just perfectly, to please Dad. It took us a week. Dad looked at it and said, 'Not bad—not good, but not bad.' " That motto, "Not bad—not good, but not bad," created in Bob Dole a certain insecurity. Bob would always feel unworthy of winning, because Doran had inculcated in him the belief that he was "not good" or at best just "not bad." In later life he would set himself up for failure, making the motto a self-fulfilling prophecy.

Like his father, Bob Dole is a workaholic and reluctant to praise. It is no coincidence that Bob has always kept a photograph of his father, in his glasses and trademark overalls, on the wall in his Senate office. Nor is it coincidental that, when asked on national television which U.S. presidents' portraits he would hang up in the Oval Office if elected, he replied: "I'd hang up a picture of my parents—of my father in his overalls."

Watching his affable and popular dad deal with farmers and merchants every day, the bashful young Dole picked up the skills he would later master as a national politician: offer the moneymen something they wanted. "Doran would empathize with every farmer who came into his station," Dean Banker recalls of Bob's father. "During the 'Dirty '30s,' when the price of wheat plummeted, the farmers would come in and rail against 'the interests' who 'rigged' the price of wheat. Doran would nod in agreement, smile, and commiserate with them. 'You know, I think maybe you got a point there,' he would say. And Bob, standing behind his dad, would take it all in."

Dole's mother, Bina, was as unusual as her name. In the 1930s, when women were expected to limit themselves to kitchen, children, and church, Bina went into business for herself as a roving saleswoman for Singer sewing machines. An outstanding seamstress, she struck upon the brilliant (and hitherto unheard of) idea of offering sewing lessons to anyone who bought a Singer sewing machine from her. "I think she started the first sewing classes in the country," Kenny recalls. "And she traveled all over Kansas."

"She even sold the products received from her patrons to Dad, at his cream and egg station," Kenny says, explaining that Doran would buy the products from his wife with cash and would then try to sell them to the farmers and merchants who came into his station. "Mom and Dad had a partnership."

Bina impressed Bob with a saying he later echoed: " *Can't* never could do anything,' she would say." If you set your mind to winning, self-reliance and aggressiveness would bring success, and that was that. Like Doran, Bina Dole had a seemingly inexhaustible reservoir of energy. Unlike Doran, she seemed affectionate and warm, and she was particularly fond of her oldest son. "Bob was very close to her," sister Gloria recalls. "Even when he went to Washington, he used to call her once every week at least." Bina worked hard on her son's election campaigns, nailing his posters on trees, hosting tea parties, and touring the state for him.

What is most striking about the Dole family, apart from its devotion to work, is the almost total lack of strong emotion, intense conflict, or hostility. Bob received no praise from his parents, but he experienced virtually no anger either. His siblings recall their parents as silent work machines who communicated the values of perfection and work through example, and who kept their anger pent up. In such a family, one didn't gain affection just for being *oneself;* rather, one gained admiration and respect *by being a hard worker.* Yet neither his brother nor his two sisters ever approached Dole's fanatical ambition or work habits. Kenny became an oil-lease broker and Gloria opened a beauty shop in Russell; sister Norma Jean married and moved to nearby Derby. Kenny became an oil lease broker in Russell (he died of cancer, at the age of sixty-eight, in 1993).

When the stock market crashed in October 1929, Bob was only six years old. The Great Depression devastated the local economy. The terrible drought of the "Dirty '30s" exacerbated economic woes. Throughout Kansas, hot winds swept across the parched fields, raising clouds of dust and darkening the sky each day by four in the afternoon until the land was one great dust bowl where nothing grew. The dust wiped out wheat fields, poisoned cows and other livestock, and even killed thousands of people with "dust pneumonia." "It got so bad, they actually found a cow with a plant growing inside its belly," recalls Dean Banker. "The cow had swallowed so much dust that a seed had actually germinated inside its stomach." Bob Dole helped his parents place rags underneath their doorjambs and put a wet rag into his mouth when the dust storms became particulary strong.

Nevertheless, Doran managed to keep his cream and egg station, and Bina continued to sell sewing machines. "Everybody's got to eat and everybody's got to wear clothes," Bob later said of this period.

"Everybody was poor, even if they didn't know it," says Russell Townsley, then publisher of the *Russell Daily News*. "There was really no social class structure in Russell, never had been," he adds. "Sure, there were disparities in wealth, but it was never a question of one social class refusing to talk to you because you were 'below' them or anything like that. Russell was just like one big family; people cared after you in those days."

"Russell is an extended family," said Kenny Dole. Dean Banker agrees. "If you tried to use your talents and met us halfway, we'd all chip in and help; that's how it was here in the '30s."

Bob recalls that in the 1930s "there really weren't lots of wealthy families in Russell. Poverty is a relative thing. I remember my clothes were handed down to my brother Ken, and Gloria's were handed down to Norma Jean. My father had an old car." Dole's family was not down-and-out and his parents were never unemployed. Bob found ample opportunities to work after school in the local drugstore and the cream and egg station. "Bob's father was a merchant," explains John Woelk, who lived in Russell in the '30s and later helped get Bob started in politics. "During the Depression, those hardest hit were the workers, who lost their jobs; next were the farmers, with wheat at twenty-five cents a bushel; then came the merchants, like Doran Dole." Woelk considered Dole's family actually upper middle class compared to other families at the time. The house in which Bob grew up is physically quite impressive for Russell. It is quite large and, though it has been remodeled in recent years, it must have been a status symbol of sorts for Doran Dole and his family.

Dean Banker, however, describes the Dole family as "lower middle class." Yet Kenny remembered his family's situation as even more desperate. "Every time Bob and I walked to school, we looked around for pieces of old cardboard on the street so we could put it inside our shoes and cover the holes."

In 1937, the Doles were forced to rent the main floor of their home to oil companies, which used it to house oil workers. The Doles, who needed the rent in order to survive, moved into the basement of their own home, a situation that was particularly humiliating for Bob and Kenny. "I was ashamed to go to school every day," Kenny said, adding that he never learned the details about the renting because "Mom and Dad didn't discuss finances with us."

Bob felt particularly bitter, realizing that everything was for sale, even one's own home.

Bob and his family were poor during the Great Depression, but they were not as poor as the millions of unemployed in the big cities of America. Bob tasted hard times, but not so hard as to make him bitter toward the rich or susceptible to the wave of populist oratory coming over the radio. He identified with Russell as an extended family, a small heartland community sufficient unto itself. His parents were Democrats, and Bob was treated to frequent doses of populist rhetoric from destitute farmers. Certain populist sympathies would reappear in Dole's political career, when he would side with "the little man" against "the interests."*

Ever since wheat had first been planted in the state in 1874—by Mennonites, who brought in turkey red wheat from the Russian Ukraine—"hayseed orators" had

---

*In Bob and Elizabeth's 1988 book, *The Doles: Unlimited Partners,* Bob says that his parents were originally Republicans, became Democrats when Bob was young, then switched back to the GOP when Bob ran for county attorney in 1952.

crossed the plains and the prairies like itinerant missionaries, preaching the homespun virtues and rights of the common man, denouncing capitalism, and sometimes espousing a virulent brand of anti-Semitism. The Great Drought of the 1890s had savaged the once-productive wheat fields, embittering Kansas farmers and filling their minds with fears of conspiracy and demands for government aid. Forty miles from Russell, in the tiny town of Lucas, a Civil War veteran named S. P. Dinsmoor invented a unique formula for concrete, sculpted a striking collection of statues, and placed them for public view in what he called the Garden of Eden. One of those statuary groups depicts Capitalism smashing Labor, a basic theme of populism.

Since the turn of the century, populist orators like "Sockless" Jerry Simpson and Mary Elizabeth Lease had rumbled through Kansas with fiery tongues. Fiery spellbinders, they told hungry-eyed farmers that "Wall Street owns the country. It is no longer a government of the people, by the people, and for the people, but a government of Wall Street, by Wall Street, and for Wall Street. The great common people of this country are slaves, and monopoly is the master." Some of the populists blamed Jews for the Depression. They echoed the anti-Semitic views of Father Coughlin, the demagogic "radio priest" whose fiery anti-Semitic harangues swept across the Midwest airwaves.

But in the '30s, Bob was too involved with sports, work, and school to take an active interest in politics. His acquaintances from this early period remember him as popular but "hard to get close to," a hardworking young man who wanted to be liked and thirsted for recognition and admiration. Hauling cream cans for his father helped Bob build up a muscular body and an obsession with physical strength. He began jogging around Russell at five-thirty every morning, and continued to do so for as long as anyone can remember. "Nobody else ran at five-thirty in the morning except Bob," Banker recalls. "You could always see him running through the streets, like a messenger, a man going someplace. He was huffing and puffing, going at it, like a man in a hurry . . . that and basketball and football and track . . . he wanted to be a Charles Atlas." He became a "magnificent physical specimen," according to Kenny. By the time he was a teenager in Russell High School, he was six feet, two inches tall and weighed 190 pounds, all of it muscle. "He was a Rambo before that name was invented," a neighbor explains. He ran while delivering newspapers and handbills, too, and never seemed out of breath.

His high school basketball coach, Harold Elliott, remembered Bob as "not the best athlete, but a fierce competitor. If you told him to climb a wall, he'd climb the wall." George Baxter, Bob's high school football coach, remembered a game in the late 1930s in which Bob "threw and caught his own pass and scored a touchdown." When asked later why he had played quarterback and receiver simultaneously, according to Baxter, Bob replied somewhat sheepishly, "I guess the ball just stuck to my hands."

When I worked for him in the Senate, Dole repeatedly asked, "Do I have to throw and catch my own passes?" as he furiously chided staffers for failing to live up to his high expectations. He sacked one campaign manager after another for failing to "catch his passes."

During the 1930s, according to Dean Banker, "Everyone in town came out to see the high school games, because in those days there were no professional or college teams, and the rivalry between Russell and Hays High was the most important topic of discussion, more important than the price of wheat." For weeks, people would be heard in the streets of Russell discussing the game in which Dole had been the hero.

In high school, Bob also had a job at Dawson's Drug Store, where he worked for a dollar a day. Wearing a white uniform, he helped the pharmacist fill prescriptions and dispensed sodas at the store's fountain.

He began asking questions of the doctors who came

into the drugstore, and he listened to their answers. "He saw that in the hard times the doctors were always the best-dressed men in town, the most respected members of the community, and the most secure," a friend recalls. "Bob was fascinated with the power over life and death that doctors had and with the fact that they were the most respected men. He wanted to be like them. He wanted to be liked."

"The soda fountain at our drugstore was the social center of town in those days," Bub Dawson recalls. "It was the town watering hole. Every afternoon, it would fill up with school kids and shoppers who stopped to have a Coke or some ice cream or food. Bob had a real following then. Kids and other people liked him; he got along well with people of all ages. He would come in after practicing football and basketball after school, and he would work until ten or eleven at night. I think he picked up a lot of his humor, his bantering wit, at the soda fountain . . . but he was hard to get close to." The soda fountain job helped Bob overcome his shyness. "The Dawson brothers, Chet and Bub, would always insult patrons," Dole recalled. "I thought I'd add in a few jibes to make sure they got what they paid for." Dole would later hone this talent on the political stage.

Alice Mills, who was principal of his school in the 1930s, recalled in the town newspaper, "He was not a leader or a follower—he was independent. When called upon [in class], he was always ready with the answer. He was not a show-off, nor did he seek special attention. He was alert and dependable, and he always looked right—exceedingly neat."

Mabel Lacey, Bob's seventh-grade English teacher, told the paper that he was a "splendid student. He always paid attention. Bob was there to learn what was before him. He was better than any of the others in his class, and I never saw anyone who didn't like him. He was always already in the classroom when I got there."

Faith Dumler, Bob's high school Spanish teacher, echoed these praises in the *Russell Record,* remembering

Bob as "a leader among the kids. He was well liked. I don't remember him dating. Bob and one of his very good friends, Bud Smith, who was killed in action, were both so good-looking. Bob was lots of fun. He had that banter wit that he still has, [that] put-down wit [that's] a prevalent area-type humor."

Bob's talents as a comedian are well remembered in Russell. A typical example is given by Faith Dumler: "Someone remarked they had just been to a beauty shop, and Dole would quip, 'Oh, you didn't get waited on, did you?' This put-down wit does indeed seem to be quite prevalent among Russellians." In Russell, the target of Dole's humor would generally counter with an even stronger insult, and a game of one-upmanship would ensue, whether at the soda fountain or in the courthouse. As his first wife, Phyllis, remarked, "When he started using that wit around people who didn't know him, he offended. But once you know him, you're not offended by it."

The versatile Dole got several other jobs, dug ditches for a while, and continued loading and hauling cream cans at his father's cream and egg station.* In addition, Dole managed to work as sports editor for the Russell High School newspaper, the *Pony Express*.

In the summer of 1941, Dole graduated from Russell High School, as a member of the National Honor Society and a star athlete. One of Dole's rivals for the 1996 GOP presidential nomination, Senator Arlen Specter (R-PA), also lived in Russell, Kansas, and attended the same high school several years after Bob.

"Our parents could give him only $65 for the whole year at KU [Kansas University]," Kenny recalled. "So,

---

*Doran Dole maintained his cream and egg station until the late 1940s, when such stations gradually faded away in the face of competition from large companies and farms. Doran then became an employee of the Norris Grain Company, managing its grain elevator next door to his old cream and egg station, until he retired.

he had to get a loan on his own." Resourceful as always, Bob asked a Russell banker, George Deines, to lend him $300 and promised to earn it back by waiting tables in Lawrence. According to Kenny Dole, Deines presented it to him along with the advice to wear a hat because "guys who move up in the world always wore hats." He went off to KU with his best friend, Bud Smith, sporting a fedora and suit. He joined a fraternity, worked as a waiter, and pursued undergraduate pre-med classes. He also made the team in football, basketball, and track, but found the competition at KU far keener than at Russell High School. "I realized I wasn't quite the athlete I thought I was," he later said.

Track became his true love. He came very close to breaking an indoor track record for the quarter-mile at the university, competing even harder than he had at Russell High and earning block letters for his college sweater. As high school coach George Baxter said, "Bob never competed in the easy track events." He went in for the 440- and 880-yard events and continued jogging alone at 5:30 A.M.

To Bob Dole, running in the early-morning mist of Lawrence in the fall of 1941, the war raging in Europe seemed a million miles away. He would sweep through KU and medical school and then become a respected and secure country doctor.

7

CAPTAIN AHAB AND LIEUTENANT DOLE

Dole's most formative experience occurred on April 14, 1945, when he was shot on the battlefield in northern Italy, abandoned by his fellow soldiers, and left to die. Dole has never felt "whole" since. Like Captain Ahab, who embarked on a lifelong vendetta against Moby Dick, the whale that had bitten off his leg, Dole has embarked on a lifetime crusade for revenge against the loss of the use of his right arm.

At virtually every 1988 presidential campaign speech he recounted his war injury and recovery and seemed lost in a daze. His audiences, bewildered yet mesmerized, went away wondering why he was talking about 1945 instead of 1988. In his most recent Senate campaign in 1992, Dole again regaled crowds with the recounting of his grievous injury, unfair fate, and brave comeback. When some veterans of more recent wars complained that he was improperly exploiting his ancient war wounds, Dole froze in anger, wondering why they could not appreciate his "sacrifice."

What really happened on that terrible day?

Dole was enrolled as an athletic, carefree student at Kansas University (KU) when the United States entered World War II in 1941. Unlike many gung-ho youths of his generation, Bob was not interested in rushing to sign up for military service. Instead, he wanted to finish up his studies and attend medical school.

He finished his freshman year in May 1942, while hundreds of thousands of boys his age were either enlisting in the armed forces or being drafted. That summer nineteen-year-old Bob lived at home and worked odd jobs, looking forward to his return to KU, but he could hear the rumble of the Union Pacific passenger trains streaking past his house at night, carrying troops now as well as civilians, as the arsenal of democracy shifted into high gear for the war effort.

At the start of his sophomore year, the dean called him into his office and told him, "You're not doing very well; you might be better off in the army." Never academically inclined, Dole was just "sowing oats," as he later confided.

Dole, who had been priding himself on being the only member of the family to go to college, now realized that he had to put his academic plans on ice. Horrified at the thought of being drafted into the army, mixed in with the faceless, uneducated masses of the U.S. war machine, Dole set out to find a way to serve the country as an officer. By joining the medical corps, he figured he would come out of the war with credit toward his medical license and follow in the footsteps of his father, who had been in the Army Medical Corps during World War I.

In December 1942, Bob enlisted in the U.S. Army's Enlisted Reserve Corps but spent the next six months finishing out his sophomore year at KU, far from the din of gunfire. His brother Kenny also enlisted and the two were called to active duty in June 1943 and headed for army training at Camp Barkley in Texas.

At the time of his departure from Russell, Bob was an Adonis, young and athletic, but he would return two years later in a body cast, unable to look at himself in the mirror—the withered shadow of a man destined to spend the rest of his life trying to recapture what he had left behind.

After his stint at Camp Barkley, Bob went on to study engineering at Brooklyn College in New York. In early 1944, Bob finished his classes at Brooklyn College, moved on to Camp Polk in Louisiana, and was trained as an anti-tank gunner at Kentucky's Fort Breckenridge. He was accepted for Officers' Candidate School (OCS) and entered Fort Benning in Georgia with the rank of corporal.

While Dole was training to become an officer, the Allies invaded Europe. On D day, June 6, 1944, the Allies launched the long-awaited second front under the unified supreme command of another Kansan Dole had heard much about—General Dwight David Eisenhower. By the end of August 1944, Paris had been liberated, the third U.S. Army under General George S. Patton had stormed across France, and a kind of festive spirit pervaded the U.S. Army as its forces tightened the noose on Nazi Germany. Rome was already liberated, but the German troops, retreating into northern Italy, continued to mount a fierce resistance to the Allies. Mussolini, deposed by his own Italians in 1943 and then reinstated by Hitler as a puppet ruler, now directed shadow armies.

Bob's OCS crash course training lasted three months. On graduation as a second lieutenant, he found himself headed for Naples, Italy, on a troop ship that arrived shortly before Christmas 1944. From Naples, Bob went to a replacement depot near Rome, where he awaited assignment to a combat unit.

He was a second lieutenant now, and he realized that in combat, second lieutenants held the most dangerous position of all, because they led their platoons into the thick of battle and were the most visible target to the enemy. "Second lieutenants were the real cannon fodder of World War II," says Al Nencioni, Dole's sergeant at the time.

On February 25, 1945, Dole was assigned to I Company, 3rd Battalion, 85th Regiment in the legendary 10th Mountain Division. Now fighting in the northern Apennine Mountains of Italy, this was one of the most formidable fighting units in the U.S. Army. Back in 1940, a full year before Pearl Harbor, the head of the National Ski Patrol, coincidentally named Charles Minot "Minnie" Dole (no relation to Bob), came up with the idea of establishing a unique elite army unit of mountain troops whose purpose would be to wage mountain warfare in places as diverse as Norway, Burma, and the Alps.* Minnie Dole convinced the War Department to organize the mountain unit and began recruiting volunteers who were mostly experienced skiers and athletes, many from the ski slopes of New England, Utah, and Colorado. The glamorous crack unit attracted recruits thirsting for adventure and glory.†

One of the first such recruits was Devereaux Jennings, a young skier from Utah. Jennings, unlike Bob, emerged from the war unscathed and went on to compete in the 1948 Olympics. He remained close to Bob Dole and served as national cochairman of Veterans for Dole in the 1988 presidential campaign.

The 10th went into action in early 1945 in the Italian Apennines, and had just successfully battled the Germans for Mount Belvedere when Bob Dole joined it as a replacement officer in late February 1945. Dole was assigned to lead the second platoon of I Company. "We had the highest esprit de corps you could find," Nencioni recalls. "A lot of those guys were college guys; they'd been on their college skiing teams, including the captain of the Dartmouth skiing team. They had an esprit de corps from their school, and I think it just went right into the unit.

"We had a lot of guys who were great big athletic, boxer types," says Nencioni, and these men made Dole, who was then a second lieutenant, look almost wimpy. Along with Jennings, another future Olympian, Ollie Manninen, was in the company, but there were also a lot

---

*Being superstitious, Bob Dole always felt fate had played a big role in his life, and he pointed to the fact that Minnie Dole had the same name and played a major role in creating the army unit that would cost Bob his arm.

†The 10th Mountain Division still exists. Its most recent assignment, in 1994, was to invade Haiti under President Clinton.

of intelligent, college-educated athletes. "The first two regiments probably had the highest IQ of any infantry ever in the history of the army," Nencioni says. "They told us the regiment I was in had an [average] IQ of 122, which meant that everyone could go to OCS, but hardly any of them went because they wanted to stay enlisted."

Walt Galson, then an enlisted soldier, remembered, "I was approached by an MP and told, 'Here's this young lieutenant fresh out of OCS; could you give him a lift?' He had only fuzz on his chin and seemed so young."

"He [Dole] came in as a replacement, which isn't easy," Dev Jennings recalls. Jennings, who served directly under Dole as a sergeant in the 2nd Infantry platoon, and who was very close to Bob throughout his combat tour, recalls that the young Dole "started asking questions as soon as he got there. He really adapted himself and learned what was going on very quickly. He was always cool about things and very human. He never intimidated people or got outwardly tough. He was brave and very respected by the staff and the whole company. He was the best officer I ever had, he listened and really wanted to know what was going on. Before we made a move he'd call us to come and take a look, and he'd show us what the plan was and make sure the communications were right and that we understood things."

I Company was referred to as a "suicide squad" because it took staggering losses. From the time Dole joined the unit, I Company was "pretty much under fire all the time," Jennings says. Dole's troops were "subjected to artillery fire all night when you're in defensive positions and along ridges and when you're out on patrols. There wasn't any real time in between when it was 'sweet.' We didn't bivouac, we just lay there in the hole [at night]." I Company served as the spearhead of attack, often encountering Germans ensconced in dugouts on the sides of the rugged mountains.*

_____

*According to Jennings, I Company began in early 1945 with 6 officers, 188 enlisted men, and 3 medics. By the time the

Al Nencioni, who handled the mortars in the platoon, recalls Dole as a particularly brave and even reckless officer who showed no hesitation in charging into combat. Nencioni and the other troops found they could trust Dole and rely on his judgment and bravery "right down to the nitty-gritty. I'd rather have this guy [Dole] lead a company than these other type of guys," Nencioni says to this day. Dole seemed to fit in well with the troops. "I think some of our spirit rubbed off on him," Nencioni explains.*

Dole's leadership qualities were an important ingredient in the 10th Mountain Division's relentless drive to mop up the tail end of German troops still clinging desperately to the mountains of northern Italy. The 10th became legendary for never giving up a foot of ground it had captured and for being willing to sustain severe casualties in order to achieve its objectives.

Dole's suicide squad saw some of the fiercest fighting in the European theater. "The battalion lost between 60 and 70 percent of its men," Nencioni recalls. Dole himself suffered a slight leg wound in March 1945, and earned a Purple Heart, but he went right on leading his platoon as the 10th launched Operation Craftsman, a massive assault on German positions in the Po Valley.

But in the early hours of April 14, 1945, American bombers began dropping their bombs over a German-held area not far from Bologna, in the hills along the Pra del Bianco Valley.

---

company finished off the Germans in early May 1945, it had received the following replacements: 5 officers (including Dole), 181 enlisted men, and 4 medics—striking evidence of a huge casualty rate. Dole later called I Company a suicide squad.

*Nencioni, who would suffer a concussion shortly after Dole's injury, went on to become an FBI agent for twenty-six years. Operating out of the Washington field office, he frequently visited with Dole during the latter's congressional tenure in the 1960s. A talented musician and composer, Nencioni won a music performance prize in Italy after the end of the war and went on to compose the "FBI March" under J. Edgar Hoover.

Postponed for two days because of bad weather, the massive ground assault was now about to begin in full fury. Dole and his platoon had camped along the ridge of a mountain during the night where they had received reinforcements. Their objective that morning was to cross the valley and storm the German-held Hill 913, about a thousand yards away. Mines posed a major hazard to the troops.

U.S. planes blasted the area with bombs until "the hill looked like a cloud of smoke filled with dust," according to Nencioni. "We didn't think it would be too bad, so we took off." Dev Jennings, Dole's sergeant, recalls that "we jumped off at about ten-thirty or eleven in the morning, on the front side under very heavy fire." The hill erupted like a volcano as the orange of exploding gunpowder permeated the land and the *rat-a-tat-tat* of machine-gun fire crackled across the air.

"Our objective [that day] was to go three miles," Nencioni recalls. "There was a hedgerow and other obstacles in the way." "When we got there, we were met with heavy artillery, machine-gun and sniper fire," says Jennings, who was leading his own squad to the right of Dole's unit, when Dole's squad found itself ambushed. The Nazis threw everything they had at the Americans— machine guns, rifles, mortars, even a "rocket that was the first I'd ever seen," says Jennings. "It looked like a cigar."

Dole was filled with raw anger and a protective instinct for his comrades as he saw them mowed down like bowling pins. He spotted a farmhouse near the base of Hill 913 from which Nazi gunfire crackled. The original orders called for Carafa to lead the men across the clearing while Dole remained behind, but, according to Technical Sergeant Frank Carafa, Dole altered the orders and personally led a squad of men toward the enemy gunfire.*

---

*There may have been something self-destructive in Bob's seemingly reckless quest to flirt with disaster by charging into battle.

In the din of the assault, Dole saw his radioman go down. Dole hauled the radioman back into a hole, then charged out again when something suddenly hit Dole in the back and right shoulder. "He was hit twice, I believe," Nencioni says. Whether it was bullets or mortar fragments, Dole went down for good.

Platoon Sergeant Stanley Kuschick ran to Jennings, shouting, "The lieutenant's been hit!" Kuschick ordered Jennings to lead his squad to Dole's left flank, where help was badly needed.

According to Nencioni, Kuschick administered a shot of morphine to Dole and then "he took Bob Dole's blood and made a big M on his forehead, so nobody would give him any more morphine" (thereby preventing a dangerous overdose). Dole "didn't look good," Kuschick told Nencioni at the time, adding that he didn't know whether Dole would "make it or not."

Combat troops are trained to keep driving forward toward their objective and to leave the killed and wounded behind. But Stanley Kuschick ignored these rules and ordered a soldier who had been shot in the leg to stay with the fallen Dole until help arrived. Nencioni says, "Because our objective was three miles out, we had to keep going. So, in that sense, he [Dole] was 'abandoned.'" The platoon made it to the top of Hill 913 that night, wondering what had become of its fallen lieutenant.

The 10th Mountain Division pushed on to crush the Germans and bring about the surrender of the Italian front commander at the Brenner Pass on May 2, 1945. According to Nencioni, the German commander, who had seen action on the eastern, western, and Italian fronts, stated that the 10th Mountain Division "was the best division he'd ever faced."

Dole lay on the battlefield in a semiconscious stupor, unable to feel his legs or arms, miles from any medical facility. As his whole past life raced before his mind's eye, he claims to have "seen" his old dog, his parents, and childhood friends. "It was a long day," he would later remark.

He might well have died had it not been for a wonderful stroke of luck. As dusk set in, a twenty-five-year-old U.S. Army private named Bill Roberts spotted him. Roberts, whose detail was about to march down a winding ten-mile road to an ambulance pickup spot with seven German prisoners, noticed the red M on his forehead, and checked for signs of life. Dole was still breathing but paralyzed (two of his vertebrae had been crushed, and his right arm was a mangled, bloody mess).

Private Roberts ordered two German prisoners to carry Dole on a litter down the mountain road. Once the small detail was shelled by the enemy. Later, a U.S. tank driver saw the Germans carrying the litter, and ordered his tank crew to fire. Roberts barely managed to countermand the order by identifying himself. Finally, Roberts's detail inched its way to the ambulance rendezvous, and Dole was driven to a medical aid station. "I think Jesus was with us that night," Roberts said forty years later when he learned for the first time that the nameless young lieutenant he had brought down the mountain on a litter that night was in fact Bob Dole.

He was treated at an army evacuation hospital and transported to a base hospital at Casablanca, Morocco. His parents were informed of their son's injuries in a chilling telegram sent to them in Russell, Kansas, by J. A. Ulio, the adjutant general, which stated:

THE SECRETARY OF WAR DESIRES ME TO EXPRESS HIS DEEP REGRET THAT YOUR SON 2LT DOLE ROBERT J WAS SERIOUSLY WOUNDED IN ITALY 14 APRIL 1945 PERIOD HOSPITAL SENDING YOU NEW ADDRESS.

Bob dictated letters to his parents from his hospital bed. A month later he was shipped to a Florida army hospital in a body cast, "like furniture in a crate," he would later recall.

A hospital train then bore him home to Kansas, and he was admitted to the Winter General Hospital in Topeka. When his parents arranged to bring him home for a brief stay, the entire town was on hand to greet the wounded hero.

"He looked like someone who had just come out of Dachau," said Bub Dawson, one of his old Russell friends. The strapping young athlete who had been a magnificent physical specimen at 190 pounds when he had left Russell two years earlier had come back a shrunken invalid weighing only 120 pounds. And yet he had a positive mental attitude, a cheery outlook that amazed practically everyone who saw him.

Back at Winter General Army Hospital, Dole faced long months of painful recovery. "That damn army almost killed him," his friend Bub Dawson would later recall. Kenny Dole added, "They kept him in that body cast, didn't bother to move him at all, so the sulfa drugs they gave him crystallized in his kidney, and he lost the kidney."

Dole developed a severe infection in his kidney, and his temperature rose to 108.7 degrees. "I remember going to visit him in his hospital room," Kenny Dole said. "He was so badly infected, his arms hung out over the sides of his bed, and the pus dripped from under his fingernails and into buckets they had on the floor." The doctors told Bina that Bob had only a few hours to live. She rented an apartment near Winter Hospital to be near her son and visited him night and day, giving him encouragement throughout this difficult time. On July 11, 1945, doctors operated to remove Dole's right kidney, which had developed kidney stones as well as an infection due to the crystallization of the sulfa drugs. Amazingly, Dole recovered from his surgery, but he never forgot nor forgave the army.

In the meantime, the army gave Dole what he later called a "bedpan promotion" to captain. He began to recover, and each day his mother helped him relearn to walk, though it was many months before he could stand up without assistance. Doran also regularly came to visit his son, shuffling onto crowded trains, where he had to stand up, and arriving with his ankles swollen because of an edema.

As has happened to so many wounded and crippled war veterans, the bedridden Dole found himself haunted by the question, "Why me?" As he admitted more than forty years later, his faith was shaken as he found himself wondering "if anyone was looking out for me up there. With only three weeks left in the war, why did I have to get hit?"

During this time, he was "completely helpless . . . I couldn't feed myself for almost a year or do anything with my hands." He required assistance even to go to the bathroom and to dress, and when he got the first real look at himself in a mirror since he'd been wounded, he was shocked. Kenny quoted Bob as vowing to "get back the ten years he lost" because of his injury by living extra hard and driving himself with all the more determination and by fighting the specter of "dependence." Bob himself said he "lost three years" in army hospitals, and so claims he is three years younger than his real age.

In the army hospital, his bitterness toward his doctors—"the experts," as he would derisively refer to them—was compounded when they told him he would remain a cripple for life. He rejected their professional opinion, and for years refused to believe that he would never regain full use of his limbs. Still quite helpless as 1945 drew to a close, however, Bob was moved in his plaster body cast from the Topeka hospital to the Percy Jones Army Medical Center in Battle Creek, Michigan. The hospital, bursting with 11,000 patients, was a major amputation, orthopedic, and neurosurgery center.*

There he remained for the next two and a half years. Whether this move from Topeka to Battle Creek was

---

*Dole's ex-wife, Phyllis, says that Bob was also treated at Hines Army Hospital near Chicago during this time, but Dole has never mentioned this.

medically necessary is debatable. Certainly, it could not
have helped his morale, for it took him far away from his
parents and friends, particularly from his mother, who
had practically moved in with him in Topeka's hospital.

Just before Christmas 1945, Bob developed a dangerous pulmonary infarct, which lead to severe chest pains.
Menacing blood clots, which easily could have killed
him, developed and dicumarol was administered to dis-
solve the clots. The doctors insisted on total inactivity
and then inexplicably and abruptly terminated the dicumarol treatment. The consequences of this decision were
nearly fatal. Bob developed a severe infection, producing
a 106-degree fever. Penicillin failed, and Dole would have
died had it not been for a new, experimental antibiotic
called streptomycin. Because the new wonder drug was
considered dangerous, Dole's parents had to consent to
its use.

While streptomycin saved Bob's life, there would be
no medical miracle to restore his atrophied, virtually
useless right arm. For the next two years, Dole struggled
to regain mastery of his body.

Initially put in traction, he advanced to a wheelchair
and then tried to struggle to his feet. Falling often, he
disdained assistance and tried to pick himself up—a
discipline of extreme self-reliance that would carry
through to his Senate years when he tried to do everything by himself and kept aides at an arm's length.

Dole also occupied himself with tasks as diverse as
reading everything from Plato to military history, selling
cars to fellow patients (for a commission), and making up
jokes for them as he was wheeled around to various
wards to cheer them up. His talent as a comedian, impressive in Russell before the war, was now honed to a
razor's edge. Humor became his antidote to the grim
realities of his physical condition, and a shield to camouflage his true feelings of being a "victim."

Dole's brother, Kenny, believed Bob's fierce drive was
further honed by his struggle against falling back into
helplessness. "He just can't stop; he can't slip back at

anything in life," Kenny noted. "He won't dare wear a clip-on tie or loafers, he won't let others do things for him, because he knows that if he ever stopped, it'd be all downhill, and he'd wind up where he started." Dole would always act with fierce independence, shunning assistance and refusing to delegate tasks to his staff, an extreme self-reliance that is both a strength and a weakness.

Dole spent the long, lonely days at the hospital in a desperate campaign to strengthen his legs, learn to dress himself, eat, and write with his left hand. At first, it took him half an hour to button a shirt and even longer to knot a necktie or tie a shoelace. He challenged himself by playing a little game: each day, he would mark down the number of minutes it took to perform a task, then try to beat his own record. The game rekindled his competitive energies, and he pretended that he was "competing against another guy. If I hadn't tried," the author heard him say more than thirty years later, "I'd still be in a wheelchair now, drawing disability."

While he regained the use of his legs and left arm and hand (though the fingers of his left are partially numb to this day), his shattered right arm and shoulder remained physically grotesque and useless. The muscles in his arm and shoulder had atrophied horrendously and Dole remained intensely uncomfortable about the useless arm that hung from his shoulder. Photos show him with the arm permanently bent as if in an invisible sling.

A less determined or vain man might have been content to carry his arm in a sling for the rest of his life, but Dole demanded that the army operate, feeling that the country owed him at least that much. The same Dole who would later object to being photographed wearing eyeglasses (which he occasionally uses for reading) now shuddered at the thought of going through life as a Captain Ahab, a cripple.

When the army rejected his request for special surgery to cure the arm, Dole refused to give up. With the characteristic thoroughness that would mark his later years, he began making the rounds among the patients, asking each one whether he'd heard of any appropriate doctors. Finally, he struck gold: a patient named Bill Eilert, injured in Okinawa, had heard of a Dr. Hampar Kelikian in Chicago, a surgeon who might be able to help.

Dole's uncle made contact with Kelikian, an Armenian immigrant who had risen from poverty to become one of America's top surgeons, who volunteered to operate on Dole without charge.

But the Chicago hospital told Dole that he would have to pay a hospital fee of $1,800, and Dole had no money. At this point, the Russell VFW started a Bob Dole Fund, placing a cigar box on the counter of Dawson's Drug Store. Some people contributed $100, others a few dimes.

The cigar box drive enabled Dole to go to Chicago in 1947 for three operations, which left him only with *partial* use of his right arm. At least, he could now hold a piece of paper or a pencil in his right hand, but he would never be able to write with it or do anything heavy. For many years, he had difficulty controlling his right arm; it would sink to his side, so he would have to reach over with his left hand and lift it back up, like Dr. Strangelove. It remains permanently angled at his waist. Although he can move it a little, he cannot lift it high on its own power. His right hand is permanently gnarled as well, which is why he always holds a pen, pencil, or some other light object in the hand as camouflage.

Dole would be forever grateful to Dr. Kelikian for the "miracle" operation that enabled him to feel, at least, "sort of whole again." Kelikian, too, kept in touch. When Dole married the following year, the Armenian surgeon sent him a telegram: USE THAT ARM I FIXED LOVINGLY. Later, Dole had to go back to the hospital for additional surgery on his arm, and he experienced severe pain for years, but in terms of physical appearance the operation was a stunning success.

For many years, Dole remained self-conscious about his withered arm and studiously avoided discussing it. But in 1983, when Kelikian died, those suppressed feelings came gushing forth in a mighty torrent. On the Senate floor he delivered a moving eulogy. Midway through his speech, however, he was overcome with emotion and had to leave the Senate chamber.

When he discovered that Kelikian had paid all the hospital fees, Bob returned the $1,800 to the local VFW. Kenny says that the citizens of Russell then decided to apply the money to a "Chevrolet especially made for Bob, with a gear stick on the left," which a local welder and car buff had pieced together.

After his three operations, Dole returned to the Percy Jones Army Medical Center in Battle Creek at the end of 1947 to finish his long convalescence. By this time, he had been presented with a second Purple Heart for his injury in combat and with a Bronze Star with Clusters for heroism and bravery under fire, and had been promoted to captain.

By a curious twist of fate, in the hospital Dole found himself in the company of two other wounded servicemen who would join him in the U.S. Senate twenty years later—Daniel K. Inouye of Hawaii (who also lost an arm in the war) and Philip A. Hart of Michigan, for whom the Hart Senate Office Building, housing Dole's office, would one day be named.

As he lay in his hospital bed, day after day, Dole pondered what kind of a future he had now, with one good arm and a precarious medical condition, a college education half completed, his dream of becoming a doctor shattered. "You think nobody could have it worse than you, why did God do it to me," he recalled many years later. "I didn't do anything, it's unfair. . . . You think, 'I'm never going to get married, never going to amount to anything.' Might live off a pension, might end up selling pencils for a living. You change the way you measure everything. Life becomes a matter of learning how to use what you have left."

"What he had left was his head," Kenny recalled. In a phrase he often repeated to explain his seemingly impulsive actions, Bob said of this period, "You have to make a decision." He made that decision with the savage intensity and tenacity that would mark his entire career. He resolved to compensate for his physical deficiencies by "running at 110 percent," to race by "at seventy-five miles per hour while everyone else was doing fifty-five." His drive became phenomenal.

From his hospital bed, the young man who had once aspired to be a track star now watched some of his comrades from the 10th Mountain Division competing in the 1948 Olympic Games. Now that Dole could no longer excel in sports, politics seemed a perfect outlet.

Early in 1948, Dole made two decisions that would help lift him out of the hospital bed: to look for a wife and to complete his college education. With characteristic determination, he began appearing at social functions at the Officers Club in Battle Creek while still at the hospital. One day he spotted a young occupational therapist named Phyllis Holden and asked her to dance. A rather plump, modest-looking woman who held a bachelor's degree from the University of New Hampshire, Phyllis had been working in the psychiatric ward of the Percy Jones Medical Center. Hailing from a Concord, New Hampshire, upper middle-class family, she was socially a cut above Bob. She wasn't Miss America, as he later noted, but she was "something."

Within a few weeks, he asked for Phyllis's hand and she agreed. They were married June 12, 1948, a bare three months after meeting.

The wedding took place in Phyllis's hometown in New Hampshire, at the Episcopal Church attended by the bride's family. Phyllis recalls that the only member of Bob's family to attend was Bina. The newlyweds honeymooned at Lake Winnipesaukee, New Hampshire, and then headed west.

After his marriage, Bob arranged for his discharge with what the army called a "total and permanent disability." He began receiving a veteran's disability pension and financial assistance on the GI Bill for his college work.

Dole would go on to collect an army disability pension for the rest of his life.

That fall, Dole and his new bride took the train across the prairie. He enrolled as a junior at the University of Arizona, and once again resolved to become the first member of his family to get a college degree. Phyllis worked in occupational therapy, her specialty being psychiatry, and helped pay the rent. Contrary to myth, she did not attend classes with Bob. "I attended classes only occasionally," she told the author, "and only showed up to write his exams, as he dictated them to me, if the professor didn't allow him to take oral exams. But usually they let him take orals."

Dole went to classes armed with a sound-scriber machine, a heavy box with two little plastic records, obtained from the Veterans Administration. He sat in a chair near a wall, plugged his sound-scriber into the socket, and recorded all of the professors' lectures. At night he played the records and meticulously took notes on the lectures with his left hand. "It would take him hours to transcribe all the notes each night," Phyllis recalls, "because he wasn't naturally left-handed."

Dole enrolled in a course in German, a deeply symbolic choice. Instead of blaming Germans for costing him an arm, he blamed the enemies of Germany.

"He set goals for himself in every class," Phyllis later recalled. "He always had to get A's. Once, while he was studying German, I asked him, '*Why* do you have to get all A's?' He answered, 'You tell me how to study a B or C's worth and I will. . . . I gotta study until I get it all.''

The University of Arizona had no law school at the time. It did offer Arizona residents a reciprocal law school education at the University of New Mexico, but since Dole was not an Arizona resident, he was ineligible. Once again, society had shut the door in his face, and he was furious. By the spring of 1949, the young Kansan faced the prospect of returning home to law school, just when he had grown accustomed to the haunting desert scenery and the climate of Arizona. He had set himself the goal of going into politics and resented the bureaucratic mentality of the university, which seemed as unreasonable and unfair as the army medical bureaucracy he had battled for the previous three years.

Frustrated, he ran harder into the desert winds, which Phyllis believes to be the reason why blood clots began reappearing in his lungs. That spring he was forced to check into a Veterans Administration hospital in Tucson, where he was subjected to a battery of blood tests and given medication to thin his blood. The problem, a recurrence of the lung obstruction that had nearly killed him in the army hospital in Michigan, made his future all the more uncertain. This time, however, his hospital stay was relatively brief. He emerged from Arizona feeling like a carpetbagger and returned to Kansas in the summer of 1949.

His lung and blood problems persisted, and he was obliged to bypass Kansas University because there was no medical lab in Lawrence sophisticated enough to give him the ongoing blood tests he needed. The only Kansas city that had both a lab and a college was Topeka, so Dole enrolled at Washburn Municipal University in the fall of 1949 and pursued a joint bachelor's and law degree.

During Dole's first year at Washburn, America was embroiled in an anti-Communist hysteria that swept the country like wildfire. Following Truman's upset reelection victory over Thomas Dewey in 1948, the president had found himself on the receiving end of a savage political assault by the right, which accused the Democratic Party of losing China to the Communists and of giving away half of Europe to Joseph Stalin. The Soviet Union had exploded its first atomic bomb and imposed the Berlin Blockade, initiating the Cold War. Truman had countered by announcing the program of foreign aid and containment called the Truman Doctrine, and young right-wing Republicans like Congressman Richard Nixon were earning a name for themselves in Washington by blasting the "party of treason" in sensational hearings of the House Un-American Activities Committee.

In the Midwest, anti-Communist hysteria ran especially high, with Republican Senator Joseph McCarthy of Wisconsin announcing to the world in 1950 that he had a list of countless "card-carrying Communists" working in the State Department and other government agencies. As McCarthy ranted, a whole army of real Communists invaded South Korea, and the beleaguered Truman ordered U.S. troops into action in that far corner of the world in the summer of 1950. The president's approval ratings in the polls plummeted to an all-time low of 26 percent. As Dole later put it, 1950 "was not a very good year to be a Democrat," especially in a state like Kansas. The ambitious law student who had his own ideas about the incompetence of the government and the army listened excitedly.

John Woelk, who was Russell County Attorney from 1949 to 1953 and a Republican, was looking for a good man to challenge incumbent Democrat Elmo J. Mahoney for the seat in the Kansas House of Representatives, representing Russell County in the Eighty-First District. Since the Kansas legislature met in Topeka, and since Dole was a law student there with an interesting past, Woelk and several other Republicans tried to recruit him.

"I didn't know back then whether he [Dole] was a liberal or a conservative," noted Woelk, "and I still don't know, and I don't think he knows, either."* Nonetheless, it seemed logical to Woelk and his friends to back Dole. "Besides," Woelk noted, "he needed the money, and the legislature does pay something," although that salary was small.

Knowing that Kansas GOP voters outnumbered Democrats two to one, Dole agreed to run. "It didn't take much persuasion," Woelk recalls. "Whenever it came to running, he was more than willing. He enjoyed campaign-

*Woelk, who still lives in Russell, told the author, "Bob doesn't have any strong philosophical beliefs; he's a practical politician." He added that Bob was "very good in dealing with people; he knew how to handle people."

ing.'' Dole worked night and day on his race for a state seat.

Dole's immediate and wholehearted embrace of the Republican Party served a deep psychological need. Now he had a vessel in which to chase his Moby Dick. He energetically defended his newfound party in a manner that struck observers as fanatical.

His first Democratic opponent, incumbent Elmo J. Mahoney, was a colorful homespun character with a great gift of gab. But Dole won the seat for the Eighty-First District by 2,576 to 1,803 votes and became one of 125 representatives in Kansas's lower house (105 Republicans and 20 Democrats).

In the official handbook of the Kansas legislature for Dole's first team, 1951–52, Dole looks strikingly boyish. The youngest member of the legislature, at age twenty-seven, he is surrounded by colleagues, all of whom look old enough to be his father or grandfather.

Then, as later, Dole compiled an outstanding attendance record in the legislature, making certain he was present for all key votes and debates, no matter how obscure the bill or the issue. ''The legislature was in session only three months of each year,'' Phyllis recalls, ''and they met only in the mornings, when they met at all . . . Bob arranged to take his classes at Washburn University in the afternoons so he could attend the legislature in the mornings.'' He saw the legislature as a part-time debating club when he graduated magna cum laude from Washburn with his bachelor's and law degrees, in 1952.

Just as Dole graduated, another Kansan was being nominated by the GOP for President of the United States. Dwight D. Eisenhower of Abilene was virtually certain to trounce the hapless Democratic candidate, Adlai Stevenson. Like Dole, Ike had been selected as an ''instant Republican'' because of his war record. Dole was inspired by the Kansas farm boy from Abilene, whose prominence was another good omen for his own political future.

On his first day back in Russell, Dole rented a new office and hung up his shingle. "I remember it was a very modest office," recalled Eric "Doc" Smith, another young Russell lawyer, who formed a law partnership with Dole and then became a judge. "The first thing Dole did was to go out and buy a magnificent, very expensive chair that he put in his little office. I was struck by the fact that it looked like a hundred-dollar saddle on a ten-dollar horse."

"Dole ran his law office to *please people*," John Woelk recalls, "he wanted to be liked, to impress."

An obsession with making a good appearance extended to his clothing as well. He wanted to be the sharpest dresser of all, the man who would stand out far from the competition. The adulation he had once craved and received as a high school athlete he now eagerly sought as a smartly dressed attorney. His suits were altered with padding on the right shoulder to conceal his withered arm. Dole would go to Banker's clothing store, where a chubby German tailor measured him. "The tailor would mumble, *'Ja, ja,'*" Dean Banker recalls, "and Bob would stand there for hours, insisting that every inch of the suit was a perfect fit." Dole has remained a fastidious dresser to the present day. His attire is always impeccable and elegant.

Bob's vanity and sensitivity about his appearance extended to his face. In a photograph taken with several young lawyers and politicians on Russell's Main Street in 1952, he was caught wearing eyeglasses—for the first and last time. To this day he avoids wearing glasses in public, slipping them into his pocket at the approach of a photographer.

In the same 1952 photograph, Dole can be seen with his right hand in his pocket, a ploy that worked only to a point. When a stranger offered to shake his right hand, Dole would wince uncomfortably as he held out his left hand, thumb down. Eventually, he developed various other tactics, such as holding a coat, pencil, paper, or a very light briefcase in his right hand. Al Nencioni, his old army buddy who visited him in his congressional office in the 1960s, recalls seeing Dole *always* carrying a little briefcase or pencil, even in his own office. The camouflage tactics had become habit, already second nature to Dole.

Phyllis played an important part in helping Dole live with his handicap. "Probably the most important thing I did," Phyllis said, "was not treating him as handicapped but treating him as normal. I knew when to ask if he needed help, when not to . . . I think what it has to do with is not pressuring him to help him. To perhaps notice if he needs a little bit of assistance and do it quietly without making an issue of it."

Phyllis remembered most vividly how difficult it was for Dole to shake hands with his left hand. "That took courage," she noted, "to shake hands and have people notice that he couldn't shake hands with his right hand."

One of the most embarrassing moments came when Dole tried to cut steak one night at a restaurant. Because he could not hold a knife and fork at the same time, the task was impossible. "We learned early on to have it done in the kitchen," Phyllis said. He also tended to drop glasses and spill drinks because his left hand was initially quite weak and had to be repaired in another operation after their marriage. But he learned and survived.

For Bob Dole, the struggle for survival was an ongoing war that had to be fought every day on many battlefields for the rest of his life. "I've got to confess," he said forty years later, "I think there was a time when, you know, you get depressed because you can't do things. I don't mean you go into a depression, but you're frustrated and you want to get angry with yourself. And you know when you've got to have somebody help you dress and undress when you go the bathroom, you go back to those years; now that gets pretty touchy sometimes. So, I think there probably was a time when I just had not quite half recovered when I got maybe a little too independent for my own good."

For Bob Dole, the war will never be over.

8

THE REAL WAR BEGINS

For Bob Dole, the real war was going to be fought not in the mountains of northern Italy, but in the halls of power in Russell, Topeka, and Washington. It was to be long and bitter, the enemies were Democrats, and he would take no prisoners.

Those who criticize Dole for being a senator for sale or a dirty campaigner must realize that in Dole's view, a political soldier has to do whatever it takes to win. Dole knew from the start that the ammunition needed is money. The first special interest group that Dole sought support from was the oil industry. In 1950s Kansas, wildcatters were discovering astounding quantities of black gold buried beneath the flat plains and wheat fields. Oil men flocked to Kansas from Texas, Oklahoma, Louisiana, and other oil states.

In 1952, Russell County Attorney John Woelk, the man who had recruited Dole to run for the legislature two years earlier, announced that he would not seek reelection. "The county attorney positions were always very hotly contested in the elections," Woelk explains, "because they were a stepping-stone for clients or if you wanted to go into politics."

Bob Earnest, another young Russell attorney and a Democrat who would run against Bob Dole six years later, says that Bob found the law far too mundane and always yearned for the excitement of politics. As far as

Dole was concerned, the law was just a means of earning an income and an entrée into politics, a chance to meet oilmen and Republican kingmakers who were often lawyers and judges.

The county attorney had an office in the county courthouse in Russell, and was responsible for representing the state and the county in criminal and civil matters. The salary was "less than the janitor made," Dole said, but it was an entry into the political battlefield, and Dole thirsted for battle.

Local Republican movers and shakers favored Dean Ostrum, another young lawyer and a son of a lawyer, although Woelk denies this. In the end, however, Dole won the nomination over Ostrum, the establishment candidate.

Dole was "an unusually good listener, and he sounded out people for their advice," Dean Banker recalls. "Some people advised him to declare his candidacy in the city of Russell, but another fellow suggested he announce in Bunker Hill [a small town in Russell County] because that was the hometown of Ray Shaffer, who was Russell County Republican chairman. Bob said, 'I'm gonna announce in Bunker Hill. That'll impress Shaffer, and he'll endorse me.' So we went to Bunker Hill."

Banker introduced Dole at a meeting in the high school auditorium of Bunker Hill. Banker was a "warm-up man" well known for introducing a singing barbershop quartet before Rotary Club meetings, and his family was well known countywide for its clothing store. In his announcement speech, Dole dutifully paid homage to Shaffer and his wife and won their hearts.

Dole's manners extended to the courtroom. Judge C. E. "Ben" Birney, then a district judge in Graham County and a Republican party activist, would later recall Dole's unusual politeness when he came before the bench in a trial or hearing. And Russ Townsley, the *Russell Daily News* publisher who covered Dole's trials in court, recalled his deference toward the judges. John Woelk commented, "He identifies with politicians, not with the common man."

As the August 1952 primary approached, Dole simply outcampaigned Ostrum, managing to overcome the latter's advantage of wealth and status. Dole beat Ostrum by a scant fifty-two votes in the GOP primary. Dole then defeated George Holland, his Democratic opponent, by a two-to-one margin, 4,207 to 2,065, on the same day that Eisenhower was elected president.

Dole was sworn into office as Russell county attorney in January 1953 by a wizened old district judge named J. C. Ruppenthal, whose son Phil had been Dole's high school pal. Photographs of Bob then depict a lean, serious-looking young man with an intense expression. Strikingly absent is the broad smile he had worn prior to his wartime injury. In photos from the 1950s, Dole looks like a man with a chip on his shoulder or, as Dr. William Roy, one of his later opponents, would say, "a man with something burning deep inside his gut."

He launched into the job with relentless energy, prosecuting criminals and traffic violators, mediating family and business disputes, and explaining the law to myriad county workers and officers. He also began to build a small private practice, but his heart was never in it. His caseload consisted mainly of real property title work, divorces, and family law—pretty drab stuff for such a volatile and energetic personality. One day, Bub Dawson recalls, Dole showed up saying he had a case. Dawson rounded up Bob's brother and friends, saying, "Hey, Bob has a case." Everyone thought it was a case of beer. But it actually was a real legal case.

In court, Dole impressed many with his fiery wit and agile mind. He was particularly effective against Norbert Dreiling, a Democrat and an attorney from nearby Hays.*

---

*Dreiling, Kansas Democratic Party chairman from 1966 to 1974, severely criticized Dole over Watergate. His hometown, Hays, has been one of a handful of Democratic strongholds in Kansas.

"Whenever those two got together for a trial," Russell Townsley recalls, "the whole town wanted to come out and see them go at it. It was the best show in town, better than watching a prizefight." Dole would watch his opponent make an oral argument before the judge and then typically brush past him and make some remark like "That was a stupid thing to say. Haven't you read the rules?"

Gradually, khakis had come to replace overalls in Russell, and oil came to rival wheat in value and importance. The oil boom reached its peak in the 1950s, when there were more than 3,000 oil wells in Russell County alone and Kansas was one of the biggest oil-producing states in the nation.* More than 60 percent of Russell County's valuation was now attributable to oil, while only 40 percent was based in farming and real estate. America was roaring into the age of the automobile with a booming economy, interstate freeways were crisscrossing the land, and oil was king in Kansas.

Dole ran unopposed for reelection as county attorney in 1954, and he defeated Democrat Clifford Holland (brother of George) in 1956 by a vote of 3,175 to 2,319. Increasingly confident, he hit upon a brilliant scheme to attract support in 1957. That year the state legislature infuriated the oil industry by imposing an oil and gas severance tax of 1 percent. The tax also angered farmers who received royalties for oil produced by wells on their land. Dole filed a quo warranto suit, asking the court to declare the law unconstitutional on several different grounds.

One of those grounds was a technicality, and Dole clearly exploited it to the hilt. Article 2, Section 16, of the Kansas Constitution provided that in order for any bill or law to be valid, its "subject . . . shall be clearly expressed in its title." The Supreme Court of Kansas, in

---

*To the present day, Russell's official emblem is an oil rig. In the 1950s, Russell County alone produced about five million barrels of oil per year (today it produces about four million).

an opinion issued in January of 1958, agreed with Dole and declared the tax statute unconstitutional because its title was "fatally defective." The oilmen and the royalty-earning farmers went wild. He had single-handedly saved them millions of dollars.

"Bob attracted the financial support of the oil industry because of his role in nullifying the severance tax," according to John Woelk. When he became a candidate for Congress, oil money would flow his way. For the first time Dole reaped the benefits of protecting a special interest group.

Dole also took an active lead in prosecuting companies and individuals who had allowed saltwater to escape into streams and then onto the soil, damaging farmers' land. He reached out to farmers, supported their interests in the courtroom and the courthouse, and appealed to their populist tendencies by speaking out against "the interests" who were "ruining your land and mine." Just as his father had done, Bob spent hours listening to farmers airing their gripes against the powers that be, agreeing with them, and promising to look after their interests.*

His popularity was not limited to rural Russell County. In towns across the county, Dole impressed common people as a brilliant, angry, and witty firebrand who deserved their votes because he was tougher and better than anything the competition offered.

Dole displayed an appetite for work as impressive as his ability to pull rabbits out of hats for the oilmen. "Every night," Dean Banker recalled, "I would walk by the county courthouse and see only one light still on—Dole's. Even the janitor left before he did." Often Dole would appear at a party at seven o'clock and leave by eight so that he could return to the office to work until

---

*One of the most disheartening tasks facing Dole as county attorney was that of approving monthly welfare benefits for his paternal grandparents, former tenant farmers who had been kicked off their land. This is a story Dole frequently tells in his stump speeches in order to emphasize his humble roots.

midnight. "He'd come home at midnight, sleep in the basement, and then be off by five the next morning," Bub Dawson recalled. "It didn't make for much of a home life."

One night the hours paid off and he struck pay dirt. McDill "Huck" Boyd, publisher of the weekly *Phillips County Review* in Phillipsburg and a Republican power broker (he subsequently became state GOP chairman and a GOP national committeeman), drove through Russell near midnight and noticed Dole's lights still burning. Deciding that he wanted to meet the government official who worked that late, Boyd went up the stairs and introduced himself to Dole. He'd also heard about Bob's work for the "oil boys" and wanted to shake his hand. Thus began a thirty-year relationship that would help propel Dole to the pinnacle of national politics.

Dole finally gained entry into the old-boy network that ran the state GOP, the old "Alf Landon machine," which had originated in the '20s and '30s and dispensed political patronage.* The '50s were a transition period between machine and independent political processes in Kansas. With the advent of television and the decline of political parties, especially after 1960, the bosses' clout declined.† But Dole liked what he saw. One day, he would create his own fearsome Kansas machine, which would dwarf Landon's and make him the Kingfish of Kansas.

In the 1950s, if you wanted to get elected in Kansas, you still had to have the endorsement of the old Landon machine bosses—men such as Boyd, Dane Hansen, Lacy Haynes (editor of the *Kansas City Star*), Harry Darby,

*Landon was governor of Kansas and the GOP presidential nominee in 1936. Landon reached his one hundredth birthday in September 1987 and died one month later. His daughter, Nancy Landon Kassebaum, has been a U.S. senator from Kansas since 1979.

†In the mid-1960s, for example, the Kansas Republican Party lacked coherent leadership and became badly factionalized. Dole steered an independent course during this period and acted as his own political mentor, according to Russell Townsley.

and Landon himself. They operated by word of mouth: if they liked you, they would call their friends at the newspapers, oil companies, and the financial power-houses.

Dole, again playing the role of dutiful son, buttered up Boyd. He made known his strong interest in running for Congress, and Boyd encouraged him. He became increasingly active in Republican Party organizational and promotional activities all over west-central Kansas, collecting political IOUs, and building a personal network of supporters. He made a personal pilgrimage to secure boss Dane Hansen's support.

Dole was more ruthless among his peers. According to Norbert Dreiling, Dole "just took over" the local Russell County Republican political machine in the mid-1950s. He ruthlessly pushed out John Woelk, his first patron, who was part of the liberal wing of the Kansas Republican Party and a rising state senator. "He just cut the support from under Woelk and took it over himself. That was the end of Woelk's political future," notes Dreiling. Woelk never forgave Dole for this and remained bitter thirty years later.*

Dole ran for Russell county attorney for the last time in 1958, beating Democrat Bob Earnest, 2,807 to 2,195. Earnest, who later took over some of Dole's private practice caseload after his election to Congress, says that "Bob channeled his competitive energies from athletics into politics. He made his brain act as his arms and legs."

Harry Morgenstern, who was Russell County sheriff when Dole was county attorney, recalled Dole as "kind and personable, but if a person was wrong, he was wrong—no matter who he was. Bob hated to see children abused; that was one thing he didn't tolerate, if he knew about it. He had a good personality, was very neat, and always got everything done. He was businesslike, but had time for everybody. He had a good sense of humor, yet could be real stern when he had to be."

*Dole's ruthless trashing of Woelk is similar to his abandoning of Dave Owen thirty years later. See chapter 27.

As the '50s came to a close, the aging two-term President Eisenhower prepared to leave office and the congressman serving in Dole's Sixth District was getting tired. A huge and gregarious man with strong ties to the oil industry, Wint Smith had represented Kansas's Sixth District in Congress since 1947. Nicknamed "The General," Smith had always been a man of action, serving as a Kansas highway patrol commander before embarking on a frustrating congressional odyssey. He had defeated the hapless Elmo J. Mahoney, Dole's first opponent back in 1950, in the 1958 congressional election, in which Dole campaigned for Smith. Smith had become frustrated with what he called a "do-nothing, stalemate Congress."

Traveling around the state in his khakis and a huge cowboy hat, Smith quietly put out the word among Landon's old boys that he would gladly retire in 1960 if the right man could be found to replace him. Smith handpicked Bob Dole.

Dole became known as "Wint's Golden Boy," and the Alf Landon machine went busily to work endorsing him, lining up oil money for his campaign, and otherwise spreading the word among the largely conservative, Republican newspaper editors to endorse Dole.

It was 1960, the year of Francis Gary Powers's ill-fated U-2 flight over Russia, the aborted summit meeting between Ike and Khrushchev, and the rise of John F. Kennedy. The Cold War was raging, Nixon was about to be nominated as Ike's successor, and the nation's voters were trying to decide whether they wanted four more years of staid Republican rule or the "new frontier" offered by the young Catholic senator from Massachusetts.

The Sixth Congressional District of west-central Kansas was a huge, largely rural area with considerable anti-Communist as well as anti-Kennedy sentiment. Dole kicked off his campaign at Topeka's Jayhawk Hotel, the political hub of both political parties in Kansas at the time, on Kansas Day, January 29, 1960. On March 2, 1960, Mary Humes, a clerk in the Russell County courthouse, wrote a letter to the editor of the *Salina Journal* endorsing Dole for Congress. Humes praised his "integrity, character, intelligence, and capacity for public service." Humes's letter gave Dole a populist hue, which he exploited cleverly by presenting himself to poor farmers as "one of you."

In photos from this election campaign, however, Dole sports a perpetual scowl. Dole might have been a shoo-in had it not been for a charismatic young Republican state senator named Keith Sebelius, who denounced Dole as "the candidate of the special interests," specifically big oil. Sebelius, who hailed from Norton, in northwestern Kansas, displayed considerable gumption in taking on Dole. He had unsuccessfully challenged Wint Smith himself in the 1958 GOP congressional primary election and was something of an iconoclast. Sensing that there was something sinister about Dole that bothered a lot of voters, Sebelius tried to exploit latent Populist sentiment by painting Dole as a puppet of "the interests," while presenting himself as the independent and conscientious champion of the common man.

Dole was infuriated. As the August primary approached, Dole was particularly incensed when a third candidate named Phillip J. Doyle of Beloit, Kansas, appeared on the ballot. Dole was convinced that Doyle had been put up by Sebelius as a ghost candidate to confuse voters with his similar-sounding name. "In those rural areas," Dole's first wife Phyllis recalls, "people often pronounced 'Dole' and 'Doyle' the same way, so they were confused as to which one Bob was. In addition, Doyle's first name was Phillip, which was similiar to mine, and he had the middle initial J, which was also Bob's middle initial."

In an effort to eliminate the confusion, Dole hit upon the novel idea of stocking his campaign rallies with cans of Dole pineapple juice. Dole publicized his rallies and meetings by announcing that Dole pineapple juice would be handed out to anyone who showed up. "We had to get special clearance from the Dole Corporation to use their name and their product," Bob's brother, Kenny, recalled. "They said to us, 'Anything that promotes the sale of Dole pineapple juice is fine with us. Go ahead and use all you want.' And we sure did." The pure, wholesome image of pineapple juice also had great voter appeal in Kansas, which was still a dry state.

Supporters of Dole began spreading rumors that Keith Sebelius was an alcoholic. This stemmed from a visit of Sebelius to a church carrying a box filled with groceries for the needy. Unfortunately for Sebelius, the box happened to bear a whiskey label and insignia, and a photographer managed to snap his picture as he entered the church. Soon there were rumors that Sebelius was bringing whiskey into a church for drunken parties.

In retrospect, the mudslinging sounds similar to later Dole campaign tactics. Sebelius's widow disliked Dole for the rest of her life. When her husband died in 1982, she refused to invite Dole to a reception at her house, and declined to even talk to him.

Though federal prohibition had been repealed in 1933, liquor was permitted by law in Kansas by the drink only at certain private clubs and could be sold only in specially licensed liquor stores; not even beer could be bought off the shelf. It is easy to understand why even the mention of booze in association with a political candidate would make fundamentalist voters shudder.

Dole had a talent for coming up with original slogans and techniques. His two campaign slogans were "Young Man on the Move" and "Roll with Dole"—which accurately captured his incessant activity and indefatigability. He designed a wheel-shaped campaign business card that he and his aides handed out on every street corner and on every farm they could reach. The card was three inches in diameter. On one side was his photograph, surrounded by the words R. J. BOB DOLE—REPUBLICAN—CONGRESS. On the other side was a colorful blue-and-red wheel with twelve spokes. At the hub was the name BOB DOLE; on the rim were the words PUT YOUR SHOULDER TO THE WHEEL AND ROLL WITH DOLE IN '60. On each of

the twelve spokes were the candidate's achievements:
BORN 7-22-23 . . . KU & WASHBURN . . . METHODIST . . .
RUSSELL NATIVE . . . LEGISLATURE 1951 . . . WON 7
ELECTIONS . . . BOY & GIRL SCOUTS . . . SEC. 4-H FAIR
ASSOCIATION . . . SER. OFF. VFW & AM. LEG . . . ELKS-
MASON-KIWANIAN . . . CO. ATTY. 4 TERMS . . . TWICE
WOUNDED VET.

The Bobolinks were another popular campaign tool,
and originated when Mary Humes was working at the
Russell County courthouse and mentioned to Dole that
her daughter, Nancy, and her friends—students at nearby
Fort Hays State University—sang in a barbershop quartet. Dole eagerly seized on the idea and formed the
Bobolinks. The original group consisted of four girls from
the Russell area: a pair of twins from Lucas, Dorothy and
Delores Voss; Nancy Humes, who played the ukulele;
and Bonnie Langdon, who went with Dole to Washington
as his secretary after he won his election. The girls were
later called Dolls for Dole.

"We traveled around with him from town to town,"
Dorothy Voss recalls. "We would go door to door and
sing a song for the voters. We would go into stores and
meetings, too."* Dole organized several other groups of
singing girls in different towns. When he showed up, they
would greet him with a campaign song. One song went:
"Knick, knack, paddywack, Roll along with Dole. . . ."
Childish, but it worked.

Phyllis and Bina Dole sewed special dresses and skirts
for the Bobolinks and other young women and girls who
appeared with Bob at campaign rallies and posed with
him for photos. In one such photo, dated July 23, 1960,
Dole is crouching down, surrounded by twenty-four females wearing identical dresses and huge buttons in the
shape of a sunflower sporting Bob's face and name. His
own daughter, Robin, wore a dress with the message I'M

---

*Dorothy was so devoted to singing for Dole's campaign that
she stood up her future husband on their first date in order to
show up with the Bobolinks at a Dole campaign rally.

FOR MY DADDY. ARE YOU?* Dole continued to use the Bobolinks and Dolls for Dole as late as his 1974 Senate campaign.†

At the GOP primary in August 1960, Dole got approximately 16,000 votes, Sebelius 15,000, and Doyle only 4,400. In the heavily Republican Sixth District, defeating Sebelius virtually guaranteed Dole a victory in the November general election. Against Democrat William Davis, of the far western Kansas town of Goodland, he won a seat in Congress by a three-to-two margin.

Bob went to Washington at the same time that John F. Kennedy entered the White House. In the Capitol, Dole felt like a true outsider, a backbencher who occupied himself primarily with agricultural issues. He won a seat on the House Agriculture Committee, where he excoriated Kennedy's farm policy and questioned the wisdom of selling American wheat to the USSR.

Dole championed anti-Communism, the rights of the handicapped and veterans, and farming interests during his years in the House. He compiled an impressive overall attendance record of more than 90 percent, one of the highest in Congress.

Garner Shriver, also a congressman from Kansas in the 1960s, remembers Dole as attending "only those social functions where there would be people who had come a long way from Kansas to see him. . . . He used to work the phones a lot, and we used to call him a workaholic back then. Because of that, he was a loner; he didn't have many close friends. When he wanted something accomplished, he was relentless and aggressive in hanging on until he got what he wanted." In addition, like so many others who knew him, Shriver recalled that Dole "used his handicap politically, to an advantage" by appealing for a sympathy vote.

Another Kansas congressman, Larry Winn, who rep-

*Robin was born in October 1954 and is Bob Dole's only child.
†Sebelius later won this same congressional seat when Dole moved up to the Senate in 1968.

resented the Third District in the 1960s, recalled Dole as "the hardest-working person I ever met in my life" and noted that "his humor often gave the impression that he was a smart aleck, but he was so good that he could be a stand-up comic if he weren't in politics."

In 1962, Kansas lost one of its six congressional districts through reapportionment, due to its population decline. As a result, Dole's Sixth District was merged with the old Fifth into a new First District that now included fifty-eight counties. Spanning the entire western half of the state, the new First was one of the largest districts in the country, presenting Dole with quite a challenge as he sought reelection.

He faced a tough opponent in incumbent Democrat J. Floyd Breeding, a popular congressman from the old Fifth District. Realizing he needed a big issue to earn name recognition in this still largely rural, conservative, and anti-Kennedy area, Dole decided to publicize some shady dealings that Billie Sol Estes had been involved in.

On March 29, 1962, the FBI arrested the thirty-seven-year old Estes, a crony, fund-raiser, and former aide of Vice President Lyndon Johnson, on fraud charges involving forged mortgages. In February 1962, Dole introduced a House resolution calling for a congressional investigation into the Department of Agriculture's handling of Estes's cotton allotments and other matters. Dole accused the Kennedy administration of suppressing evidence linking Estes to Lyndon Johnson. On June 8, 1962, a Republican congressional committee, echoing Dole, charged that a counsel on a House subcommittee had been fired when he found out Estes had been bribed by Johnson, and the whole affair led to Senate and House investigations. Estes was subsequently convicted of mail fraud and of conspiracy to swindle farmers by selling them nonexistent liquid fertilizer storage tanks on the installment plan.

Dole gained considerable publicity, becoming nationally known after articles appeared in *The New York*

Times, and earning kudos back home. He defeated Breeding in November 1962 by 21,000 votes.

His popularity was not universal, however. Jim Parrish, who was then a high school student interested in politics, recalls attending a Dole congressional campaign rally. "I was really interested in meeting him," Parrish said. "I went up to him and offered my hand. He looked at me with disdain, then quickly moved away to mingle with the more 'important' voters. At that instant, I became a Democrat." Parrish went on to become Kansas state Democratic chairman and has never forgotten this incident.*

Following the October 1962 Cuban Missile Crisis, President Kennedy made dramatic strides toward rapprochement with the Soviet Union. But this did not play well in conservative western Kansas. On September 30, 1963, Dole and nine other conservative congressmen wrote Kennedy a letter asking for clarification on his policy of selling wheat to Russia, and hinting that they would oppose it. Nevertheless, on October 8, Kennedy approved the wheat sale. Dole represented the largest wheat-producing district in the country, and on November 6 he stated on the House floor, "It is hard to justify fighting Communism with the one hand and feeding it with the other," and railed, "We are dealing with an international Communist conspiracy."

Two weeks after Dole's speech, on November 22, 1963, Kennedy was assassinated in Dallas. Dole's speech on the House floor on December 5 affords an insight into the qualities of Kennedy that Dole admired. "Kennedy was a politician in the finest sense," Dole told his colleagues. "He laid *careful plans for winning*—and serving in—the presidency."† After quoting laudatory editorials from

---

*In 1994, Parrish admitted a grudging admiration for Dole's success in the rough-and-tumble world of politics. He admires Dole, as do so many other critics.
†Dole's remarks sound eerily similar to his eulogy for Richard Nixon thirty-one years later.

western Kansas newspapers, Dole concluded his speech by praising Kennedy as a successful professional politician.

Kennedy's assassination elevated Lyndon B. Johnson to the presidency. Johnson was a man whom Dole both loathed and admired, and to whom he himself would later be compared as Senate majority leader and as a senator who bent over backward to help his campaign contributors, the moneyed special interests.

In the 1964 congressional campaign, Dole faced Bill Bork, a Democrat who felt the full force of Bob's tongue. Dole ran radio and TV ads stating, "Bork is a jerk." Dole was cocky, crude, and rude. But he was a winner. Richard Nixon campaigned for Dole in Kansas, sizing up the congressman for a future Senate seat, and Dole supported Barry Goldwater for president. During the campaign and throughout the '60s, Dole continued to capitalize on the reactionary views of his constituency—and continued to please Nixon and Goldwater—with his fair share of red-baiting. According to Norbert Dreiling, "Dole out-Nixoned Nixon. He was always looking for Commies under every rock—especially every Democratic rock."

Lyndon Johnson made a special effort to defeat Dole, not only because of his role in the Estes matter and his vociferous partisanship and criticism of the Democratic administration, but also because of Dole's vehement opposition to Johnson's Great Society programs in 1964 and 1965. Bob voted for the landmark Civil Rights Bill of 1964 and for the Voting Rights Act of 1965 but voted against an Open Housing Bill of 1966 and virtually all of the Great Society programs, including the bills establishing food stamps, Medicare, Judicare, federal educational assistance, and other programs aimed at helping the needy.

Bob was presented with a plaque given annually to the most conservative congressmen by the right-wing Americans for Constitutional Action. He received this award every year from 1961 to 1968 and became the

darling of the right wing. Dole was a ferocious red-baiter
in his House days, branding a Kansas newspaper he
didn't like the "*Prairie Pravda*," and painting his opponents in flaming red colors. Dole's reputation from his
House years contrasts sharply with his later reputation
as a pragmatic opportunist. Was he truly a conservative
in the 1960s? Norbert Dreiling has remarked, "Dole will
do what it takes to get elected. He has always accurately
reflected the constituency he happens to represent. In
the '60s, when he represented the First District in Congress, he reflected their views: anti–Great Society, anti-
Johnson, anti-Kennedy. Then, after he expanded his base
to cover all of Kansas [when he became senator in 1968],
he moderated his views. Then, when he began running
for president [in 1980], he modified and moderated them
again."

Dole easily won reelection to the House again in 1966,
this time using a more low-key approach in this race
against a woman opponent, Bernice Henkle of Great
Bend, Kansas.

Dole served on a U.S. congressional delegation to
survey the food crisis in India in 1966 and on another
delegation to study the Arab refugee problem in the
Middle East in 1967.* He favored sending wheat to the
starving masses in India and elsewhere but other than
that showed little interest in U.S. foreign policy then.

While compiling this impressive conservative record in
the House, Bob remained in close contact with Frank
Carlson, the senior Republican U.S. senator from Kansas
and one of the powers of the old-boy network. Carlson,
who had been governor of Kansas from 1947 to 1950 and
a U.S. senator since 1951, treated Dole as his fair-haired
boy, much as Wint Smith had done eight years earlier.

*In his House years, Dole also served on the Republican Task
Force on Urban Affairs and as an adviser to the U.S. Delegation
to the United Nations Food and Agriculture Organization at
Rome in 1965. His interests in foreign affairs, during those
years, seemed limited to agriculture.

Not surprisingly, Carlson chose him as his successor when he retired from the Senate.

Dole faced a tough primary fight for the GOP nomination against former Governor Bill Avery. Dole secured the support of Dave Owen, a key fund-raiser and boss of pivotal Johnson County, and won the primary in August.

On October 10, 1968, a month before the general election, his Republican colleagues rose in the great well of the House chamber to shower praise on the man who had stood in their ranks for eight years. Virtually every congressman who spoke assumed that Dole would be "promoted" to the Senate. As Representative Burt Talcott of California said, "I am pleased to participate with the friends and colleagues of my colleague from Kansas in wishing him bon voyage into the political maelstrom of the other body [the Senate]." "I know his [Dole's] arrival in the Senate will brighten, enliven, and enrich that body," Representative Paul Findley echoed. "I am confident he will continue this same splendid record in the other body," Representative Alex Pirnie chimed in.

His House colleagues were right. Dole bounced into the Senate three weeks later with a resounding election victory over Democrat William I. Robinson for the first of five legendary terms.

9

"NIXON'S DOBERMAN PINSCHER"

During the presidency of Richard Nixon, even after Watergate, Bob Dole was a staunch supporter of all of the president's policies. He can hardly be accused of inconsistency during these years in the Senate.

Bob Dole was elected to the Senate on the same day that Nixon attained the presidency on November 5, 1968. They first met in 1964, when Nixon had come to Kansas to campaign for Dole in the latter's race for congressional reelection. The two men met again at the Republican National Convention in Miami in 1968, when Nixon was nominated for president, with Dole's avid support.

In January 1969, Nixon began a stormy reign as "president of all the people." Like Dole, Nixon was a workaholic with enormous drive and a lifelong loner who pursued his own agenda with fanatical persistence. Unlike Dole, however, Nixon was reluctant to emerge from the shadows and directly assault his opponents. He preferred to let others fight his battles. The senator from Kansas eagerly volunteered.

In January 1969, Dole brought his acid tongue into "the world's greatest deliberative body," the United States Senate. After eight years in the House of Representatives, where he had never had much of an audience outside of west-central Kansas, Dole suddenly found himself in the stratosphere of American politics.

Though the Democrats still held a majority there, the

Senate, more often than not, merely reacted to Nixon's initiatives. Lacking any coherent leadership, the Democratic senators found their most articulate torchbearer in Ted Kennedy, who was regarded as a political idol until Chappaquiddick crippled his political career in July 1969.

Dole perceived himself as a product of the working class who had been snubbed by the likes of Kennedy all his life, and he particularly resented the hagiographic portrayal of the Kennedy brothers by what he considered the liberal press. Well aware that Nixon shared his antipathy for the Kennedys, Dole saw a vacuum to be filled in the Senate: point man for Nixon and foil to Ted Kennedy and any other critic of Nixon. He surprised his colleagues by immediately becoming, as many called him, a one-man "Dole Patrol."

In contrast to most of his Republican Senate colleagues, Dole frequently visited the White House, and unofficially became Nixon's direct line to the Senate floor. Notwithstanding this, there was something chillingly mechanical about the way in which Dole defended Nixon in the Senate. Never questioning any of the president's policies in any way, he was furiously defensive and bitter toward anyone who dared to oppose the commander in chief.

Having campaigned in 1968 by claiming he had a "secret plan" to end the Vietnam War, in 1969 Nixon revealed that plan to be Vietnamization, a painfully slow process of replacing half a million U.S. combat troops in Vietnam with ineffective, unmotivated, corrupt South Vietnamese ARVN troops. The bogus nature of Vietnamization was evident when Nixon announced in June 1969 the withdrawal of only 25,000 U.S. troops, less than 5 percent of the American force there. By early fall 1969, massive antiwar demonstrations were occurring all across the country and many colleges shut down with "Vietnam moratoriums."

In the press, Nixon was lashed severely. He was attacked by hawks for withdrawing any troops at all and by doves for prolonging the war for no purpose except "saving face." Nixon unleashed Vice President Spiro Agnew on the press and Dole on the Senate.

Dole attacked his colleagues in harsh personal terms, both on and off the Senate floor. Often, he would chase departing senators off the floor and into the cloakroom or hallway, where he would yell at them for opposing Nixon. Republican Senator William Saxbe of Ohio gave Dole the nickname "hatchet man" and applied it to him in no uncertain terms. "Dole is so unpopular here," Saxbe said, "that he couldn't even sell beer on a troop ship." "If you like Richard Nixon, you'll love Bob Dole," said many irate colleagues sarcastically. But Nixon had few followers in the Senate except Dole.

Dole's fanatical, unquestioning defense of Richard Nixon extended beyond the Vietnam War to tax bills, economic policy, and Nixon's two doomed Supreme Court nominees, Clement Haynesworth and G. Harrold Carswell.*

Dole in his early Senate days saw himself as a "sniper," always thirsting for a fight, "one of the toughest men I've ever met, the kind of guy I'd like to stand back to back with in a knife fight," according to Senator Bob Packwood, and "the first man we've had around here in a long time who will grab the other side by the hair and drag them down the hill," according to former senator Barry Goldwater. With his lean six-foot, two-inch frame and dark hair and sideburns that reached to his earlobes, Dole actually looked like a gunslinger.

Paradoxically, Dole could sometimes wax eloquently and sensitively. Rising to address the Senate on April 14, 1969, he bared his soul. Calling handicapped people an "exceptional group which I joined on another April 14, twenty-four years ago,"† Dole described the handi-

---

*In his 1988 autobiography, Dole wrote, "I voted for both men. In retrospect, I was right on Haynesworth, wrong on Carswell."
†Dole has always been superstitious about the significance of April 14. As recently as April 14, 1994, he organized a Capitol lunch commemorating the twenty-fifth anniversary of his maiden Senate speech. President Clinton attended.

capped as "a minority group whose existence affects every person in our society and the very fiber of our nation. . . . As a minority, it has always known exclusion. Maybe not exclusion from the front of the bus, but perhaps from even climbing aboard it; maybe not exclusion from pursuing advanced education, but perhaps from experiencing any formal education; maybe not exclusion from day-to-day life itself, but perhaps from an adequate opportunity to develop and contribute to his or her fullest capacity."

Asserting that "at least one out of every five Americans" is handicapped, Dole spoke eloquently of the unique problems facing them and demanded the creation of a presidential task force to "review what the public and private sectors are doing and to recommend how we can do better." The goal of all handicapped people, he said, was to "achieve maximum independence, security and dignity for the individual."

Dole saw the handicapped and farmers as his two key constituent groups in his early Senate days. He won a seat on the Senate Agriculture Committee. He also sat on the Senate Select Committee on Nutrition and Human Needs, the Small Business Committee, and the Public Works Committee.

Cocky and aggressive, Dole was always willing to pick a fight. When Arkansas Senator William Fulbright objected to his unorthodox rupture of normal Senate floor procedure, the brash Kansan shot back acidly, "Is it a rule of the Senate that one must clear everything with the senator from Arkansas?" Dole took on Nixon's defense with a zeal that infuriated his colleagues. The Republican minority leader, Senator Hugh Scott of Pennsylvania, a moderate who was lukewarm on Nixon, and who epitomized the despised Eastern establishment—or as Dole called it, the "Rockefeller wing" of the GOP—was deeply irritated that Dole constantly defied his authority. But to Dole, Scott was just a figurehead. His loyalty was to Nixon and Nixon alone, and this did not go unnoticed by the man in the Oval Office.

The senator's biting criticism of GOP minority leader Hugh Scott intensified. He said Scott should be replaced by "younger and more aggressive leadership." Nervous that Dole might split the party by challenging Scott for the post, Nixon decided to offer him the position of Republican National Committee (RNC) chairman in January 1971, replacing an ineffective Rogers Morton, who had been nicknamed "Nixon's Saint Bernard." Dole's impending selection created a storm of protest among the Senate's forty-three Republicans. Some claimed he was too conservative, while others objected to his abrasive personality. Hugh Scott opposed Dole's selection on the grounds that the job required a full-time chairman, not someone who already had a job as senator. H. R. Haldeman, Nixon's chief of staff, noted how difficult Dole was to deal with. But Nixon loved Dole and installed him as head of the RNC to help prepare for the 1972 reelection campaign.

Dole took on his new role with enthusiasm. Flying around the country three or four times a week, then rushing back to Washington to cast key Senate votes, he became a human whirlwind, putting in eighteen-to-twenty-hour days on a regular basis. Seldom home except to sleep, his marriage to Phyllis literally atrophied. His real mistress was politics, his real "mate" was Nixon, and his real love was power. Dole finally walked out on Phyllis in January 1972. The woman burst into tears, but agreed to file the petition for divorce herself, sparing him embarrassment.

The technical distinction between the Committee to Reelect the President and RNC turned out to be immensely important to the senator's political survival in 1972, for it enabled him to dodge Watergate bullets by insisting that he knew nothing about the burglary or its subsequent cover-up by Nixon. In 1972, Watergate was still being called a "third-rate burglary" and was not yet linked to Nixon. It played little role in the presidential election between Nixon and Democrat George McGovern.

During the 1972 campaign, Dole attacked George Mc-Govern as "an opportunistic politician who has engaged in one of the dirtiest political campaigns ever to cover up a record of questionable conduct," and accused *The Washington Post* of being McGovern's "handmaiden" in the campaign.

Nixon won the election by the largest landslide in history, in November 1972. But the self-destructive Nixon felt depressed and bitter. On the day after the election, he called a meeting at the White House with Haldeman and announced that he would "purge" many of his top aides, because he wanted to start his second term "with a new team." Astonishingly, one of his targets was Bob Dole.

Just as Dole himself was later to dismiss his own longtime aide Dave Owen, Nixon now began freezing Dole out, to solve what he called "the Dole Problem": his "abrasive" outbursts and unpopularity with many Republicans. One night, Dole spoke to a top Nixon aide, who asked, "Would you like to *see* the president?"

"Yes!" said Dole eagerly.

"Then turn on the television. The president is speaking in ten minutes," hissed the aide.

Dole himself believed that the president still liked him but that a "nameless, spineless, faceless few" in the White House were conspiring to bad-mouth him.

On November 28, 1972, Dole was summoned to Camp David, where Haldeman conveyed Nixon's decision to fire him as RNC chairman. "My chopper had barely left the pad when Haldeman began pushing me down the hill," Dole bitterly complained. It was the first time he had ever been fired from any job.

To add insult to injury, Haldeman ordered Dole to fly to New York to ask George Bush to resign his position as United Nations ambassador, so that Bush could replace Dole as RNC chair. In addition, Nixon assigned Dole to ride at the end of his inaugural parade behind the horses on January 20, 1973.

In 1994, when Haldeman's *Diaries* were published, the

true story was told: The paranoid Nixon evidently felt threatened by Dole as well as other politicians. He issued orders to "eliminate the politicians, except George Bush. He'd do anything for the cause." Nixon wanted "good hacks" and "loyalists." "Give us the names of loyalists," Nixon told John Ehrlichman, saying he wanted, "Not brains, loyalty." Nixon clearly saw Dole as too ambitious and abrasive.

In 1973 the Nixon presidency unraveled. *The Washington Post* had kept up a steady drumbeat of attack as the Watergate scandal was revealed by reporters Bob Woodward and Carl Bernstein. They discovered Nixon's cover-up of Watergate and pushed Nixon aides H. R. Haldeman and John D. Ehrlichman into early retirement in April 1973. The story had been picked up nationally, and the media churned out an almost daily barrage of damaging news reports relating to a criminal cover-up and the obstruction of justice. In the summer of 1973, the Senate Select Watergate Committee, under the chairmanship of Senator Sam Ervin (D-NC), held sensational televised hearings that daily implicated Nixon and his top lieutenants further.

Dole has praised Nixon as a "Man of Vision" and has trivialized Watergate, but he watched the gathering developments with mounting apprehension. Reports surfaced that James McCord, the head Watergate burglar, had been on the payroll of the RNC during Dole's chairmanship, and that he may have once taken orders from Dole.* Dole came dangerously close to being burned by the Watergate flame that would ultimately consume Nixon. Onetime RNC employee James McCord, who had met Dole on many occasions, joined Nixon's Committee to Reelect the President, dubbed CREEP by Dole, as a security consultant. McCord's real mission was to install bugs. On June 17, 1972, McCord and several assistants were arrested for illegally breaking into and

---

*According to Bob Brock, Dole's RNC "paid half of McCord's salary" (the other half was paid for by CREEP).

entering the Democratic National Committee (DNC) headquarters in Washington's Watergate building and installing electronic eavesdropping devices. Dole joked, "Thank God it was my night off." But privately, he worried about the ties between McCord and the RNC. McCord, facing a stiff prison sentence at the hands of federal Judge John J. Sirica, began implicating other key figures in CREEP and the White House. Nixon's lieutenants began falling like dominoes, particularly after ex-White House counsel John Dean testified about Nixon's personal involvement in the cover-up, and the embattled president himself squirmed and declared defiantly, "I am not a crook."

Particularly dangerous for Dole was the testimony of Hugh Sloan, treasurer of CREEP, at the Senate Watergate hearings in August 1973. Sloan testified that he had given Dole $3,000 for a trip to South Vietnam: "Internally, within the staff, we could not understand why we were paying for Mr. Dole's trip." Watergate Committee investigators found a CREEP memorandum stating that Dole had been selected by Nixon as a spokesman for the administration's Vietnam policy in the summer of 1971. The memorandum noted that Senator William Fulbright, the severest critic of Nixon's war policies, had never been to Vietnam and implied that Dole should go in order to observe the war firsthand and thereby enhance his own credibility as a defender of the policy. The memorandum estimated that the trip would cost $2,000 or so and stated that Dole had rejected payment for his expenses from Republican Party and Senate committee funds. If the trip were paid for with party funds, the memo said, then Dole might be criticized for playing politics, while if Senate funds were used, he might be criticized for misappropriating government money.

On August 5, 1972, the *Congressional Quarterly* published Dole's report on his 1971 travels. The report noted, "August 17–22: Japan, South Vietnam, Cambodia, Thailand, to observe the progress of the Vietnamization program, treatment of POWs, and drug abuse problems among servicemen, personal expense.''

The $3,000 came from the same secret cache that was later used to finance the Watergate burglary, and this cache was filled, allegedly, with secret corporate campaign contributions. The significance of the $3,000 used by Dole for the August 1971 trip to South Vietnam is that Dole's office first claimed that he paid for the trip with his own money, and then, after Nixon campaign officials admitted they gave him the money, Dole admitted that the money came from the campaign. Dole probably knew that the source of the money was the same safe kept by Hugh Sloan, Nixon's campaign treasurer and a major Watergate figure. Dole's aide, Mike Baroody, admitted that Dole accepted the $3,000 from Nixon's campaign coffers rather than from the Republican Party official fund, which raises more questions.

According to Hugh Sloan, the secret slush fund contained about $1.8 million in unreported campaign contributions. Yet Dole was never called as a witness before the Senate Watergate Committee, and there is no record that the committee investigators ever interviewed or investigated him on this matter. Senators were then still treated as sacred cows, immune to interrogation. And, in fairness, there were much bigger issues at stake.

Dole managed to sidestep another scandal involving the Nixon administration that did result in Senate investigations. The scandal concerned ITT (International Telephone & Telegraph) Corporation's alleged 1971 attempt to influence Nixon's Justice Department in its handling of an antitrust case involving ITT. In mid-1971, according to *The New York Times*, while Dole was still chairman of the Republican National Committee, the ITT-Sheraton Corporation "offered the committee a $400,000 'guarantee,' ostensibly as part of an effort to attract the 1972 Republican National Convention to San Diego, where the corporation was building a hotel. At the same time, the Justice Department was considering whether to require the conglomerate to divest itself of several of its major,

profitable holdings'' because of possible antitrust violation. John Mitchell, who was Nixon's key political adviser (and in 1968 and 1972 his campaign manager), was
U.S. attorney general at the time.

According to the *Times,* Ed Reinecke, then the Republican lieutenant governor of California, received the ITT
offer of money for the convention in May 1971 and
transmitted it by telephone to John Mitchell. Reinecke
testified about his role to the Senate committee and was
later tried and convicted of perjury. The conviction was
overturned on the technicality that no quorum was present at the Judiciary Committee when he gave his testimony, but Reinecke was finished politically.

ITT's offer was made public in February 1972 by
columnist Jack Anderson, who published a memorandum
allegedly written by Dita Beard, a consultant for ITT,
which suggested that the $400,000 was offered as a bribe
to Nixon to pressure the Justice Department to make a
decision favorable to ITT on the antitrust divestiture
issue, over which Nixon had control. Beard later denied
writing the memorandum, and it has never been con-
clusively determined whether the memorandum was
genuine.

At this time, the Senate Judiciary Committee was
considering Nixon's nomination of Richard G. Klein-
dienst to succeed John Mitchell as attorney general and
reopened its hearings to investigate the ITT matter. Incredibly, Dole was not called as a witness here either,
although he had been chairman of the Republican National Committee when the ITT offer was made in 1971.

There is a question about whether or not Dole was
informed of the ITT offer of convention money at the
time that Reinecke and Mitchell handled it. According to
The New York Times, Reinecke later told a grand jury in
Washington that he had personally informed Dole and his
assistant at the RNC, Daniel Evans, about the offer.
Josephine L. Good, another of Dole's RNC assistants,
testified under oath that she personally gave Dole a
memorandum on July 2, 1971, that completely outlined

ITT's offer, but said she was "not certain" that he had read the memo or spoken to Mitchell about it.

In March of 1972, Dole held a news conference in which he said that the Republican Party had received ITT's offer but that this offer had no connection with the antitrust case. He insisted that he had rebuffed an effort by Dita Beard to meet with him in 1971. However, in 1974, when he was running for reelection to the Senate in Kansas and the ITT affair became a campaign issue, the *Kansas City Times* quoted him as saying he had never known about any ITT offer at all. Characteristically, his public comments were contradictory.

Nixon's viability and credibility as president collapsed rapidly after he fired Watergate special prosecutor Archibald Cox in the Saturday Night Massacre on October 20, 1973. Cox had insisted that Nixon turn over tape recordings of Oval Office conversations; Nixon refused and then ordered Attorney General Elliot Richardson to fire Cox. When Richardson refused and resigned, Solicitor General Robert Bork then followed Nixon's orders and fired Cox.* By early 1974, Congress initiated impeachment proceedings against Nixon.†

As more and more leaders from both parties called for Nixon's impeachment or resignation, Bob Dole found himself in the familiar position of straddling the fence and remained officially noncommittal. He was one of the last Republican senators to jump ship on Nixon.

Dole faced a tough reelection campaign for the Senate in 1974 when a strong contender, Congressman William Roy, announced his candidacy. Roy was a popular two-term congressman from Topeka who held both a medical

---

*In 1987, Dole supported Reagan's nomination of Bork for the Supreme Court, introducing him to the Senate Judiciary Committee. Bork was rejected by the Senate.

†Interestingly, one of the staffers on the House Judiciary Committee at this time was Hillary Rodham Clinton. Her boss was Bernard Nussbaum, who would later become Clinton's White House counsel in 1993, only to be driven out of that post by Dole's sharp attacks over the Whitewater scandal.

and a law degree and had specialized in obstetrics and gynecology from 1955 to 1970. He was also a gentleman.

Life breathed into Dole's campaign in June 1974 when the Senate Watergate Committee gave him a clean bill of health and stated categorically in its final report that the Watergate affair had not been the workings of the Republican National Committee. Nonetheless, back home in Kansas, some of Dole's Democratic opponents began smearing him with Watergate mud. Norbert Dreiling, Kansas State Democratic Chairman, challenged Dole to confirm or deny that James McCord was on the payroll of the RNC "on or about" June 17, 1972, the date of the second Watergate break-in.

Two former top officials of the RNC, Tom Evans and Barry Mountain, stated that Dole had not been involved in the RNC's hiring of McCord, however, and this helped to clear Dole's name. Evans stated that the RNC, not Dole personally, had hired McCord Associates and that Dole had called him after the Watergate break-in and asked him about McCord's status on the committee. "I told him, 'Senator, there is no status to report. He's been terminated,' " Evans maintained.

In 1974, when Dole returned to Kansas, everywhere he went he was asked whether or not he favored the impeachment of Nixon. "It's an impossible dilemma," Dole complained. "One guy gives me hell for betraying Nixon. The next guy comes up to me and says, 'I'm for you, Bob, but you've got to get Nixon off our backs.' There's no way to stay on that tightrope." In February 1974, Dole stated publicly that "a legal case against the president has not been made." Later he retreated slightly from that position but maintained until the bitter end that he hoped that Nixon would be proven innocent. At one point, he toyed with the idea of calling together all the Republican senators to draft a "statement of independence" from Nixon but gave that up as impractical. He even tried humor. When asked whether he would like the president to campaign for him in Kansas, he replied that he "wouldn't mind it if Nixon *flew over* the state."

He was bailed out of his dilemma by Nixon's abrupt resignation on August 9, 1974. In September 1974, President Gerald Ford pardoned Nixon for any crimes he may have committed in office and thereby angered a large number of voters. Polls showed Kansas public opinion running three to two against the Nixon pardon.

Dole went home to Kansas to face the toughest campaign of his life. The polls showed his Democratic challenger Dr. Roy leading him by as much as thirteen points.

On CBS's "Face the Nation" that fall, however, Roy was asked if he would make Watergate an issue against Dole and he answered that he would not. This was a fatal error.

According to Robert Brock, a key adviser, campaign manager, and fund-raiser for Roy's campaign, "We had things we could have used on Dole but Dr. Roy held back. He didn't want to conduct that kind of campaign." Brock claimed that Nixon got the IRS to harass him with "jeopardy assessments" and revocation of nonprofit certificates, to punish him for opposing Dole. As for Roy, in his speeches, Roy only said that "Dole knew or should have known about the Watergate affair in his capacity as [Republican] Party Chairman. . . . We need a candidate who will represent the state and the nation rather than his party and the head of his party." This was rather mild criticism, and Roy didn't go much further than that.

Dole launched a strong counteroffensive in September 1974. He fired his ineffective campaign manager, replacing him with the indefatigable David Owen.* Owen accused Roy of mudslinging and devised a clever television commercial in which Dole's face was depicted on a

---

*Owen, a banker from Stanley, Kansas, went on to become Dole's protégé and close adviser for the next thirteen years, until his abrupt resignation from Dole's presidential campaign staff in January of 1988. He was convicted of subscribing to false tax returns, a felony, in 1993 in a strange trial, claimed "political harassment" and wound up in federal prison in March 1994, when he received even further harassment by authorities. He is the subject of a separate chapter in this book, chapter 27.

billboard, as a voice whined, "Bill Roy says Bob Dole is against old people," and mud was splattered on Dole's face simultaneously. Then the voice groaned, "Bill Roy says Bob Dole is against the farmer," and more mud splattered on Dole's face. This pattern was repeated on several other issues, presenting Dole as a victim. Then another voice cheerfully proclaimed, "Bob Dole voted thirty times for Social Security," and mud came off; the voice then announced, "Bob Dole served the Kansas farmer on the Agriculture Committee," and the rest of the mud disappeared to reveal Dole's famous face. "Dole's a great crier," Roy complained years later. "He's very good at complaining about how poor Bob Dole is being whipped by the opposition."

Owen told me that polls revealed this commercial had a sensational effect on resurrecting Dole's standing: "Every time we ran it, Dole would gain three points in the polls."

With his career on the line, Dole hunched over a bench in a high school stadium on a chilly Halloween night just before the election, begging for votes, wondering if he would survive. Dole's standing in the polls began to improve graudally. Going into the weekend before the election, in some polls Roy was slightly ahead, but the election was considered a toss-up.

In 1974, abortion was a very heated topic in Kansas, which is a Bible Belt state. Abortion was of interest to only about 15 percent of registered voters, most of them Catholics and fundamentalist Protestants, according to the polls, but to those people it was crucial. The year before, the Supreme Court had issued its controversial *Roe v. Wade* opinion, which essentially declared it unconstitutional for any state to ban abortions outright during the first trimester of pregnancy. Dole said that he would support a pro-life constitutional amendment to overturn the opinion.

The right-to-life people flocked to Dole and opposed Dr. Roy because as a physician he had performed about ten abortions (done legally under Kansas's restrictive laws, which required independent second medical opinions for an abortion to be performed), and because he believed that the decision to end pregnancy should not be subject to criminal law, as long as it was performed by a licensed physician in a licensed hospital. His position favoring a very restricted use of abortion as a medical procedure was seriously distorted by Dole in the campaign, and Roy was painted as favoring "abortion on demand" in "any trimester." Roy was even called a "baby killer."

On the Sunday just two days before the election, an avalanche of leaflets depicting dead fetuses in garbage cans appeared on automobile windshields outside Catholic churches and on hotel room doorknobs all over Kansas, especially in Catholic church parking lots. In addition, voters were assaulted with a barrage of hand-delivered pamphlets and direct mail, radio, and newspaper ads attacking Roy's position on abortion. Ads placed in major Kansas newspapers at this time depicted a skull and crossbones: one crossbone held the word *abortion* and the other the word *euthanasia,* and the ad read VOTE FOR LIFE—BOB DOLE WILL SUPPORT A HUMAN LIFE AMENDMENT. VOTE FOR DOLE. In addition, Roy was picketed and harassed by hecklers at virtually every campaign stop. "Sometimes there were so many pickets that you couldn't get into or out of the building," Roy recalls.

On November 5, 1974, Kansans went to the polls and gave Dole a victory by a bare margin of 13,000 votes; the final tally showed that he received about 393,000 votes (50.8 percent) compared to Roy's 380,000 (49.2 percent). Dole later said that the turning point in his campaign had come in late September or early October, when he had regained confidence in his ability to win. But Roy blamed his defeat on the unfair, last-minute campaign against him by the state's anti-abortion forces. During his concession speech, Roy said, "I was flat out beat on the abortion issue." It was unfortunate, he said, that the people of Kansas, "not many of them, but some of them," took that negative and harsh position on the abortion issue. He decried the distribution of anti-abortion literature by the right-to-life organizations. He also said that the right-to-life groups were unusually well-financed "by mysterious sources."

At a news conference covered by the Associated Press the day before the senatorial election in November 1974, Dole did *not* specifically disavow any ads. *The New York Times* reported that, according to the federal election records filed after the 1974 campaign was over, Dole accepted in-kind contributions worth $288.56 from a Shawnee Mission, Kansas, woman for five insertions of an ad in separate newspapers. She signed the skull and crossbones ad placed by the Eastern Kansas Right to Life Organization. In addition, Dole accepted an in-kind political contribution for "postage" from a Shawnee Mission man who was also affiliated with the Kansas right-to-life organizations.

The *Times* also reported that, according to the Right to Life Affiliates of Kansas, an umbrella group of the anti-abortion forces in that state, Dole had assigned a full-time staff member to coordinate with this group. "On October 5, 1974, less than a month before the election, Senator Dole appeared before the right-to-life state convention in Hays, Kansas. He is quoted as telling an audience of 150: 'If you want a human life amendment [to the Constitution], then elect those who will support your position. The people must be asked to speak. We must ask the American people what they want.' He also reportedly told the group, 'I say I am against the interruption of human life and the law ought to oppose this interruption.' He went on, 'That's what right to life is all about—the interruption of human life.' " In *Lifetime*, a pamphlet of the Right to Life Affiliates, which was published after the Hays convention, its members were urged to place newspaper ads supporting Dole. According to the *Times*, the pamphlet stated, "The last week before the election is the right time for ads. Run six small ads (one each day) and a larger one on November 5

[1974]." A sample copy of the skull-and-crossbones ad was shown as an example, along with others that read DOLE FIGHTS ABORTION, ROY PERFORMED ABORTIONS. The pamphlet urged its readers to "get some sponsors (don't be shy, it's not for yourself), then with money and ad in hand, go place your ads." Other leaflets said, "Dr. Bill Roy is an abortioner."

According to federal election law regulations in force in 1974, it was perfectly legal for individuals to place ads opposing a candidate without having to set up a political action committee or report the cost. Any ads placed or contributions made or services performed on behalf of a candidate, however, had to be authorized by the candidate and deducted from the amount allowed for media expenses. Dole insisted that he had never authorized ads and therefore had never deducted their cost from his expenses.

Bob Brock told me that "after the 1974 elections, we traced the source of the money financing the abortion leaflets, and we traced it directly to Dole's campaign money." He also insisted that a Dole staffer acted as a liaison with the anti-abortion activists. But Dole's brother Kenny and Owen have denied any connection. A Kansas right-to-life publication also denied that the leaflets were funded by the Dole campaign.

Shortly after his victory over Roy, Dole joked sardonically, "They said that since my opponent has a medical degree and a law degree that he was one in a million. Now he's one in ten million—he's unemployed." Bob Dole had learned his lessons well from Richard Milhous Nixon.

III

THE ART OF SELF-DESTRUCTION: DOLE AS PRESIDENTIAL AND VICE-PRESIDENTIAL CANDIDATE MANQUÉ

I went for the jugular—my own.
—Bob Dole

10

"I WENT FOR THE JUGULAR— MY OWN": GOP HATCHET MAN IN 1976

As we will see, in 1980 and 1988 Bob Dole sabotaged his own presidential races, but in 1976 he was blamed for bringing the entire GOP ticket of Ford-Dole down to an ignominious defeat. The same personality traits doomed him each time.

The story of how Dole came to be selected as Ford's running mate in 1976 is one packed with high drama and political maneuvering.

Gerald Ford, the bland, long-term Republican congressman from Grand Rapids, Michigan, was selected by President Nixon to be the nation's only nonelected vice president in history on October 12, 1973. He replaced Spiro Agnew, who had resigned in disgrace upon pleading nolo contendere to tax evasion charges. One of the reasons Nixon gave the nod to Ford was the latter's reputation as a lightweight. Dole told me that Nixon had felt that "he'd never be impeached [during Watergate] if Jerry Ford was next in line." Ford might have seemed to be a bumbler, but, nevertheless, Nixon was forced to resign from the presidency on August 9, 1974. After a month in office, Ford pardoned Nixon for all Watergate crimes he may have committed, and this single act sank him in the polls.

Ford compounded his mistake by selecting Nelson Rockefeller to be his vice president. Rockefeller's unpopularity as a plutocrat further sank Ford in the polls. (To salvage his presidency, Ford announced in late 1975 that Rockefeller would *not* be his running mate in 1976.)

In November 1975, Ronald Reagan announced his own candidacy for the 1976 presidential nomination, splitting the GOP down the middle during the bitterly contested primary season the following spring.

Ford and Reagan were neck-and-neck in the delegate count as summer approached. The Kansas Republican Party held its caucus convention in Topeka in the summer of 1976 to call for a vote as to whom their delegates would support at the Republican National Convention in August. The national media zeroed in on Kansas as a critical arena. "As Kansas's delegation goes, so will go the nation," said a popular slogan. Considered "America's heartland" and "Eisenhower Territory," Kansas was regarded as a bellwether state.

Most of the Kansas GOP establishment delegates supported Ford because they disliked and distrusted Reagan as a "right-wing extremist" who was "unelectable." But Reagan had a strong minority following. Reagan flew to Topeka and personally addressed the convention, creating much enthusiasm. Alarmed at this prospect, Owen, Dole's alter ego and fund-raising whiz kid, managed to secure the Kansas delegation overwhelmingly for Ford, upon Dole's insistence, by several controversial means. He promised delegates various things, twisted arms, and pulled some rabbits out of hats. He out-organized Reagan and produced a lopsided, ringing majority for Ford. To this day, Kansas Reaganites remain bitter about Owen's pressure tactics.

Although the national delegate count would remain close up to the convention, the pendulum now moved inexorably toward a Ford nomination for president.

Meanwhile, Jimmy Carter won an impressive series of primary victories by attacking Ford over the recession, the Nixon pardon, and the "Misery Index"—a combined figure of the high unemployment and inflation rates. In July, when the Democratic convention met in New York, Carter won the nomination easily, selected Walter Mondale as his running mate, and held a commanding thirty-point lead over President Ford in the polls.

Though the GOP party establishment, which then was "moderate," backed Ford, both he and Reagan went into the national convention claiming enough delegates to win the nomination on the first ballot. Dole went to the convention as a Kansas delegate pledged to vote for Ford, spurning Reagan's emotional address to the Kansas Republicans shortly before the convention began. He urged delegates from other states to support Ford as well.

Selected to act as temporary chairman of the convention, Dole impressed delegates and a national television audience with his no-nonsense, take-charge, tough-guy demeanor. The tall, dark, lean Kansan, who reminded many of the actors Humphrey Bogart and John Forsythe, seemed to breathe fire as he excoriated the Democrats and their nominees. (In later campaign speeches, he referred to Carter as "Chicken-fried McGovern" but subsequently said, "I take that back—I've learned to respect McGovern.") Dole, as chairman, controlled the agenda in an early convention floor fight, while Owen maneuvered delegates for Ford. On August 18, 1976, on the first ballot, Ford won the nomination with 1,187 votes to Reagan's 1,070. It took 1,130 to win, so Ford escaped with a bare fifty-seven delegates above the needed number.

A few hours before the vote, Senator Dole had been walking through the lobby of his hotel in Kansas City when he spotted Dorothy Voss Beecher, one of the original Bobolinks who had performed for his first congressional campaign in 1960. "He came up to me and told his friends, 'Hey, there's one of my Bobolinks!'" Dorothy recalls. "I couldn't believe he still recognized me. My hair was up and I looked so different; my friends were stunned."

Running into a ghost from his first race turned out to be a good omen for the superstitious Dole. At 3:15 A.M. an exhausted Ford gathered with his aides in his Crown Center suite to deliberate on his running mate. The list was soon narrowed to four names: Anne Armstrong, ambassador to Britain; former Deputy Attorney General William Ruckelshaus; Senator Howard Baker of Tennessee, who had sat on the Senate Watergate Committee; and Bob Dole. Ford chose Dole. This selection was not exactly a bolt out of the blue. For weeks, he'd been put forward by Owen and members of the Landon old-boy network. "Senator Dole takes a backseat to no one in his ability to communicate with people," Owen wrote to Ford a few days before the convention. "He is capable of taking the attack to the Carter-Mondale ticket. Dole is a real cage-rattler."

Ford was impressed that Dole was a more aggressive, slashing campaigner than the other contenders, as he had shown in his 1974 campaign against Dr. Bill Roy. The colorless Ford wanted to spend much of the fall in the White House Rose Garden looking presidential, while his running mate vigorously stumped the nation, launching missiles at Carter and Mondale. Ford also thought that Dole would help in the farm belt, where he had inherited a real problem thanks to Republican policies.

Dole accepted eagerly, later joking that "When I got the call, this morning, I thought Ford had the wrong number." He also quipped, "The vice presidency is a great job—it's all indoor work with no heavy lifting."

But Bob Dole's sardonic personality had already alienated many delegates. On August 19, 1,921 of 2,259 convention delegates voted for Dole's nomination: while 103 delegates abstained, mostly as a protest. Another 235 delegates voted for thirty-one seemingly random choices instead of Dole.

The press attacked Dole with a vengeance. A *New York Times* editorial called him "Ford's Doleful Choice," and political cartoonists ridiculed him as a snarling dog, a mudslinger armed with cans of black tar, and the like. Dole never forgot or forgave the press for what he called its "smear campaign" against him. He spoke of being "ambushed" by the press.

Even Richard Nixon criticized Ford's selection.

"They're going to have trouble with that guy," Nixon growled. "He's able, but his personality's abrasive as hell, and he's going to cause a helluva lot of problems with the press. They better get somebody good to handle him, someone who can control him, limit his appearances to select audiences, or this guy's going to alienate a helluva lot of people." Nixon was right.

As disillusioned with Dole as Nixon were some civil rights leaders, one of whom, Roy Wilkins, denounced him as an "enemy of blacks."

Just after the convention, Bob approached Ford, telling the president, "If you want to start the campaign in the heartland, I know of a little town in heartland America where we can start it." The next day, August 20, Dole managed the first presidential visit to Russell, Kansas, since 1905, when Theodore Roosevelt had spoken for a few minutes from the rear platform of a Union Pacific train.

Dole's hometown went wild, putting up a huge home-made banner that proclaimed in red letters: WELCOME HOME, BOB: GLAD YOU COULD COME ALONG, JERRY. The *Russell Daily News* printed a banner headline declaring BOMBSHELL HITS RUSSELL.

A grinning Dole rode with Ford in a motorcade through a crowd of several thousand on Main Street and then onto the lawn of the courthouse, where he had once worked as a county attorney earning a lower wage than the building's janitor. He mounted the platform and made his speech. As he began to express his appreciation to the town, recalling "the time I needed help, and the people of Russell helped," his words suddenly stopped, tears welled in his eyes, and he lifted his left hand to cover his face.

But the sensitive man with tears in his eyes was soon to become an acerbic, aggressive opponent. According to top Ford aide Lyn Nofziger, Dole flew around the country, like an "unguided missile," aiming at the Carter-Mondale ticket. "We're not on a leash; we're sort of on our own. If we do something wrong, I suppose Ford will rein us in," he said at this time. Dole's campaign speeches were written by his own aides, not by the Ford organization, and Dole said what he liked.* He kept Owen as his campaign manager.

In the early part of the campaign, the senator showed little evidence of having a coordinated strategy. "The trouble with this campaign is that no one is in charge and Dole does not know how to delegate responsibility," one insider told *The Washington Post*. Ford campaign aide Jim Baker referred to the Dole campaign as a "rough spot."

One of Bob's Republican speechwriters was George Gilder, who recalls Dole's nasty temper and chaotic disorganization. Once, Dole hurled the pages of a speech Gilder had drafted across the room and onto the carpet. "Bad . . . bad . . . bad," Dole snarled. Then, turning to Gilder, he thundered, "Pick up the papers and get out!" Dole made "little effort to control his temper, relate to his staff, research his positions, or uplift his rhetoric," Gilder recalled. He struck Gilder as a dark, pessimistic, and cynical tyrant with a "gloomy view of the world" and a "hostility to ideas and affirmative visions."

Gradually, Dole found his stride, slashing mercilessly at Carter and Mondale. "It took Jimmy Carter a long time to decide how many debates to have," he snapped. "He finally decided to have three so he can tell each of his positions on each issue." When asked at a press conference if he would play the role of a "one-man truth squad" stalking Carter around the country, Dole quipped, "It would take more than one." He attacked Carter as a "hypocrite," a "waffler," a "man of contradictions and false promises" who "gets his orders from George Meany," who was then president of the AFL-

---

*Later, particularly during his 1988 presidential campaign, Dole claimed to have just been doing what he was told in the 1976 campaign, fulfilling the role of hatchet man that he had been assigned by the Ford organization. This is his standard response when queried by the press about his hatchet man image.

CIO. "Would you buy a used peanut from Jimmy Carter?" Dole asked his audiences. When Carter admitted to *Playboy* magazine that he had occasionally "lusted in [his] heart," Dole said, "We'll give him the bunny vote." Dole referred to George Meany as "Walter Mondale's makeup man." When asked why he was savaging his opponents so viciously, Dole replied, "You want to leave a little raw meat in the audience."

On October 15, in the first such televised debate, Dole debated the Democrat vice-presidential nominee, Walter Mondale. Bob looked especially hostile that night, leaning against the podium and blinking his eyes at an astoundingly high rate. One outburst stands out in memory. "If we added up all the killed and wounded in Democrat wars in this century," Dole taunted Mondale before millions of viewers, "it would be about 1.6 million Americans, enough to fill the city of Detroit." Evidence of Dole's self-destructive and irresponsible mentality, the remark was absurd and insensitive.

Mondale looked solemnly at his opponent and declared, "I think Senator Dole has richly earned his reputation as a hatchet man tonight." Dole looked away.

Dole's wisecrack offended millions of veterans and families of war victims. According to Owen, who was present, the remark had not been rehearsed. It was "off the wall." "None of us could believe he said that," Owen recalls. Shortly afterward the Ford-Dole ticket sank in the polls, and the tide turned.

As with his 1988 campaign, the 1976 one was also wracked by scandal related to campaign fund-raising. The most damaging charge was Gulf Oil Corporation lobbyist Claude Wild's statement in early September 1976 that he had illegally given $2,000 to the senator in 1970 to pass on to other Republican Senate candidates.* After Dole vehemently denied the charge, Wild recanted his statement a few days later, saying he had been "in error." No further explanation was given.

---

*Since 1907, federal law has banned corporations from directly contributing money to political candidates.

From 1960 until 1974, Claude Wild had been in charge of dispensing about $4 million in political contributions from a slush fund. Many of these were illegal. In January 1976, the Watergate special prosecutor's office gave Wild a grant of immunity and compelled him to testify about $170,000 in Gulf slush funds that he had dispensed in 1973. Wild told a federal grand jury that he had made a Gulf corporate contribution to Dole of $5,000 in 1973. Wild refused to comment publicly.

On March 8, 1976, Dole himself testified before a grand jury. "They were concerned about whether I had received any money from Gulf Oil, and the answer was no," he said in September 1976. He went on: "They were concerned about whether I had received any money from Senator Scott [Hugh Scott, Republican Senate minority leader in 1973], and the answer was no." The senator said he had voluntarily offered to turn over his records to the special prosecutor, but insisted that "they've never asked for them" except for "one little book." That book was Dole's cash ledger.

In September 1976, *The Washington Post* alleged that the first ten pages of the "little book" were mysteriously missing and that the ledger "has drawn renewed interest from the Watergate special prosecutor, who is investigating the alleged 1973 $5,000 Gulf Oil cash contribution to the reelection campaign of Senator Bob Dole."* The ledger, purported to record all cash received and spent during 1973 and 1974 in Dole's Senate reelection campaign, had been kept by Jo-Anne Coe, Bob Dole's office manager.†

*Under the federal election laws in effect in 1973, an organization spending cash was required to file with the secretary of the Senate's public records any expenditures above $50.
†Coe has held several positions with Dole since 1967, including chief assistant and political operative, as well as administrative director in his Senate office. In 1985, when he became majority leader, Dole made her the first woman secretary of the Senate. She returned to his Senate office in 1987, and now is chair of Campaign America, Dole's leadership PAC.

The *Post* reported that Wild had testified to the grand jury that he had given $5,000 in cash to Dole's then administrative assistant, William Kats. Questioned several times by the special prosecutor, Kats said he did not recall receiving any money from Wild.

The ledger's list of cash contributions began on page eleven, and the first date listed was April 17, 1973. *The Washington Post*, citing "informed sources," said that Wild's contribution would have been made before that date. On the inside cover of the ledger book, Coe had written that the record of cash receipts began "on page nine." Page nine, however, was one of the missing pages. Dole claimed that the ten pages were "always missing. They were never there. Nothing was taken out. . . . I didn't keep the records." Coe explained that she had made some "mistakes" on page nine and, after tearing it out, had begun recording the contributions on page eleven. To some, this episode bore an eerie resemblance to Nixon's infamous eighteen minutes of missing tape.

As Dole plodded along in his campaign, he found himself on the defensive about more Watergate-related allegations. On October 20, just two weeks before the election, *Washington Post* columnists Jack Anderson and Les Whitten published a searing column accusing Dole of being a middleman in the notorious milk producers' 1971 campaign contributions to Nixon at a time when they were trying to persuade the Nixon administration to approve more milk subsidies and increases in the price of milk.

Anderson and Whitten claimed that "evidence still buried in Watergate files" revealed that Dole himself received $15,600 from the milk producers in 1973 and then returned it after the Watergate scandal broke out. Anderson and Whitten alleged that Dole pressured the Nixon White House to accept money from the dairymen.

Anderson and Whitten wrote about a secret February 2, 1971, memo marked "confidential" from Haldeman to White House aide Chuck Colson, which mentioned Dole trying to channel the milk money into Nixon's hands.

Haldeman said in this memo that Dole, then RNC Chairman, "sent me a note at the cabinet meeting (in early 1971) regarding the milk producers and is apparently being pressured by them. They have told him that they are unable to work out a means of getting their activity regarding their support for us. Would you please get in touch with Dole and follow up on this?"

A Nixon official involved in the milk scandal claimed that Dole "went back and forth . . . on behalf of the milk producers," pushing their contributions on nervous White House aides.

Nixon's White House tapes showed that at a secret meeting chaired by the president, the dairymen's situation was discussed, and Dole's name came up twice. Top Nixon aide John Ehrlichman said that Dole should be brought in, while Nixon commented, "I think you have a good game plan."

After this meeting, Nixon's supporters set up committees that transmitted hundreds of thousands of dollars from the milk industry to Nixon's campaign, while the Nixon administration ordered the milk price increases and subsidies demanded by the dairymen.

Dole denied any involvement in the milk scandal, noting that he "wasn't involved in the milk price distribution," and said that he could not recall sending any note to Haldeman.

These Watergate allegations against Dole undoubtedly hurt his ticket, just as the Dave Owen scandal in 1988 took its toll.

In the final tally, Dole and Ford lost the election. The Democrats won 40,827,394 votes, compared to the Republicans' 39,145,977. Carter won 297 electoral votes, while Ford picked up 240 (one elector cast a vote for Reagan, who was not even a candidate).

After losing, Dole lashed out mercilessly at his staff, blaming them for his defeat. "He was like a snake," said a close aide at the time.

Dole later said with great wit that he "went home and slept like a baby—I cried all night." The day after the election, he received a phone call from another sore loser, Richard Nixon, who commiserated with him over the defeat.

Dole reported that for months after the November 1976 defeat, he would order his driver to drive past the White House each day so that he could stare at the massive white portico and pillars and dream about what might have been, but for his self-destructive faux pas.

11

DON QUIXOTE RIDES FOR THE WHITE HOUSE: THE 1980 PRESIDENTIAL CAMPAIGN

W hen I worked for Dole during his 1980 presidential campaign, the same flaws that were apparent in his earlier vice-presidential bid were still in evidence. Dole failed to exploit opportunities, held back his forces, failed to organize any coherent campaign theme, hired Senate aides who supported other Republican candidates, and failed to delegate responsibility properly.

The senator should have been the front-runner. Dave Owen told me that Dole began running for the 1980 presidential nomination "two days after" the November 1976 defeat of the Ford-Dole ticket. But instead of making any serious effort to promote himself as titular head of the Republican Party, Dole hid in the comfortable womb of the U.S. Senate.

Dole realized in early 1977 that Ronald Reagan would be his main rival in 1980, because Reagan had mounted a strong insurgent challenge to Ford for the 1976 nomination. But Reagan was very vulnerable in 1980 because he was still seen as an extremist Barry Goldwater clone by large elements of the Republican establishment, and because he was far older than any other man ever elected president (Reagan was born in 1911).

Having supported Goldwater's campaign in 1964 and Reagan's in 1976, I advised Dole to link Reagan with Goldwater and to attack Reagan as an extremist who could not win an election. Dole was in an excellent position because at the Kansas State GOP convention in May 1976, he'd thrown his support to Ford and knocked the wind out of Reagan's sails. But Dole would not listen.

His chief administrative aide, Bill Fritts, was a strong Reagan supporter who took coffee breaks with Reagan strategists in the Capitol cafeteria. Pete Velde, Dole's chief counsel, was a strong Bush supporter, as were many others on his Senate payroll. Only Jo-Anne Coe and Betty Meyer, his secretaries, and Sheila Burke, his nurse-turned-aide, took him seriously.

Dole enrolled in a course called Speech Dynamics, run by Dorothy Sarnoff in New York. Speech Dynamics was a personal training program to restructure the presence, image, and style of politicians, corporate executives, and other public figures. It cost $3,500 and involved extensive training before cameras, lengthy discussions, and other techniques. "We change behavior very, very fast," Sarnoff boasted, noting that "My father was a surgeon, and I like to think of the camera as a surgeon's knife." So Dole went under her knife. Of him she said, "He was a wonderful student. We discussed his sense of humor. We changed that. We took the snideness away from him. We changed the way he dressed to more of a classy look." The truth, though, is that the veneer of slickness quickly rubbed off his craggy, rough-hewn image.

By 1979, the general consensus among Republican political observers was that Dole didn't have a prayer. But Elizabeth resigned her seat on the Federal Trade Commission on March 9, 1979, in order to campaign full-time for him, and sold her Exxon stock to avoid any appearance of conflict of interest while her husband voted on oil industry tax bills. Elizabeth also loaned Bob $50,000, prompting the Federal Election Commission investigation that will be discussed in chapter 27. "I think you'll see a different Bob Dole from the one who was assigned the bad-guy role in 1976," Elizabeth told reporters in a voice as sweet as molasses.

Elizabeth strongly supported the Equal Rights Amendment, and, in contrast to his more conservative rivals,

Bob sometimes shared her view. He also tended to support her purported commitment to consumer rights, anathema to big business. Dole's Senate staff disapproved. "The senator's wife is too liberal," complained Dole's aide Bob Lighthizer when he was interviewing me for a job. "We need some good conservatives here to convince him to vote the right way."*

Dole often seemed unable to hold a position in response to conflicts between Elizabeth's position and that of his staff. On one highly controversial bill affecting consumer rights in the antitrust field, the *Illinois Brick* case, Dole remained undecided for months.† The bill was a brainchild of Ted Kennedy, which made it ipso facto loathsome to conservatives. But Dole didn't know what to do.

Another antitrust bill sought to prohibit large oil companies from using their vast resources to merge with or acquire other non-energy companies. This was another brainchild of Kennedy's, who ranted against big oil for using windfall profits to buy up department stores. Dole offered to support the bill but only if the committee accepted his compromise amendment. But the amendment, which would have given oil companies a loophole permitting most mergers, got nowhere. The media and his fellow senators ignored Dole completely.

With virtually no support outside Kansas, and his political base eroding even there (some were saying he had sold Kansans down the creek in order to pursue his national ambitions), Dole set out like Don Quixote against Reagan, Senator Howard Baker, George Bush, John Connally, Congressmen Phillip Crane and John

*Bob Lighthizer worked for Dole in 1979–83, then joined his presidential campaign in 1987. Lighthizer became the treasurer for Dole's third presidential bid in 1995.
†The Supreme Court decision had restricted the consumer's right to sue a manufacturer for violations of antitrust laws. Kennedy's bill sought to amend the statute to permit such suits. The bill never came to a vote on the Senate floor.

Anderson. Referring to himself as "jousting with a tooth-pick" and backed by a pauper's pence, he bitterly complained about his wealthier and more popular rivals.

In 1979, the polls showed the senator from Kansas to be the choice of fewer than 6 percent of Republican voters nationwide. He seemed undecided about the seriousness of his candidacy, pointedly staying away from key primary states, such as Iowa and New Hampshire, except when he had to do some last-minute campaigning. The pragmatic Dole realized that by running for president, he was jeopardizing his chances for reelection to the Senate in 1980. But he enjoyed flirting with danger.

In the early weeks of 1979, Dole made several tactical moves in the Senate aimed at buttressing his unannounced presidential candidacy. He dropped his position as the ranking Republican on the Agriculture Committee in order to become a ranking member on the more visible Finance Committee, a move that antagonized many Kansans, who charged he was shortchanging his home state in order to seek national office. He also took a newly available seat on the Judiciary Committee, hoping to attract media attention by needling its chairman, Ted Kennedy. "Wherever Kennedy is, there goes the press," Dole would hiss. On another occasion he whined to the *Kansas City Star,* "I know I'll never be a Kennedy." Dole hated the Kennedys and the press attention Ted Kennedy could garner. "These Kennedys—what frauds," he would remark acidly, over and over again.

In 1979 Dole believed that Ted Kennedy would run for president against Carter, and would win the Democratic nomination. If he could "beat Kennedy," as he liked to say, he would accomplish a lifelong dream by out-Nixoning Nixon. This decision to target Kennedy was a strategic mistake, because his real rival was Reagan, not "Chappaquiddick Ted."

Dole also hurt himself by frequently taking on unpopular positions over controversial issues. In November 1978, 913 followers of the Reverend Jim Jones's People's Temple committed mass suicide in the jungle of Jonestown, Guyana, killing California Congressman Leo Ryan and some members of his entourage in the process. The People's Temple had been one of numerous religious cults that had sprouted up all across the United States in the 1970s, recruiting young people and convincing them to give all their money and possessions to a cult leader. Dole became fascinated with the cult phenomenon, especially after some of his Kansas constituents spoke to him about their children being brainwashed. In February 1979, he chaired a sensational day of televised hearings of a temporary, ad-hoc Senate committee formed to look into the cult problem. The hearing attracted considerable publicity—but of the wrong type. Dole was accused of staging a witch-hunt on Capitol Hill and was besieged by many groups who defended freedom of religion.

Upon encountering serious opposition, the senator withdrew from the spotlight and dropped the whole issue, never again chairing such a hearing. In the Senate Judiciary Committee nine months later, however, upon the author's recommendation, he introduced an amendment to the comprehensive Criminal Code Reform Act, S. 1722, which made it a felony for any cult to harass people in airports and on federal property. Dole received little credit because he adopted a low profile on this bill.

On a warm May 1979 morning in his hometown of Russell, Dole announced his candidacy for president. "Everything I have ever become I owe to Russell," he told the audience, and then went off to celebrate what the town had declared "Bob Dole Day." In this maiden campaign speech, Dole spoke vaguely of his dream "to let America be America again," chided the federal bureaucracy for vitiating the "small-town values of America," and promised a return to those very values. But he offered no specific prescriptions. Voters, though generally disenchanted with Carter's uninspiring performance as president, saw little promise in what Dole had to offer.

Appearing nationwide on "The MacNeil/Lehrer Report" a few days after opening his campaign with campaign manager Tom Bell in tow, Dole came across as a man uncertain of his beliefs and unwilling or unable to justify his candidacy. He scoffed at the polls showing him with single digit support, and insisted he would win the nomination against all odds.

Tom Bell was a former Senate aide to Bill Brock of Tennessee and head of his own political consulting firm, Response Marketing.* Bell set Dole up with a package strategy that included aggressive use of his Senate office to gain publicity on key legislation and a schedule of key appearances in primary states. Bell assigned an experienced political operative, David Chew, to work as Dole's administrative assistant in his Senate office and to get free publicity through sponsorship of conservative legislation. But the senator resented being managed. "I'm my own manager," he boasted, and he distrusted and resented anyone managing his campaign. Less than three months later, Dole fired Bell, blaming him for spending money without his authorization and for failing to raise his standing in the polls. In a nasty war of words, Bell sued for unpaid fees and Dole countersued.

Bell was the first of five campaign managers to walk the plank. "He's impossible to plan for, we never could articulate a clear position, and could not decide on a strategy," said Gerry Mursner, Dole's Midwest campaign coordinator. "We had five different strategies that could have beaten George Bush in Iowa, but Dole didn't stick with any one."

From the opening of his campaign in May 1979 to the first presidential caucus in Iowa in January 1980, Dole virtually vanished from public sight and became an invisible candidate. He made few campaign trips outside of Washington and Kansas, choosing to attend to his Senate duties. His name rarely appeared in print or on the television screen. He told his disbelieving Senate staff

---

*Brock became Dole's presidential campaign manager in 1987. Lighthizer became the treasurer for Dole's third presidential bid in 1995.

that they were his "only real staff" and that he would
win the presidential nomination by impressing voters
with his record of accomplishment and high attendance
in the Senate. As one veteran GOP strategist said to the
author, this was a "mighty peculiar campaign." Wherever he went, Dole called himself "the working candidate," and contrasted himself with Bush and Reagan,
who were not employed. "I'm the one with the full-time
job, I'm the guy who has to work for a living," he would
tell audiences. Nobody cared. Some laughed.

Many of his Senate aides secretly supported his opponents. "I hope he withdraws soon, so we can wear
our Reagan buttons to work," they joked. Dole's real
campaign office was his Senate office. His Senate staff
doubled as de facto campaign aides. Dole was the only
senator who carried on his Senate duties with no administrative assistant at all for a long while, as his office
management duties were divided among several aides.

Many Kansans criticized Dole for failing to declare
whether or not he would run for reelection to the Senate
and attacked him for putting his personal ambition above
the interests of Kansans. The press outside of Kansas
totally ignored Dole. Meanwhile, it lionized Kennedy,
whom it forced into challenging President Carter for the
Democratic presidential nomination.

"They [reporters] are attracted to Teddy like flies,"
Dole complained to me, branding Kennedy "a phony, a
limousine liberal, a big spender raised on a silver spoon."
In August 1979, Dole startled and amused the media by
announcing, in a National Press Club speech, that he
would run his campaign "against Kennedy" even before
the latter had officially announced his candidacy. On the
Senate floor and in Judiciary Committee hearings, he
harassed Kennedy with snide remarks. Kennedy ignored
him, turning up his nose at the Kansas bumpkin and
treating his candidacy as a joke.

After Kennedy declared his candidacy in early November, Dole worried that reporters would wander down the
hall and catch his Senate staff in some activity, such as

campaign work, that "might look bad." Dole complained, "The media will let him [Kennedy] get away with anything, but if I did it, they'd cordon off my office and shut me down the next morning." Instead, the surprisingly fickle media turned on Kennedy and resurrected the ten-year-old scandal of Chappaquiddick. As Kennedy fumbled and sputtered, Dole privately ridiculed him as "needing a bridge over troubled waters" and "making a big splash."

Kennedy's decline did nothing to revive Senator Dole's own invisible candidacy, however. Bob remained silent and broke. His Campaign America PAC existed on paper, but could not raise money. When a mob of Iranians seized the U.S. Embassy in Tehran and took fifty-two Americans hostage in early November 1979, Dole toyed with several controversial anti-Iran legislative proposals that might have won him some publicity. He held back for fear that the press would say, "Dole's going to get us into a war." He ordered his staff to draft tough bills imposing sanctions and embargoes on Iran, but he never saw them through.

As Dole stood idly by, other candidates stole his ideas and got the credit. On the Senate floor, on November 8, Dole accused Carter of failing to stockpile oil because of Saudi Arabian threats, thereby leaving the country dangerously vulnerable to another Arab oil embargo. Dole told the clerk of the Senate that he wanted to introduce an amendment to an energy bill that would force the president to stockpile oil in the nation's "strategic petroleum reserve," an amendment that I originated. Then Dole retreated to the GOP Senate cloakroom.

When the clerk of the Senate called out his name on the loudspeaker and told him it was time to fish or cut bait, Idaho Senator Jim McClure went up to him and said, "Come on, Bob, make up your mind. What if you were president and the Russians were attacking? What would you do?" Thus goaded into action, he finally did walk onto the floor and introduce the legislation, which passed on a roll-call vote. But the oil lobbyists opposed the amendment, and Dole played possum, while other senators introduced their own versions and took the spotlight away from him. As a result, when it passed and was signed into law by President Carter in June 1980, Dole got little or no credit for this important amendment.

On national television late in the year, Johnny Carson ridiculed Dole in a famous line: "Bob Dole is not the most exciting, charismatic personality around. He recently willed his body to science, and they contested the will." In the "parking lot of life," Carson quipped, "Bob Dole is a Chrysler."

The insubstantiality of Dole's campaign became painfully evident on January 5, 1980, when six of the seven GOP hopefuls gathered in Des Moines, Iowa, for a nationally televised debate two weeks before the "baptismal font" of the Iowa precinct caucuses. At the Iowa debate, Dole wallowed in self-pity:

> I've been wondering for some time as I stood on the Senate floor day after day after day, if the voters in Iowa really appreciate my nineteen years' experience in the House and Senate. I've wondered from time to time whether Iowa voters were aware of my role in World War II, and the strength I've gained through adversity. I've wondered sometimes if the Iowa voters know about my chairmanship of the Republican Party, my work in the party, and my campaign with Jerry Ford in 1976.

Dole's plaintive plea for support fell on deaf ears.

Two weeks later, the Kansas senator finished in last place in Iowa, with less than 3 percent of the total vote. His dismal showing was particularly humiliating since Iowa was a farm state contiguous to his own. Virtually all of his political advisers—except his wife—counseled him to withdraw, but Dole rushed headlong into New Hampshire. With a strong grassroots organization, Bush had upset the early front-runner, Reagan, in Iowa and was now the leader in the polls. If Bush won in New Hampshire, he would probably sew up the nomination.

"We have to stop Bush," Dole told his staff the next day. His eyes glowered at the prospect. Determined to demolish Bush in New Hampshire at all costs, Dole spent $50,000 on a mad, negative, last-minute campaign blitz. He suddenly moved into New Hampshire with staffers in tow. Casting off the mask of "compassion," he now seemed like Captain Ahab chasing Moby Dick.

In his search for an issue on which to harpoon Bush, Dole hit on the fact that Bush had once been a member of the Trilateral Commission, an elitist "Eastern establishment" organization founded by David Rockefeller in 1973 as a forum for promoting economic and political cooperation among the United States, Europe, and Japan. Dole identified Bush as a "card-carrying member" of this "supranational" group. Slipping easily into the role of witch-hunter, hinting at treason, Dole said that the Trilateral Commission was a conspiracy to undermine American sovereignty. Noting that Carter and all of his cabinet secretaries had been Trilateralists, Dole denounced both Bush and Carter as bankers' puppets and "Rockefeller candidates" who wanted to put foreign interests before American interests and who would subvert the Constitution.

Reagan declined to savage Bush personally and let Dole do his dirty work. Dole's attacks found a receptive audience in William Loeb, a staunch Reagan supporter and right-wing publisher of New Hampshire's influential *Manchester Union Leader*. Though he had completely ignored Dole for the past nine months, Loeb suddenly gave the Kansan an arena. News stories and op-ed pieces that appeared were followed by savage editorials lambasting Bush and echoing Dole's allegations of "conspiracy." Such attacks damaged Bush's credibility with conservative voters in the Granite State.

On February 23, 1980, three days before the crucial New Hampshire primary election, the *Nashua Telegraph* sponsored a televised debate between Bush and Reagan, because the *Telegraph* editors considered these two the only "serious" Republican candidates. Furious, Dole filed a complaint with the Federal Election Commission. He and the other candidates came up with a plan to sandbag Bush by secretly flying up to Nashua just before the debate started and demanding to participate.

At the debate, following a carefully written script, Reagan feigned righteous indignation when "the Nashua Four" suddenly appeared out of nowhere and were denied the right to participate in the debate by Bush and the *Telegraph* sponsors. Reagan seized the microphone and declared, "I'm paying for this microphone, Mr. Green" (paraphrasing a line from *State of the Union*, an old Spencer Tracy movie about a presidential campaign) and insisted he wanted the other candidates to participate. When a pro-Reagan technician turned off the power in the microphone to make the situation appear more oppressive, Reagan started yelling. Television cameras recorded everything. Caught off-guard, Bush objected, looked dazed, and was booed off the stage. "Bad, bad!" Dole shouted while someone in the audience called Bush "Hitler."

As it turned out, the Nashua Four had to stand on the sidelines and watch Reagan debate Bush alone. But Bush never recovered from the fall he took that night. His poll standings plummeted, and three days later Reagan won 51 percent of the primary vote to Bush's 22 percent.

While these gunslinger tactics helped demolish Bush, they did not salvage Dole's own campaign. Out of a total of more than 100,000 votes cast in the New Hampshire Republican primary he received a puny 608, less than 1 percent. As after every defeat, Dole reacted with anger and bravado. He strutted about the Senate like a conquering Caesar, recounting how he had turned the tide against Bush. He steadfastly refused to withdraw from the race. He continued to attack Bush, even while jeopardizing his own chances for reelection to the Senate from Kansas. "He's committing political suicide," said his Senate press secretary, Bob Waite. "If he keeps this up, he won't have any credibility left in Kansas." Everyone else on his staff echoed this view, but no one dared broach the subject of withdrawing. Dole was attacked by Kansas Democratic Congressman Dan Glickman for "pursuing the impossible dream" in seeking the presidency. "At some point," Glickman warned, "the Kansas voter is going to believe that Bob Dole is acting foolishly. He is going to start asking questions about his credibility."

Two days after the New Hampshire debacle, a reporter who had written critical anti-Dole articles asked Dole if he had a statement. Dole thundered, "Not for you—not now, not tomorrow, not ever!"

As the full magnitude of the New Hampshire disaster became apparent, the senator became increasingly isolated, dejected, and caustic. He lashed out indiscriminately at his staff, blaming them for his defeats. Lapsing into a bunker mentality, constantly saying he would "quit the Senate," he wallowed in self-pity. This withdrawal alternated with outbursts of anger, especially at Glickman.

With the Kansas primary filing deadline just ahead, Dole flirted with political disaster up to the last minute by *not* putting his name on the ballot for reelection to the Senate and toying with the idea of running only as a presidential candidate.*

Fate treated Dole to embarrassment on two further counts: his health and his creditors.

Because he had only one kidney, a nearly useless right arm, and experienced occasional numbness in the fingers of his hand, Dole worried that his health might become a campaign issue. On February 18, 1980, the *Medical World News* published a report on the health of each major presidential candidate. The magazine referred to a vectocardiography (VCG) as indicative of an "old inferior

---

*Dole had until February 12, 1980, to file for the April 1 Kansas presidential primary—which he did not do. A second primary, for the Senate office, held in August, required that he file by June 20, which he did.

myocardial infarction," and stated that Dole "seems to have had a silent heart attack three years ago." Dole hit the ceiling at this charge, denying having any cardiac problems.

The medical issue became moot because he was never taken seriously as a candidate, but Dole's problems with his creditors did not. In late 1979, Computer Business Supplies Inc. filed a lawsuit against Dole and his campaign committee for unpaid bills of $166,000. His former campaign manager Tom Bell's organization, Response Marketing, sued Dole for total lawsuit damages of $237,000 for unpaid bills.

Dole had refused to pay these bills, claiming that Bell had not gotten Dole's authority for certain expenditures. In February 1980, Dole filed his own counter-lawsuit against Bell and Response Marketing for $1 million in damages, alleging fraud, breach of contract, and negligence. Bell was infuriated and threatened Dole with a new suit for slander and libel. "This is typical Bob Dole," Bell was quoted in the press as saying. "His attorney said all along they were going to file some kind of suit to try to scare us out of our money. . . . I'll be damned if I'll let him slander me . . . and get away with it." Dole eventually dropped his suit.

On March 5, Senator Howard Baker became the first GOP candidate to quit the presidential race. Quipping that Baker, the shortest candidate, "can always open up a tall men's clothing store—in Japan," Dole felt he now could bow out gracefully. On March 15, at a news conference in Lawrence, Kansas, he finally announced his withdrawal from the presidential race. He bitterly complained, "My greatest asset, my experience and performance as a senator, turned into my greatest liability" in the presidential campaign. Deploring that "campaign skills are valued more highly than leadership skills," he gave up his fantasy with great reluctance.

Even after his withdrawal from the presidential race, Dole's Senate office felt like a sinking ship. He said he might give up his Senate seat to his wife before the term expired, then remarked, "I haven't decided if I'm going to run again." Newspapers reported the rumors and in late April a Kansas newspaper said that Dole had categorically decided to retire and join an East Coast law firm.

But what truly bothered him was the prospect of Congressman Dan Glickman, a liberal Jewish Democrat, winning his Senate seat. Finally, on May 22, he announced that he would seek a third Senate term after all. In November, Dole easily won reelection.

THE TAX MAN COMETH: BOB DOLE AS SENATE FINANCE COMMITTEE CHAIRMAN, 1981–1984

Senator Dole's appointment as Senate Finance Committee Chairman in 1981 honed his talents for logrolling and jawboning. The Finance Committee is susceptible to control by one man, like the skeletal Kansas party structure that Dole controlled. Many senators don't even bother to show up for committee hearings, and because each senator sits on two or three different committees that have conflicting schedules, Dole was able to schedule Finance Committee hearings at times that excluded his enemies and included his friends.

Long before he became its chairman, Dole's main interest in the Senate had been the Finance Committee, especially in its role in manipulating the Internal Revenue Code by clever and "creative" amendments. When I worked for him, Senator Dole spent almost all of his committee time in the Finance Committee. He was obsessed with the minutiae and esoterica of federal tax law, and commanded a truly impressive knowledge and understanding of it. He realized that because the tax code was so large and diffuse, he could put in multimillion dollar tax giveaways in esoteric legal mumbo jumbo that few would understand or even notice. "Who's gonna look at Section 2034, section B, subsection C of the code?" he would say.

Dole vowed to work closely with President Reagan, who in 1980 had been elected primarily on a "Down with

Taxes'' platform, which was supposed to benefit not only business but also Joe Six-Pack.

Following his inauguration on January 20, 1981, Reagan quickly instituted his new program, dubbed "the Reagan Revolution" by his supporters. He froze all federal hiring and sent up a package of legislative proposals to Congress that would cut back the bloated federal bureaucracy by lowering taxes, targeting "waste, fraud, and inefficiency," and by systematically cutting back on a wide array of social programs. Corporate welfare was in and social welfare was out.

Critics and admirers settled on the term Reaganomics to describe the president's attempt to balance the federal budget, increase defense spending dramatically, and slash income taxes by 30 percent over three years. Reaganomics, the most radical tampering with the national economy since the New Deal, sought to effectuate three fundamental shifts in the allocation of the nation's scarce resources: from the public sector to the corporate, from the civilian sector to the military, and from the social programs for the poor to the wealthy via tax cuts. According to Reagan's trickle-down theory, greater revenue would ultimately accrue to the government through tax breaks because a vibrant economy would produce more overall taxable income. Thus less social welfare spending would be needed, since almost everyone would have a job. Ultimately, the tax cuts (and the consequent slashing of social programs) could be justified as incentives given to the rich for the benefit of all.

Reagan obtained cuts of $35 billion in programs thanks to a coalition of Republicans and conservative "boll weevil" Democrats in both the House and Senate. Then he turned to reducing taxes, for which Dole would be his point man.

Reagan soon faced grim consequences. Unemployment, which had been slightly higher than 7 percent on Inauguration Day, rose steadily upward toward 8 and 9 percent. Factories were shutting down at an alarming pace and capacity utilization was heading below 70 percent. The financial markets reflected great pessimism during the early months of the Reagan presidency. The only positive factor was a decline in interest rates from the prime rate of 21 percent Reagan had inherited.

Dole sometimes called supply-side economics "the napkin theory," because one of its founders, Professor Arthur Laffer, had allegedly conceived his theory one day at a restaurant, when he drew a curve on a napkin. When candidate George Bush had ridiculed Reaganomic theory as "voodoo economics" during the 1980 presidential campaign, Dole had remarked acidly, "Bush has his head on right, for once." But now Bush was vice president, Reagan was president, and Dole found himself codifying the economic theory by weaving it into tax law.

Dole's genuine doubts about the validity of the supply-side economic theory exacerbated his natural indecisiveness. On May 15, 1981, *The Wall Street Journal* editorial skewered him as a procrastinator and flip-flopper.

"Perhaps it is time to remind him [Dole] that he is no longer in the opposition . . . and that man in the White House, Ronald Reagan, is a fellow Republican," the *Journal* editors wrote. "He wallows in doubts . . . hems and haws. . . . Chairman Dole's performance would be a bit more understandable if he had a tax plan of his own."

When shamed into action, Dole unveiled his own plan two weeks later. His was a compromise measure that reduced the total amount of the tax cut from 30 percent to 25 (over three years), proposed a number of incentives to stimulate savings and investment, and was somewhat "leaner" than Reagan's.* Yet earlier, while publicly criticizing President Reagan for not going far enough in slashing welfare programs, Dole introduced his own draconian proposal for budget cuts, exceeding Reagan's by $1 billion.

Dole enjoyed wielding power as Finance Committee Chairman. He bullied Reagan's aides, cajoling and pres-

---

*Dole also successfully inserted in the tax bill a provision requiring income tax rates to be indexed to the rate of inflation.

suring them to embrace his bill. "He was harder on us than on his committee members," one aide complained. Reagan went along, and the bill sailed through the committee by a bipartisan 191 vote. It then moved quickly through the Congress and became law. It was called ERTA, the Economic Recovery Tax Act of 1981.

Dole's tax bill brought about huge tax breaks on oil production, capital gains, stock options, estates, interest income, IRAs, savings certificates, and other items. The tax bill even allowed companies to sell their tax breaks to other businesses if they couldn't use them in a particular year. While social spending was cut by about $30 billion, military expenditures were increased by a corresponding $28 billion—the largest single increase in U.S. peacetime history. To pay for the new weaponry, child nutrition programs and workers' unemployment insurance were reduced drastically, as were welfare payments, Medicare, and Medicaid aid to the states. CETA public service jobs were eliminated entirely, as were college education benefits previously provided under Social Security. Even the food stamp program, which Dole had previously supported, was reduced by $1.7 billion, thereby eliminating more than a million recipients.

With virtually all cuts in social spending going to military and corporate clients, the federal budget deficit remained untouched. Projected at about $49 billion, the 1981 budget deficit turned out to be even worse: $57.93 billion. Indeed, with taxes cut by a whopping 25 percent, it seemed obvious that the deficit would dramatically *increase*.

Unemployment increased by 13.6 percent in the first ten months of 1981; housing starts declined by 44 percent; new car sales were down by 30 percent; total industrial output declined by 0.5 percent. The bond and stock markets were taking a nosedive. On November 10, Reagan admitted publicly that he expected some hard times ahead. The phrase "hard times" was repeated in banner headlines around the country and, for ten million

unemployed people, became synonymous with Reaganomics.

In December 1981, *The Atlantic Monthly* magazine
published a sensational article by William Greider entitled "The Education of David Stockman." This article,
based on a series of taped interviews with Reagan's
budget director, revealed the fundamentally flawed basis
of Reaganomics. Stockman admitted that the great
Reagan tax cut was really "a Trojan Horse to bring down
the top [tax] rate" for the rich. He denigrated supply-side
economics as nothing more than a dressed-up version of
the old trickle-down theory.

The administration announced in January 1982 that it
expected the 1982 federal budget deficit to reach a record
of $91 billion; this was assuming the most optimistic of
circumstances. Other sources estimated it would exceed
$109 billion. The previous record, $66 billion, had been
set by the Ford administration in 1976.

Dole began complaining that Reagan's policies were
unfair and proposed the enactment of a minimum tax on
the wealthy. A weathervane without real ideology or
beliefs, Dole shifted his position when he sensed public
opinion changing. He said he was bothered by the fact
that many corporations and wealthy individuals paid no
tax at all, thanks to loopholes in the tax laws and generous tax breaks. Reagan, who initially opposed the idea
of a minimum tax on the grounds that it would stifle
productivity and weaken incentive, went along with Dole.

On February 19, 1982, Dole announced that he wanted
to repeal the "safe harbor leasing" rule sanctioned by his
Finance Committee the summer before. Strongly favored
by the business community, it enabled less profitable
companies to sell their tax breaks to more profitable
ones. Dole declared that "leasing is indefensible in a year
in which the federal deficit will reach nearly $100 billion"
and called it "corporate welfare."* With combative flair,

---

*Dole's coining the term "corporate welfare" is ironic, because
he has gone on to become one of the most extreme practitioners
of corporate welfare in modern history, as detailed throughout
this book.

he declared that his repeal would be applied retroactively to all leases entered into "as of the date of this speech" and warned that henceforth anyone who chose to engage in such a swap would "do so at their own risk."

Ten days later, Dole said on "Face the Nation" that Reagan would have to accept changes in the ERTA tax bill that had been enacted just the year before. He suggested a repeal of the 10 percent tax cut scheduled to go into effect in July, as well as imposition of a minimum tax on the wealthy and the closing of tax loopholes. He fingered rich doctors and other professionals who routinely used such loopholes. At about this time, the Congressional Budget Office released a report proving that the 1981 tax cut was producing very little benefit to low-and moderate-income taxpayers, while benefiting the wealthy. Dole seized on this to hammer away again at the unfairness of Reaganomics.

When Reagan claimed his programs did not hurt "the truly needy," Dole responded that Reaganomics was just helping "the truly *greedy*." Increasingly, he delivered his speeches with populist gusto that struck many observers as "radical" and "liberal." On one national television program, a well-known panelist said in reference to Dole, "If I didn't know any better, I'd think that person sitting next to me was Teddy Kennedy." Dole kept everyone guessing.

In March 1982, Dole spoke to the Chamber of Commerce, and told the businessmen to their faces, "There is a perception out there that this administration lacks sensitivity, lacks compassion, and spends most of its time dreaming up programs to help the rich . . . you see it on a daily basis, morning, noon, and night." At the same time, he kept attacking the "liberal Democratic Congress" for creating the deficit of which he himself was a major architect.

In April 1982, Reagan proposed a massive cut of $2.3 billion in the food stamp program. Dole countered with a proposal to cut back only one-third as much and rounded up enough support among his Senate colleagues to force Reagan to back down.

Dole again defied Reagan that May by proposing a crucial amendment to the Voting Rights Act, which preserved the act's provisions against discriminatory voting booth practices. Dole mustered enough support among Judiciary Committee senators to pass his "compromise amendment" and again presented Reagan with a fait accompli. As a result, Reagan was made to appear as an opponent of civil rights progress, while Dole earned the accolade of "the Dirksen of the '80s" from civil rights lobbyist Joseph Rauh, who then considered him an ally in the war against what was felt to be an insensitive Reagan administration.

But Dole's crowning achievement of 1982 was his success in proposing and spearheading The Tax Equity and Fiscal Responsibility Act of 1982 (TEFRA). In June 1982, Congress was stalemated over a budget impasse. In contrast to their eager rubber-stamping of a year before, the legislators showed no tolerance for the massive social budget cuts President Reagan proposed. His proposal was overwhelmingly rejected, and he declined to offer a substitute. Meanwhile, hundreds of different proposals were introduced in both the House and the Senate, but none stood any chance of passage.

Dole decided to step into this leadership vacuum by proposing a major tax compromise package that he judged would appeal across the board to Democrats and Republicans, liberals and conservatives. The keystone was the repeal of many of the benefits that had been given to business and rich individuals the previous year. He set a clear goal of raising $98 billion in taxes.

On June 28, 1982, Dole promised he would "step on a lot of toes in Gucci Gulch," with TEFRA. "There's a perception that we've been too hard on poor people," he said. "Now we have to make sure that corporations pay taxes." Social programs should be left alone to "stabilize for a couple of years," he said, and he vowed to direct his fire at "some of the other programs that have escaped" spending cutbacks. In addition to repealing the safe harbor leasing rule and closing corporate and upper-bracket loopholes, he proposed increasing numerous taxes that would chiefly affect the middle class: on airline tickets, cigarettes, and telephone calls. Medical payment deductions would be reduced significantly. The three-martini lunch—that is, the standard business entertainment deduction—was also targeted for repeal. In addition, Dole proposed more stringent reporting requirements for taxing waiters' and waitresses' tips, an immediate 10 percent withholding tax on savings account interest and stock dividends, and enhanced enforcement powers for the Internal Revenue Service.

TEFRA was the largest single tax-raising measure in U.S. history and these proposals shocked and angered the business community and conservative Republicans.* After all, this was the party that had promised to cut back taxes, give big business a stimulus, and get the government off the backs of the people. By its very nature, the tax bill seemed a repudiation of Reaganomics. Conservatives like Kemp said so vociferously. Dole was denounced by many as a "tax collector" who wanted to beef up the IRS's tax collecting and enforcing power. Conservative Republican Congressman Newt Gingrich of Georgia denounced Dole as "the chief, self-appointed tax collector for the liberal welfare state." Dole, however, declined to characterize his bill as a step backward and insisted that he was not reversing Reaganomics.

In a lengthy op-ed piece he wrote that appeared in *The Washington Post* on August 8, 1982, the senator said he was "not trying to make a U-turn. We are merely adjusting the route to keep from going off the road." He insisted that he was still a "conservative" and claimed,

---

*In 1990, TEFRA's tax hike would be exceeded by that crafted by Bush and Dole as part of the notorious budget compromise of 1990, which ultimately cost Bush his presidency for violating his 1988 campaign pledge to "read my lips: no new taxes." The 1990 bill raised taxes by $137 billion.

"I am not a liberal . . . neither am I a lemming." He wrote, "I never defined conservatism as the religion of the propertied few or of those whose voices carry in direct proportion to their wealth." He went on to praise "working people" and insisted that "the current debate is not one of conflicting philosophies, but over how to put conservative theory into practice in a way that won't invite popular rejection."

The flavor of the tax debate was caught brilliantly in a political cartoon by Clyde Wells accompanying Dole's piece in the August 8 *Washington Post*. The message of the cartoon was clear: Dole was trying to steer economic policy in one direction, while Reagan did not know where he was going, and was driving an ancient Model-T.

Dole convinced Reagan to actively support the TEFRA bill. Reagan went on national television to ask the American people to call and write to their representatives in Congress and urge them to pass this "necessary" measure, insisting that it was not a tax hike but just a "reform" measure needed to close the budget deficits.

The TEFRA tax bill passed the Senate, by a 52–47 vote. Several liberal Democrats who viewed the bill as an attack on the rich provided the margin of victory. In the House, though bitterly opposed by Kemp and a contingent of die-hard conservatives, the bill was finally passed in August and became law on September 3, 1982.

Several national newspapers and broadcast networks focused on Dole, showering kudos on him for his extraordinary role as the Great Compromiser. They spoke of "the new Dole," a man to be reckoned with as "a potential president," a courageous leader who was willing to stand up to big business for the good of the country, while the rest of his colleagues cowered in fear.

In late August 1982, Dole received a hero's welcome from brokers on the floor of the New York Stock Exchange. Eyewitnesses said they had never seen any politician so lionized by Wall Street, which felt that the passage of TEFRA portended a sharp drop in interest rates since the tax hike would mean less government borrowing. Interest rates did drop dramatically, and as a result, the stock market, which had hit a two-year low below 800 in June, suddenly began to rise in mid-August, marking the beginning of a long bull market. The bull market that Dole ignited was eventually to drive the Dow Jones Industrial Average to a peak of more than 2,700 in August 1987 and eventually over the 4,000 mark in 1995.

While in New York, Dole addressed a convention of the Sheet Metal Workers Union.* He was the only Republican invited, an extraordinary recognition of his reputation for standing up in the Senate for the working man. Dole followed several prominent liberal Democratic senators to the podium in what was billed as a "parade of presidential hopefuls."

Meanwhile, he was being pilloried by the business lobbyists. During the tax bill hearings before his committee, Dole had kept them at arm's length. When a whole line of such lobbyists stood outside his hearing room to plead their clients' causes, Dole remarked, "There they are, linked up Gucci to Gucci. They'll all be barefoot by morning." He attacked business lobbyists for their "high-handed tactics" and "campaigns of distortion" against his bill. When they threatened to lobby against a provision, he countered by threatening to impose an even tougher measure against them. "Nobody wants to give up a good thing he's got going," Dole said of big business. "What you don't want to do is to let some amendment slip in that helps some big corporation."

Horace Busby, a business lobbyist and former aide to Lyndon Johnson, castigated Dole for having "undergone a transformation this year" and described Dole's tax bill as being "very much in the mode of a Democratic liberal bill, lightly taxing individuals, coming down heavily on

---

*Dole said this was the first union he had addressed since his early days in Kansas. He had acquired an anti-union reputation during the 1960s and 1970s. He once blasted Walter Mondale for "never making a speech more than two blocks from a union hiring hall."

investors and businesses.'' Dole told *Fortune* magazine, ''We shouldn't favor big business over small business. We shouldn't favor any business over any individual enterprise or partnership.'' He continually criticized corporations for their abuses and wealthy individuals for their greed and their exploitation of tax loopholes. ''I think it's unfair,'' he said, ''that we have to take money away from a disabled man who's trying to get along on food stamps, so that doctors and dentists can put $40,000 away in a tax-free shelter.''

In August, Dole seized another opportunity to expose business abuses. The Johns-Manville Corporation, whose assets exceeded its liabilities by $1 billion and which had sales of $2 billion per year, filed for bankruptcy to shield itself from thousands of claims and lawsuits filed by victims of asbestosis and other lung diseases allegedly caused by Manville's products over the years. This was an unprecedented use of the bankruptcy laws. Dole attacked the maneuver as ''dubious at best'' and held hearings in his Senate Judiciary Committee to draft legislation preventing companies from exploiting the laws in this way. He featured witnesses who suffered from exposure to asbestos and who testified about the cynical legal maneuvers used against them by Manville.

Dole intensified his criticism of the enormous influence that big business was wielding over Congress through its financing of campaigns via political action committees (PACs). He told *The Wall Street Journal* in 1982, ''When the PACs give money, they expect something in return other than good government. It is making it much more difficult to legislate. We may reach a point where if everybody is buying something with PAC money, we can't get anything done.''*

---

*Later, revealing how he can change his position on an issue, he vehemently opposed Senate bills that would have placed a cap on campaign spending. He led filibusters against campaign reform bills, and became ''PAC Man,'' the largest beneficiary of the PAC system in Congress.

He drew more publicity by calling for a special lame-duck session of Congress between the November 1982 election and Christmas to deal with the Social Security issue. When the election came in November, and the GOP lost twenty-six seats in the House, Dole declared on television that "Reagan has taken a bath in the House."

Two weeks after the election, he staged another sensational media event by leading a delegation of congressmen and American businessmen to Moscow, where he addressed the Soviet Trade Council and called for more trade between the United States and Soviet Union. At a time when Reagan was denouncing Russia as an "evil empire," Dole once again reversed his earlier stance, calmly walking up to the gates of the Kremlin and shaking hands with the Soviet leaders.

With the appointment of his wife to a cabinet position as Secretary of Transportation in January 1983, Dole acquired a mystique. It raised speculation that Elizabeth, herself, might be tagged as a presidential or vice-presidential candidate in 1984 or 1988.

The recession bottomed out in late 1983. As a result, Reagan's standing in the polls skyrocketed, and Dole's dreams of a 1984 presidential candidacy faded away. No politician was willing to listen to Dole's calls for more taxes and spending cuts, and Dole was unable to articulate a clear plan that was palatable to a majority.

Just a year before he had been hailed by civil rights lobbyist Joseph Rauh as the hero of the Voting Rights Act, but now Dole found himself bitterly criticized by the same man for his role in a controversial compromise that he engineered on the membership and independence of the U.S. Civil Rights Commission.* According to Rauh,

*The Civil Rights Commission, created in 1957, was charged nationwide with enforcing the laws guaranteeing civil rights, such as voting rights and affirmative action racial quotas. It had originally been a six-member commission and had been harshly critical of the Reagan administration in 1981–83. In November 1983, the commission was "reconstituted," its membership was expanded from six to eight, and Reagan managed to appoint a

Dole had promised to support "our choice of pro-civil rights members" on the commission after its reorganization. Instead, he backed the Reagan administration's choices, thereby leading Rauh to conclude that the new commission had lost its independence and become essentially worthless.

Reagan announced he would seek a second term, and an economy now rebounding from the recession made him a shoo-in. During the Republican National Convention in Dallas in August 1984, Dole received a lukewarm reception from the delegates as he mounted the podium. His wife, who was seen as a Reagan team player, was greeted much more enthusiastically.

While the 1982–83 recession caused general discontent with the Reagan presidency and made Reagan look like a one-termer, Dole had played the part of a "Prairie Populist." But as soon as the economy recovered and Reagan resurfaced as a viable candidate for reelection, the senator quickly fell into line and thereafter supported Reagan's policies to the hilt.

---

majority that supported his policies and that, according to Rauh's personal statement to the author, was basically indifferent or even hostile toward civil rights. The White House and Dole denied that any agreement had been reached with the civil rights lobby as to membership in the newly constituted commission. Rauh claimed the commission lost its independence and was now without direction, and he seemed bitter at Dole for whatever role the latter may have played. See the *Congressional Quarterly Almanac* 1983, 292–95.

13

"DICTATOR DOLE" AND A SENATE OF "ORGANIZED CHAOS"

Dole's chaotic, quirky, and dictatorial personality fully emerged when he became Senate majority leader in November 1984. This was his first chance to run a large organization, offering perhaps the most accurate preview of a Dole presidency. Dole sought to run the Senate with an iron grip, yet paradoxically he generated an atmosphere that can best be described as "organized chaos."

The November 1984 Republican landslide gave Ronald Reagan a second term in the White House, and left the Republicans firmly in control of the Senate. Dole, who had crisscrossed the country on behalf of GOP candidates during the election, had busily collected political IOUs.

Dole's predecessor as GOP Senate leader, Howard Baker, retired from the Senate in 1984 in order to run for president full-time and "make a lot of money" practicing law. Now it was time to elect a new majority leader, and nervous GOP senators looked worriedly toward the 1986 elections, when twenty-two of them would be up for reelection (compared with only twelve Democrats), with control of the Senate very possibly hanging in the balance. They needed a strongman as Senate majority leader.

Dole lobbied for the position by approaching his colleagues one by one, promising to back their interests if they voted for him and reminding them of his effectiveness as a parliamentarian. One of the senators Dole sought support from was Jesse Helms, the arch-conservative Senate veteran from North Carolina, known as Mr. Tobacco on Capitol Hill. Dole had never previously been particularly supportive of, or interested in, bills favoring the tobacco lobby. Now he needed Helms's considerable influence. In exchange for Helms's support, Dole ultimately supported increased federal subsidies to tobacco farmers, helped kill a proposal to raise taxes on cigarettes, and (unsuccessfully) urged Hong Kong not to restrict its tobacco imports from the United States.

Dole was opposed by Republican Senators Jim McClure of Idaho, Ted Stevens of Alaska, Richard Lugar of Indiana, and Pete Domenici of New Mexico, who had more consistently conservative voting records and were thus more palatable to the right-wing majority of the Republican senators. But these men lacked Dole's drive and opportunism.

Voting took place in four "last-man-out" ballots. McClure, Domenici, and Lugar were eliminated in that order, in the first three ballots. In the third ballot, Dole was tied with Stevens, each winning twenty votes. On the fourth ballot, Dole nosed out Stevens by three votes, winning by a margin of 28–25, becoming the first Kansan to hold the Senate majority leader position since Republican Charles Curtis in 1924. Curtis, who went on to serve as Herbert Hoover's vice president in 1929–33, had always been a favorite icon for Dole.*

When the new Senate convened in January 1985, the Republicans held a slim 53–47 majority. Dole immediately vowed to reduce the massive "twelve-digit" federal deficit he had helped to create by sponsoring Reagan's

---

*Upon Dole's election as majority leader, Elizabeth and his daughter, Robin, presented him with a schnauzer puppy wearing a big red bow and a sign bearing its name, Leader. A photo captured the moment: Wife and daughter kissing Dole, one on each cheek.

massive tax cutting and corporate welfare bills. Stating that he would look out for "Senate interests" and that he had "enough independence that I won't be a lapdog," he set out on a brutal plan to slash social spending, promote business interests, and mandate the chimera of a balanced budget.

At this time, Bob created the Dole Foundation, a nonprofit organization headquartered in Washington whose purpose was to raise money for programs to help the handicapped and disabled people find jobs. He became a virtual Washington institution as a fund-raiser, and as majority leader was earning constant attention and space from an attentive national press corps—all of which had implications for his upcoming presidential campaign.

In addition, Dole controlled his own political action committee, Campaign America. Unlike the foundation, it could not accept donations of more than $5,000. Nevertheless, its coffers now filled, and Dole used the money liberally to support his favorite candidates and garner political favors.

Years before, when he was still in the minority, Dole used to complain that "the Senate is a zoo, it's chaotic, it needs a strongman at the helm." Now he was able to act as that strongman, tightening the rules, inhibiting the proliferation of myriad committees and subcommittees, forcing his colleagues into frequent marathon nocturnal and weekend sessions, making them follow his chaotic schedule and bend to his will as far as parliamentary rules permitted. By installing his longtime Senate staffers Jo-Anne Coe as Secretary of the Senate and Ernie Garcia as Senate Sergeant-at-Arms, Bob assured himself of control over the day-to-day administration of the world's greatest debating club.

The senator knew that support from the right wing of his party was necessary for the presidential nomination. "I'm perceived as a moderate Republican for all the work I've done on tax reform, voting rights, food stamps, all the stuff for veterans and the handicapped," Dole admitted in early 1985. Then, characteristically referring to himself in the plural, he declared: "We're going to make a play for the conservatives. I think I deserve a shot at them."

But he had a reputation as a tax collector for the welfare state because of his role in raising taxes and support for food stamps and other projects. The Kingston Coalition, one of the most vociferous and powerful conservative groups in the country, had greeted Dole with stony silence when he became majority leader in 1984. "He was given a very unpleasant reception," according to Paul Weyrich, a New Right leader, "there was a great deal of hostility toward him from the right wing." "Dole was not number one on any conservative's hit parade during the 1982–83 period, when he was involved in the tax increases," according to New Right guru Richard Viguerie, who considered Dole's election as majority leader a "disaster."

So, in 1985, Dole decided to compete seriously for the right wing's allegiance. He began a process of transformation that led one major political analyst to call him "the Zelig of American politics."

Dole continued to harp on the swelling budget deficit, but with Democrat Walter Mondale's 1984 election disaster on a pro-tax platform, and the right's opposition to all taxes in mind, he carefully avoided any specific proposals for tax hikes. Instead, he chose the "slash and burn" approach: ruthless cuts in social spending programs.

He became furious when Senate committee chairmen initially rebuffed his efforts to reach a consensus and failed to announce a budget deficit reduction plan by February 1, 1985. He then turned to the Senate Budget Committee to draft a plan, but Reagan supporters refused either to cut the defense budget or to freeze Social Security cost of living adjustments (COLAs), as Dole proposed.

During the tedious bargaining sessions, which numbered six or eight each day and sometimes overlapped, Dole buttonholed his colleagues in countless cloakroom caucuses, and used all his powers to coax, wheedle, and harangue them into supporting the package. In a fashion unseen in the Senate since Lyndon Johnson's wheeler-dealer days as majority leader in the late 1950s, Dole cut deals in which money was restored to senators' favored pet programs in exchange for their votes. Senators who voted for the deficit-cutting plan got money for everything from Amtrak to Urban Development Action Grants to farm programs. In many cases, Dole agreed to introduce amendments he had previously adamantly opposed. He forced the Senate into lengthy, interminable night sessions, flourishing in the chaos and workaholism.

Dole finally managed to scrape together a bare one-vote majority for his budget plan by wheeling in California Senator Pete Wilson from a hospital bed with an intravenous tube attached to his arm to cast the forty-ninth vote, for a 49–49 tie. Vice President Bush then cast the deciding vote for the compromise package on May 10, 1985.

But Dole's budget failed to pass both houses of Congress. Although his deficit reduction plan never became law, during the 1988 presidential campaign he called the resolution one of his biggest achievements in Congress and asserted that it set the climate for the subsequent Gramm-Rudman-Hollings deficit-reduction bill, which was enacted in 1986. It is significant that he viewed his draconian measure as his "greatest Senate accomplishment."

Because Reagan refused to budge an inch from his swollen defense budget, however, Dole found it impossible to craft a politically palatable deal to trim an annual deficit then hovering around $200 billion.

He even called for cuts in defense, which did not endear him to the right-wingers he now courted. However, for the first time in years, he refused to back a tax hike as a means of reducing the deficit, and he took several steps to make his new ideology known to the zealots of the right. As majority leader, he brought to the Senate floor several issues popular with conservatives, including one that actually loosened federal gun control laws, as well as a bill to grant the president line-item veto power. In addition, he made himself far more accessible personally to conservatives, hired them as staffers, and appointed a favorite conservative figure, Don Devine, as head of his Campaign America PAC.

Stretching out his arms to the right, Dole convinced many that he was truly one of them. Howard Phillips, leader of the Conservative Caucus, said in the fall of 1985, "In general, Dole has been able to shed the baggage of appearing to be someone who wants to raise taxes." However, Phillips attacked Dole on another issue, this time for being "wrong on South Africa sanctions, which is the number one issue of the conservative movement in the decade of the 1980s." (Dole had supported limited sanctions to protest apartheid.) Phillips continued to criticize Dole for some of his stands in favor of civil rights and other issues, while other dyed-in-the-wool conservatives, such as Richard Viguerie, remained skeptical about the senator's overall commitment to their cause.

Dole's transformation into a conservative front man directly conflicted with the institutional role of leading his disparate GOP Senate colleagues, many of whom did not share the right-wing philosophy. "That's the dilemma he has to resolve," warned Phillips. "He has to decide whether he wants to be a national leader of conservatives who would be in a position to become the Republican nominee in 1988 or thereafter, or if he wants to be the leader of the Republicans in the Senate. He's got to decide whether he's going to be a hero in Washington or a hero to the country."

Instead he became a hero to no one.

Ted Kennedy, for one, acidly chided his shameless courting of the right. "You've done too much good for the poor, on food stamps and civil rights," Kennedy said, "to be acceptable to those right-wingers." Dole, who appeared on a daily Mutual Radio Network talk show with Kennedy, dismissed such criticism, claiming he'd always been a conservative. Yet Dole's ideological ambivalence can be seen in his hiring of Mark Bisnow, a former aide to liberal Congressman John Anderson, as his counsel in 1985.

In the fall of 1985, Dole shepherded through the Senate the controversial Gramm-Rudman-Hollings Bill, called the "Balanced Budget and Emergency Deficit Control Bill of 1985," which provided automatic budget cutbacks (called "sequestration") if Congress and the president could not agree to meet certain targets by specific dates each year. The aim of the Gramm-Rudman-Hollings Bill was to balance the federal budget by 1991. It was a doomsday machine in that it gave a computer automatic power to shut off billions of dollars of funding on programs across the board if Congress failed to reach specific budget-cutting targets by a certain date. A new approach to the deficit problem, its passage was a bleak testimony to the failure of human leadership and decision making in Congress.

Nevertheless, Dole was proud of his role in enacting this bill, for it was the first time a serious effort to trim the deficit had been made. And by the end of his first year as majority leader, he was able to point to a host of other enacted bills as well. According to figures prepared by his own staff, as of December 1985, 163 bills were enacted into law and 474 measures were approved during the first eleven months of Dole's leadership as compared to only 84 enacted bills and 413 approved measures during the first eleven months of Howard Baker's in 1981.

Dole won mixed reviews for his performance as majority leader. Kansas's junior senator, Nancy Kassebaum, characterized her colleague as "more aggressively partisan than Howard Baker. Dole is very much the eye of the hurricane. He's right there with an enormous amount of energy sort of battling through each issue as it comes up and trying hard to engineer a compromise." She also said that Dole "blows in the direction of the political wind."

With his horror of delegating authority, Dole sought to control legislation in floor debate in a dictatorial manner unseen in any of his predecessors since Johnson. For example, when Senator Helms, chairman of the Agriculture Committee, brought his 1985 agriculture bill to the floor, Dole personally took control of it and steered it through debate.* Most majority leaders permit the committee chairmen to control floor debate, but not Dole. "My view," Dole said on this matter, "is that I have the responsibility to make it happen. I make decisions on the theory that I'm elected the leader and if I make the wrong decisions, they can get a new leader. I don't wait for the consensus. I try to help build it."

This consensus-building generally took place in Dole's office just off the Senate floor. With a window offering a magnificent, picture-postcard view of Washington, this office was converted into a meeting room when Dole installed a huge conference table. He called forty-five meetings in two weeks and routinely kept the Senate in session long into the night as he tried to exert his personal control over virtually every aspect of its operations.

A top staff director for a Democratic senator, who asked for anonymity, said, "Other leaders had a more orderly process where they didn't fray tempers, waste time, and keep the Senate in late the way it is now. There was more of a sense of comity and consensus under Baker. Dole has allowed more of a . . . meanness to be rampant."

Complaints were not limited to Democrats. "There is practically no respect left for the institution," Republican Senator Jake Garn complained in 1985, "no respect for individual senators, no respect for party loyalties whatso-

---

*Although Dole continues to call reducing the budget deficit his top priority, the 1985 agriculture bill of which he was the chief architect accounted for 12 percent of the total deficit for the fiscal year 1987. (See Martin Tolchin and Jeff Gerth, "The Contradictions of Bob Dole," *The New York Times Magazine*, November 8, 1987, pp. 6288.) The bill, P.L. 99-198, gave farmers a record $52 billion in federal price and income supports over three years according to the *Congressional Quarterly Almanac*, Vol. XLI (1985), chapter 12, p. 517.

ever. The Senate has been a disgrace for months. We have no procedure. We have no order."

In December 1985, Dole called an unprecedented meeting of all one hundred senators to discuss the Senate's "internal troubles." Yet he also said disparagingly, "If you're hanging around with nothing to do and the zoo is closed, come over to the Senate. You'll get the same kind of feeling and you won't have to pay."

Why was the Senate a "zoo" under Dole? Democratic Senator Alan Cranston described the majority leader as "not very effective in reaching across the aisle" to put together bipartisan majorities on bills. He was "too partisan."

Some Democratic senators complained openly about Dole's dictatorial and chaotic style of leadership. The 1985 farm bill, for example, was scheduled by Dole for floor action without any hearings, thereby preventing senators from rounding up witnesses to testify for or against its many provisions. During the South Africa sanctions debate, Dole locked up an important document in a safe until after his colleagues had voted. "I'm the majority leader," he shouted at his critics. "I can lock up anything I want."

Senator Tom Harkin of Iowa had antagonized Dole many times during the previous year, butting heads with him over emergency farm credit legislation and corporate welfare laws. Also in 1985, the Iowa freshman had dared to call on his own for an adjournment of the Senate, thereby challenging the majority leader's traditional authority. Referring to that presumptuous move, Dole said acidly, "He doesn't run this place yet."

In March 1986, Dole mounted a personal attack against Harkin on the Senate floor. "It has come to the point now where it is flat out politics," Dole snarled, "and I think it is fairly clear where that effort is coming from." Asked if his feud with Harkin was too personal, he replied, "Almost personal, yeah. I don't mind having disagreements, but not a single soul wants to stop this [change of wording in a resolution] except Tom Harkin.

He loves all the attention. Then he runs around and does what he normally does, anyway. So," he added menacingly, "we'll keep an eye on something he wants someday."

Five months later, in August 1986, Dole was in the midst of another personal feud on the Senate floor, this time against the minority leader, Robert Byrd. Dole expressed "surprise and disappointment" at Democratic senators who had just offered a surprise amendment on the bill to override President Reagan's veto of a bill to impose sanctions on South Africa. Furious at having his control of the Senate challenged, Dole barked, "I think it is time we ask ourselves, in all honesty, what kind of game we are playing here."

Dole also suggested that Byrd had tried to "sneak in" an amendment. When Byrd rose to his feet and demanded an apology, Dole refused. Byrd shouted, "I have had enough of this business of having the majority leader stand here and act as a traffic cop on this floor." Dole shot back: "I don't intend to be intimidated by anyone in the Senate!" Dole resented Byrd because he could not tolerate dissent, and Byrd, as leader of the minority, symbolized dissent. "I didn't become majority leader to lose," Dole bellowed.

GOP Senator Pete Domenici said he heard words on the Senate floor that evening that he had never encountered in fourteen years of service. A Republican aide muttered that the Senate was experiencing "ugly times" and added, "I don't think I've ever seen anything quite like that."

Dole was a master at filing waves of Republican amendments in such a way that Democrats were blocked from offering their own amendments on key legislation. He also perfected the parliamentary trick of the "Amendment Tree," a method of voting that permitted the majority to veto a whole series of amendments proposed by the minority, in one vote, with no debate. Some Democrats tried for days to offer amendments but were prohibited by Dole's maneuvers. Dole also managed to antagonize House Speaker Tip O'Neill, who complained, "His presidential ambitions put him in a position not to come to me to compromise."

Senator Cranston recalls one incident in which Dole had promised to support Cranston's bill in exchange for Cranston supporting his. "But later, after I fulfilled my end of the bargain," Cranston recalls, "Dole increased his price for him to support me." Dole, according to Cranston, was "unpredictable" and could be "Good Bob" one day and "Bad Bob" the next. "You never knew which Bob you'd be dealing with."

Charges of unfair tactics and "distortion of the truth" were hurled at Dole during the controversial nomination of Daniel Manion to the U.S. Court of Appeals for the Seventh Circuit in June of 1986. Manion, whose father, Clarence, had been a founder of the right-wing extremist John Birch Society, was considered a conservative and was strongly supported by the conservative groups Dole courted. In a complex series of parliamentary maneuvers orchestrated by the majority leader, three anti-Manion votes were "paired" with three absentee senators' votes. Two of the absentees, Republicans Barry Goldwater and Robert Packwood, later said they had been undecided, *not* pro-Manion. Then, during a vote on June 26, Republican Senator Slade Gorton changed his vote at the last minute from "nay" to "aye," so Manion was confirmed by a two-vote margin, 48–46. Packwood complained he had been "misled," and Democratic Senator David Boren charged Dole with duplicity, saying, "The Senate has to be a place that operates on a handshake." Old charges of ruthlessness were revived, and it was whispered that the Manion incident proved that Dole would do anything to win. Dole gave Manion foes a second chance to vote, however, and on July 23 the Senate voted 50–49 against "reconsidering" its earlier vote of June 26. (Vice President Bush cast the fiftieth vote, breaking the tie.) Thus Dole won the battle for his right-wing constituents, but alienated many of his colleagues with his tactics. Moderate senators said he was confusing his duties as majority leader and presidential candidate and that because of Dole's efforts to accommodate conservatives he was forcing the Senate to grapple with controversial right-wing legislation that might have otherwise languished on the calendar.

Despite his efforts to secure conservative backing, Dole came up short on many lists. In the summer issue of *Policy Review*, a publication of the conservative Heritage Foundation, anti-feminist Phyllis Schlafly, president of the Eagle Forum, wrote, "I don't see Bob Dole as somebody who has his heart in any of the issues that conservatives care about. He is trying to do an effective job as majority leader. But he does not seem to be an issues-oriented person." On the other hand, conservative leader Paul Weyrich, in his *Policy Review* assessment, wrote that Dole was "decisive and very tough" and praised him for opening the door to the conservative movement, a door that he said had been closed during Howard Baker's reign. "Dole's isn't always in our corner, he doesn't always do what we want, but he is open to us, he listens."

The American Conservative Union gave the senator only a 64 percent approval rating in 1983, when he was still advocating tax increases and other ideas condemned by the right wing. However, in 1985 and 1986, Dole's approval rating shot up to 91 percent, a clear indication that he had indeed made a dramatic shift. The Chamber of Commerce of the United States had given Dole a mere 62 percent approval rating in 1982 and an even lower 56 percent in 1983. By contrast, he rated a 90 percent rating in 1985 and 89 percent rating in 1986. On May 7, 1986, the *National Journal*, based on an examination of senators' voting records in 1985, said Dole was more conservative than 86 percent of his colleagues in economic matters and 83 percent in social matters. Less liberal than any of his colleagues, he had earned a conservative ranking identical to that of Jesse Helms and Phil Gramm.

On the opposite end of the political spectrum, the liberal Americans for Democratic Action had given Dole a 15 percent rating in 1982 and a 0 rating in both 1985 and 1986. The AFL-CIO, which had put him at a 20 percent rating in 1983, also dropped him to a 0 in 1986.

In an effort to appeal to the right, Dole voted against a proposal to block chemical weapons production, for the MX missile, for aid to the Contra rebels of Nicaragua, and against overriding Reagan's veto of economic sanctions on South Africa in 1986, although he had originally voted for sanctions a short time before the veto.* Despite these votes, Dole seemed less than enthusiastic about supporting the very causes he had voted for. When asked by political analyst William Schneider in 1986 whether he supported the overthrow of the Nicaraguan socialist Sandinista government by the Contras, he said, "I wouldn't say yes or no. Generally, no, I don't think so." Yet he voted for aid to the Contras, and made bellicose anti-Sandinista speeches.

Before 1985, Dole had frequently been a supporter of civil rights issues, but now he sided with extreme right-wingers on other issues to which American blacks were sensitive. He joined Senator Jesse Helms in holding up the nomination of Melissa Wells, the new U.S. ambassador to Mozambique, as a way of pressuring Reagan into dealing with RENAMO, the South African-supported guerrillas there.† And he wrote a letter to a Kansas constituent denouncing the African National Congress of South Africa, an outlawed anti-apartheid organization, accusing it of espousing "necklacing," the gruesome practice of killing suspected government spies in the black townships of South Africa by clamping burning tires around their necks.

Dole's unabashed courting of the right wing found culmination in his pivotal role as a "broker of special interests" in the 1986 Tax Reform Act. The senator

*On October 2, 1986, the Senate voted 78–21 to override Reagan's veto, thereby rejecting Dole's position.
†Dole also backed the UNITA rebels fighting Angola's leftist government.

became a master at crafting special "made-to-order" tax giveaways to businesses who gave him campaign money, such as the Ruan Trucking Company and AmVestors Insurance Company. Dole also served as broker for the interests represented by many other senators, as he wheeled and dealed to conjure up more than 600 separate tax loopholes in the Tax Reform Act of 1986. In a major exposé published in April 1988 in the *Philadelphia Inquirer*, the 1986 Tax Reform Act was revealed as one of the most shameless versions of tax giveaways in American history. This act ended up costing the U.S. Treasury billions of dollars, and raised the federal deficit and national debt through the roof.

Understandably, Senator Dole seemed wary of allowing the American people to watch his performance. In 1985, he opposed allowing Senate debate to be televised. But in 1986 he changed his mind, and on June 1 of that year, television cameras were allowed into the Senate chambers for the first time in history for live broadcast.

Dole's bending over backward to please the right after 1985 disappointed many of his moderate Senate colleagues, who had voted him majority leader thinking he would prove independent of Reagan.* As the midterm elections of 1986 approached, moderates grew understandably nervous, realizing that many of their constituents outside Washington did not share their leader's newfound enthusiasm for the right. Their fears proved justified. On November 4, 1986, Republicans were trounced nationwide at the polls, losing their majority in the Senate to the Democrats, who now took over with a 55–45 majority.

While Dole cannot be blamed entirely, the fact remains that the loss did occur on his watch. He had campaigned actively for Republican candidates everywhere in the fall

---

*Dole supported Reagan's positions on Senate votes 92 percent of the time in 1985 and 1986—in contrast to 78 percent in 1983. See the *Congressional Quarterly Almanac*, 1985 and 1986, Appendix C.

of 1986, reminding voters that it was essential to maintain GOP Senate control.* Nonetheless, he was elected minority leader by his colleagues on November 20, 1986, without any serious challenge.

In his new role, effective January 1987, he continued his confrontational posture in the new 100th Congress. He openly expressed contempt for the Democrats' claims that his goals for deficit reduction could not be met, and he backed Reagan's unsuccessful veto of an $88 billion highway bill. But he now lacked the power to control the Senate's agenda, and was no longer a committee chairman. Still, he was back in his old role as attack dog for the right, chastising the "tax-and-spend liberal Democrats" who now ran the Senate show, and slavishly supporting the president.

Dole easily won a fourth Senate term in 1986, defeating self-employed investor Guy MacDonald, who didn't even campaign, with 70 percent of the vote. Dole spent more time campaigning outside of Kansas than inside and raised the vast majority of his campaign funds outside his home state. Dole didn't even bother to show up in Kansas on election night, but remained in Washington (a practice he repeated six years later).

In a Kansas poll taken shortly before that election, the question asked was "Do you think Bob Dole should run for president in 1988?" Forty-five and two tenths percent said no, 32.8 percent yes, and 22 percent were undecided. Even more startling was the Kansas voters' response to the question "If Dole is a presidential candidate in 1988, would you vote for him?" Only 34.9 percent said yes, 32.1 percent said no, and 33 percent were undecided—an amazingly poor showing for a native son of such prominence. Dole's own constituents' ambivalence echoed his Senate colleagues' feelings.

*In 1986, Dole campaigned in 43 states and 126 cities, on behalf of about 200 candidates, according to the *Kansas City Times*, November 5, 1986. His PAC, Campaign America, gave $240,000 to House and Senate candidates and $64,000 to state and other candidates, according to the *Wichita Eagle-Beacon*.

14

"DUNKIRK DOLE, THE DISORGANIZATION MAN" AND THE 1988 PRESIDENTIAL CAMPAIGN

One of the most intriguing paradoxes about Bob Dole is the stark contrast between his resounding success as Kingfish of Kansas and his dismal failure as a national candidate.

Why is this? One stark difference is the political landscape: Kansas is a uniquely "Republicanized" state with a rudimentary party structure that readily lends itself to control by one powerful man, whereas the national Republican Party is a highly structured network favoring Establishment candidates like Reagan, Bush, and Nixon. In such an environment, Bob Dole has proved notoriously inept. His abrasiveness, impatience, independence, and quirkiness have alienated national GOP figures since the 1970s. Dole is also disorganized, no handicap when running for office in Kansas or even serving in the chaotic atmosphere of the Senate, but the sheer expanse of the United States requires a highly organized campaign structure.

Another reason is Senator Dole's deep-rooted self-destructive tendencies. He seems to have a subconscious need to flirt with disaster, and to even court catastrophe, in order to create a "crisis" in which he must desperately prove himself or crash and burn. In this sense, he resembles Richard Nixon.

Finally, Dole's Jekyll and Hyde personality has also proven a major handicap. Because he has no discernible political beliefs or ideology, he finds it difficult to articulate a coherent and compelling vision for the country. An asset in the Senate, where it has helped him strike compromises with many disparate interests, Dole's vacillating has proven a disaster in the national arena. On the stump, he has often been uncharacteristically tongue-tied and mealy-mouthed, vacillating from position to position, and drowning in a sea of ambiguity. Consider his disastrous 1988 presidential campaign, when he managed to "snatch defeat from the jaws of victory."

Senator Dole began his campaign for the 1988 GOP nomination in November 1986, right after the midterm congressional elections, when the Iran-Contra scandal broke out. He blew an excellent opportunity to damage his chief rival, Vice President Bush, by failing to exploit Bush's own involvement in the scandal, and by foolishly resorting to petty and futile potshots at the vice president.

On November 3, 1986, the Lebanese magazine *Al Shiraa* reported that President Reagan and Vice President Bush had been secretly selling weapons, spare parts, and ammunition to the fanatical Iranian regime of the Ayatollah Khomeini. Subsequent reports revealed that the sales were worth about $30 million, included weapons and missiles, and were an effort to "improve" relations with Iran and to secure Khomeini's help in pressuring Lebanese Islamic terrorists to release several Americans held hostage in Beirut. The stories that the U.S. government had been secretly paying ransom for the release of hostages created a storm of controversy, as the media pilloried Reagan, who until then had seemed untouchable, and hinted that Bush also had been involved.

On November 24, 1986, Attorney General Ed Meese told the nation that millions of dollars of the profits from the Iranian arms sales had been secretly channeled to the Nicaraguan Contras in 1985 and 1986—after Congress had passed the Boland Amendment banning *all* U.S. government aid to the Contras. Meese, in a statement many found difficult to believe, claimed that Reagan and

Bush had been completely unaware of the diversion of
funds to the Contras and pointed to an obscure staffer on
the National Security Council, Oliver North. Bush was
accused of conspiring with North to arm the Contras,
and as he plummeted in the polls, Dole skyrocketed. In
November 1986, Dole was the choice of only about 10
percent of Republican voters, far below Vice President
Bush's 40 to 50 percent ranking. But he increased his poll
standing to 30 percent by January 1987, two months *after*
the Iran-Contra disaster broke. He still trailed Bush by a
narrow margin; but in Iowa, scene of the first presidential
caucuses in 1988, Dole had actually moved ahead.

Dole had heard that Defense Secretary Caspar Weinberger's personal diary and notes revealed the vice president's presence at several key meetings in 1985 and early
1986, in which Bush approved of selling arms to Iran and
the arming of the Contras.* Many other officials also
informed Dole and his staff that Bush had known more
than he admitted about the arms sales. The information,
had it been used by Dole, might have even led to calls for
Bush's impeachment or resignation as vice president.
But, misjudging the situation as he often did in national
campaigns, Dole remained conspicuously silent, blasting
the Democrats and siding with Bush. This was a major
strategic error.

A special prosecutor was appointed to investigate Iran-
Contra, and the House and Senate agreed to set up a joint
select committee to investigate the Iran-Contra affair. As
Senate Minority Leader, Dole had the power to appoint
whomever he wanted—including himself—to this committee. Although the position would have raised his na-

*Weinberger's diaries implicating Bush finally were revealed to
the press in 1992, when Weinberger was indicted for perjury.
These revelations helped sink Bush in the fall 1992 presidential
campaign against Clinton. Dole accused "Democrat liberals"
on Iran-Contra Prosecutor Lawrence Walsh's staff of releasing
the diary story a few days before the presidential election to
hurt Bush. Bush pardoned Weinberger on December 24, 1992.

tional profile, he instead appointed the lackluster Republican senators Warren Rudman, William Cohen, and Paul Trible to the panel, which began televised hearings in May 1987. Meanwhile, a special review board called the Tower Commission, appointed by the president, published its own dubious report exonerating Reagan and Bush of any complicity in the affair.

At a time when Dole should have been campaigning, he began a quirky and tedious program. Each day on the Senate floor, beginning in January 1987, and lasting for the next two years, he recited a trivial episode from the Senate's history in commemoration of its 200th anniversary in 1989. His Senate trivia speeches were called "Bicentennial Minutes" and were eventually collected in a book entitled *Historical Almanac of the United States Senate*, published by the U.S. Government Printing Office. The anecdotes were utterly trivial. For example, he commemorated the vice president's desk originally kept in the Senate chamber.

The Senate trivia routine went largely unnoticed, but consumed considerable effort on Dole's part. He did begin spending some time campaigning in Iowa, New Hampshire, and other key primary states, claiming to be running on "a record" while Bush was doing so on "a résumé." He accused Bush of being an "observer" as vice president for the past seven years, but these lukewarm attacks fell flat.

In March 1987, Bob Dole formed a presidential exploratory campaign committee with his old Kansas friend Bob Ellsworth at the helm and Dave Owen as his national fund-raiser.* When he declared his candidacy on November 9, 1987, he was the last major candidate in either party to do so.† At the age of sixty-four, he was also the oldest candidate running.

*Ellsworth was a former Congressman from Kansas and a Defense Department official under President Nixon.
†All eight Democrats and five Republican presidential candidates had declared their candidacies for the 1988 nomination

Instead of openly criticizing Bush over Iran-Contra, Dole leaked rumors to the press hinting at a longtime extramarital affair Bush allegedly had with a female staffer. The vice president was convinced these rumors were being spread deliberately by Dole's campaign staff, and George Wittgraf, Bush's Iowa campaign director, directly accused the Dole campaign of spreading rumors. In June 1987, while attending a Republican picnic near Des Moines, Iowa, Dole spotted Wittgraf and accosted him. "Listen," Dole said menacingly, "I'm tired of being stabbed by you every time I come out here. . . . If you wanna play that game, I'll be glad to play it with you." Unknown to Dole, a CNN-TV camera crew had been standing by and recorded his confrontation with Wittgraf. The incident was reported in newspapers across the country. This damaged Dole's image and did nothing to derail Bush.

A few months later, Ted Koppel announced on ABC's "Nightline" that "one of Bush's rivals" had been planting rumors with news organizations throughout Washington about Bush's alleged extramarital affair. Koppel and ABC had refused to run the story, he said, because they considered the mudslinging in bad taste. (Dole's mudslinging provoked Bush and his own hatchet man, Lee Atwater, to investigate the senator's cronies and to target Dave Owen and John Palmer over the EDP scandal, which ultimately sank Dole's campaign in early 1988.)

Dole also faced Congressman Jack Kemp, the former Buffalo Bills quarterback, who also ran for president as the "True Conservative" choice to succeed Reagan. Kemp was a doctrinaire supply-sider, who also appealed to the Jewish vote because of his staunch support for

---

long before Dole. Democrats included Bruce Babbitt, Richard Gephardt, Michael Dukakis, Jesse Jackson, Paul Simon, Albert Gore, Gary Hart, and Joseph Biden. Republican candidates included George Bush (declared on October 12, 1987), Alexander Haig, Jack Kemp, Pierre Du Pont, and Pat Robertson.

Israel. Kemp blasted Dole as "the candidate of pain, austerity, and sacrifice." But Kemp was a colorless campaigner.

Another candidate was Pierre "Pete" Du Pont, a multimillionaire conservative who had been governor of Delaware and who criticized Dole for flip-flopping on taxes.

The fifth major GOP contender was evangelist Pat Robertson, chief of the Christian Broadcasting Network who represented the "Christian Right" and called for a theocratic government to enforce Christian values on America.

Then there was Al Haig, the former general, Nixon's chief of staff (1974), and Reagan's Secretary of State (1981–82) who had become a national laughingstock by proclaiming "I'm in charge here" when John Hinckley shot Reagan in March 1981.

Because Kemp, Robertson, Du Pont, and Dole all were underdogs trailing Bush, they considered forming an alliance to attack him over Iran-Contra. But Dole always balked, insisting he had to support the president.

From the start, Dole's campaign was notorious for chaos and the total absence of any theme whatsoever. When he declared his candidacy in Russell, Kansas, on November 9, 1987, he said: "I offer a willingness to work hard, to hang tough, to go the distance. . . . I offer the strength and determination, molded in America's small-town heartland and tempered during a career of public service, to bring common-sense answers to the complex problems facing America in its third century." Comparing himself to "America's great heartland presidents," Dole proclaimed that he and they were "plain-speaking men whose clear-eyed vision enabled them to make the tough choices." But he didn't say *what* he would do if he were elected president, and acted as if he were running another typical Kansas campaign.

After his speech, Dole made a sentimental journey down Main Street to Dawson's Drug Store (now called Rogers' Drugs), where he had worked while in high school in the 1930s and where townspeople had collected

$1,800 in a cigar box to pay the hospital fees for his postwar surgery in 1947. This time he was presented with the identical cigar box, by Bub Dawson, a high school chum whose father had placed the "Bob Dole Donation Fund" cigar box on his counter. (Dole had kept the box for forty years in his desk in Washington.)

Dole's campaign was plagued by disorganization from the start. When Bill Brock resigned his position as Reagan's Secretary of Labor to come on board as Dole's full-time campaign manager in November 1987, he found that "the campaign has no record of its expenditures or even a rundown on Dole's Senate voting record." The senator's position papers on issues had not yet been released, and then Brock himself took a ten-day Caribbean vacation, with Dole's permission, at the height of the primary campaign. To some it seemed as if Dole didn't take his own campaign seriously.

Senator Dole's standard stump speech, heard all over Iowa and New Hampshire before the February 1988 caucuses and primary, was just a boring rehash of his record in the Senate and was devoid of any ideas and plans for the future. Dole also replayed his World War II injuries and repeated this to audiences wherever he went, pandering shamelessly and naively for a "sympathy vote" for his wounds of half a century earlier.

As of mid-December, Dole was the only presidential candidate who had taken no position on the Intermediate Nuclear Forces (INF) Treaty signed by Reagan and Soviet leader Mikhail Gorbachev. Though supported by a majority of Americans, the treaty was vehemently opposed by the right wing of the Republican Party. Characteristically, Dole vacillated and procrastinated, saying he "had to read it first." Finally, after realizing that he was losing support in Iowa because of the waffling, Dole suddenly appeared at the White House with Reagan to offer his enthusiastic endorsement of the treaty.

In late 1987 and early 1988, stories in *The Nation* and *The New York Times* cited Dole's sponsorship of Senate bills favoring the tobacco, ethanol, and insurance industries and listed massive campaign contributions received from executives and the PACs of companies. *Newsday* reported that Dole had regularly solicited and accepted corporate jet rides for campaign appearances from companies whose interests he supported in Senate voting.

But the most damaging blow came in January 1988. Shortly before the Iowa caucuses, Bush's campaign released some leaflets charging that longtime Dole fundraiser David Owen was under investigation for his dealings with the blind trust set up by Dole's wife, Elizabeth. The leaflets further accused Bob Dole of "cronyism," "mean spiritedness," and "single-handedly" bringing about the defeat of the Ford-Dole ticket in 1976. Ever protective of his wife and furious at Bush's "cheap shot," Dole cast off his Dr. Jekyll mask and angrily confronted Bush face to face on the Senate floor. Waving a leaflet in the Vice President's face, a livid Dole denounced Bush for "a new low in campaigning" and for "groveling in the mud" and demanded an apology—which Bush refused to give.

Dole's outburst was reported in the media, again portraying him as an unstable figure whose temper was out of control. In response, Dole wallowed in self-pity and revealed his self-destructive political death wish by declaring publicly: "I don't want the presidency if it means stooping to this level" [Bush's level of mudslinging].

Bush's anti-Dole attacks, like his later notorious Willie Horton ads, were a subtle appeal to white racism. Because Dole had gone to bat for John Palmer, a black man, Bush implied that Dole was a "nigger lover," in the words of Lee Atwater.

Atwater, the vicious mudslinger from South Carolina who engineered the anti-Dole campaign, was looking forward to the all-important Super Tuesday primaries in seventeen states in the South on March 8, 1988, and he knew the Palmer-Owen issue would lead many Southern whites to vote against Dole.* Dole's support for the 1982

---

*Before Atwater died a few years later of brain cancer, he confessed that he had distorted and exaggerated the Palmer-Owen story to discredit Dole. He also apologized for this.

Voting Rights Act, which had angered many Southern whites, was also dredged up by Atwater.

In January 1988, Dole was embarrassed by a series of revelations appearing first in the Kansas Harris News chain of newspapers, and then picked up by the national news media. The articles alleged that Dave Owen, Dole's longtime political protégé and then-presidential campaign finance director, had a conflict of interest in his role as investment adviser to Elizabeth Dole's blind trust. (These events are detailed in chapter 27.)

Though Dole was being plagued by daily media coverage over the mushrooming Owen-Palmer scandal, he managed to ride out the storm for a while. In Iowa, where he was a popular "farm senator" from nearby Kansas and where Bush had foolishly run only a brief "imperial" cameo campaign, Dole managed a commanding lead over Bush. Dole went on to handily win the Iowa caucuses on February 8, 1988, with 37 percent of the vote. Pat Robertson made a surprisingly strong second-place showing, taking 25 percent, and Bush was humiliated by a third-place finish with only a feeble 19 percent of the vote.*

Dole came out of Iowa with such momentum that he seemed on the verge of upsetting Bush in the upcoming New Hampshire primary just eight days later. His ratings rose dramatically there, while Bush's plummeted. But, incongruously, Dole struck his staff as "depressed" and "out of gas" after his Iowa victory. "He acted as if he'd *lost* Iowa," said one aide. "We couldn't rouse him up to do anything with gusto in New Hampshire."

Another aide recalls a scene in a New Hampshire shopping mall a few days after the Iowa win. Dole was mobbed by supporters and signed autographs of his newly released autobiography, *The Doles: Unlimited Partners*. "I think it occurred to him, for the first time,

---

*Jack Kemp received 11 percent, Pete Du Pont 7 percent, Alexander Haig 0 percent, and no preference 1 percent. Haig subsequently dropped out of the race, endorsing Dole as he did so.

that he might really become president now," an ex-Dole aide recalls. "And he seemed really depressed about that. He seemed like he didn't really want it after all."

The senator and many of his top supporters, including fellow Kansas Senator Nancy Kassebaum, Republican Senator Pete Domenici of New Mexico, and Senator Warren Rudman of New Hampshire, gathered for a quiet dinner at the Holiday Inn in Manchester, New Hampshire, the week before the primary.

There, Dole's aides and friends told him that he was extremely vulnerable in New Hampshire to charges that he was "pro-tax," because of his inconsistent record on taxes in the Senate. They advised him to launch a preemptive strike against Bush on this issue, by publicly "taking a pledge," an important symbolic move in New Hampshire, to veto any attempt by Congress to raise income tax rates if he were elected president. Just six days before the primary, Dole's aides prepared such a television commercial entitled "No Taxes," and shot it at a Republican dinner in Nashua. In an on-camera Freudian slip, however, Dole said that he would "veto any attempts to *lower* taxes."

Don Ring, Dole's media producer at the time, recut the tape to say that Bob would veto any attempts to "*raise* taxes." Dissatisfied, Dole acidly noted that "it isn't going to win any Oscars." Then Dole tried to refilm the ad at the University of New Hampshire in Durham, but a blizzard led television stations in the area to change their advertising deadlines, which made it impossible to get the spot on the air. Meanwhile, Dole's well-paid pollster, Richard Wirthlin, kept insisting that taxes were *not* a major issue in New Hampshire and that it didn't matter what he said.

A top Dole adviser at the time said that "Some people think those five words—'I pledge to veto taxes'—stood between Dole and the nomination. They were buzzwords. He was willing to say them, but he didn't."

He also didn't run any negative ads. Later, he would regret this decision in these words: "I was told that people didn't like negative ads. So I didn't run any. I lost.''

As if this were not bad enough, Dole repeatedly hemmed and hawed on the issue of a running mate on his ticket if he were nominated. Former Governor Lamar Alexander of Tennessee, though largely unknown nationally, was nonetheless very popular in the South, which could prove critical to winning the seventeen Super Tuesday primaries on March 8. He was also ''anti-tax'' and would have been popular in New Hampshire. In early September 1987, Alexander flew to Concord, New Hampshire, to take his daughter to St. Paul's School there, and met with Tom Rath, the former state attorney general and Dole adviser. The two men talked about the bold idea of inviting Alexander to join Dole's ticket as his running mate even *before* the 1988 primary season opened. Alexander liked the idea and even wrote a speech to announce his union with Dole.

But Dole put off the idea indefinitely. As the winter bore on, his campaign became increasingly raked with dissention, fed by Dole's own chaotic personality and lack of clear purpose.

Tension grew between the campaign manager, Bill Brock, and the huge army of advisers who had been supporting Dole for the year. Brock was the only campaign aide that Dole regarded as a peer because he had formerly been Republican National Chairman and senator from Tennessee. But Dole never really liked or trusted him. Brock antagonized some of Dole's other brilliant ''idea men,'' such as Don Devine and David Keene, President of the American Conservative Union, and Brock continued to antagonize Dole as well. Yet Dole kept him on the payroll. He also hired Richard Wirthlin to give him advice on polling and taxes, which proved disastrous. Both men had had extremely close ties to Reagan and Bush, who was the Republican establishment's near-unanimous choice for president.

Dole's strategists and aides spent more time fighting one another than battling Bush. Dole continued to make tactical decisions from the isolation of the campaign plane, rather than trusting his fate to lieutenants. Tom Rath, former New Hampshire attorney general and top Dole aide, commented that "nothing was ever final because the people who didn't prevail could always go to the candidate [Dole], where the real authority was."

Dole's campaign was initially dominated by a spend-thrift mentality. By the end of September 1987, five months before the primaries began, Dole had spent $1.4 million *less* than Bush. If he had continued to conserve his money, he might have been able to unleash it to knock Bush out during the critical early primaries in the spring of 1988. Instead, Dole went on to outspend Bush by more than $3 million, wasting money at an astounding rate. By mid-March 1988, he was virtually broke while Bush had $5.5 million in the bank.

Dole's campaign found it necessary to violate the federal election laws and accept many thousands of dollars in illegal and excessive contributions. An interesting question is where the money went. Bill Brock's attitude, seemingly, was that "the sky is the limit" and that anything could be bought and anyone could be hired, regardless of cost. Dole's campaign rented unneeded space for its headquarters, went on a hiring splurge, and spent enormous amounts of money for polling, helicopters, and limousines. The campaign routinely chartered corporate jets and paid considerable money for them. Wirthlin originally billed Dole's campaign $50,000 and then added another $420,000 in January 1988 just for polling work. Brock, who officially began his duties as Dole's campaign manager on November 1, 1987, claimed that he needed to spend all the money so rapidly because Senator Dole had failed to do any real campaigning up to that time. Bernard Windon, Brock's main aide, said that by the time he and Brock came onto the campaign "only one minor survey had been done by Dole."

A million dollars was spent on Boston television stations for ads long before the New Hampshire primary, which later required Dole's campaign to severely slash its media budget. Intending to spend $4 million on Super Tuesday states originally, Dole ultimately spent only about $1.2 million.

At a televised debate in New Hampshire on the Sunday night before the February 16 primary, during the critical weekend when Bush's "Senator Straddle" television commercials were cutting into Dole's base of support, Dole had one last chance to save himself. During the debate among Bush, Du Pont, Robertson, Kemp, and Dole, Du Pont held up a sheet for Dole to sign, pledging not to raise taxes if elected president. Dole looked at the sheet, froze, and refused to sign it. Incredibly, he suggested that Du Pont "give it to George [Bush]. Maybe George will sign it."

Televised across the state, that mistake sent a shudder down the spines of the anti-tax New Hampshire voters and it reinforced Bush's ad theme that Dole was "Senator Straddle." The senator's support in New Hampshire evaporated literally overnight. Whereas polls on February 13 had shown him leading Bush by 2 to 5 points, on Tuesday, February 16, Bush won 38 percent of the vote, while Dole got only 29 percent. This was a landslide by New Hampshire primary standards.

Dole compounded his problem by losing his temper again on national television on the night of the primary, when a reporter asked Dole if he had anything to say to Bush. Dole angrily replied: "Yeah! Stop lying about my record." The national media picked up on this angry remark and immediately resurrected the old "hatchet man" image. "I knew this guy would go ballistic the first time he lost one primary state," noted a reporter in the *New Orleans Times-Picayune*.

After being "a model of political decorum," according to the *Chicago Tribune*, Dole now served notice that "he is no longer going to be Mr. Nice Guy."

Bob Dole never recovered from the New Hampshire debacle. Though he won two small Midwestern states a week later, he went on to lose every primary election in the South two weeks later, on Super Tuesday.

Could Dole have survived the New Hampshire disaster? Possibly, if he had had any effective organization in the South. But his strategy had been to win big in Iowa and New Hampshire and to let that momentum carry him into the Southern primaries two weeks later. To many it seemed he had conceded the entire South to Bush.

Dole could have concentrated his efforts on the west coast of Florida, where many Midwesterners who liked Dole seemed to retire, such as in the St. Petersburg-Tampa Bay area. Instead, Dole spread himself too thin over the entire state. He lost big in Florida on March 8. And in South Carolina, having been endorsed by the legendary Senator Strom Thurmond, Dole campaigned very little and lost. Donald Devine, one of Dole's strategists, said in March, "This is an example of a campaign that lost an election by making a terrible decision, wasting money and not targeting resources." Yet Senator Dole stubbornly refused to throw in the towel, bitterly blaming Owen, Palmer, Bush, Atwater, and others for his own mistakes.

In an eerily self-destructive mood, Bob fired two top campaign aides, Dave Keene and Don Devine, and then posed for a photograph at a Universal Studios lot in Florida, flanked on one side by an actor playing Charlie Chaplin and on the other side by Frankenstein. The media quickly captioned the photo, "Dole with his two fired aides."

The senator went on to perform more silly circus tricks as he plunged into chaos. Shortly before the Illinois primary in mid-March, Dole challenged Bush to a debate in Chicago. When Bush refused to show up, Dole paraded up a cardboard Bush figure and debated it by himself. When his microphone malfunctioned Dole wound up looking even more disorganized. He was trounced by Bush three days later.

Dole finally gave up the ghost in late March at a press conference in the ornate Senate Caucus Room where Nixon's fate had been sealed in the Watergate committee hearings fifteen years earlier.

When Bush clinched the GOP presidential nomination in April, Dole gave a bitter speech on the U.S. Senate floor, in which he excoriated the media for "nit-picking" and focusing on trivia while ignoring the real issues in his campaign. In a mighty burst of invective hauntingly reminiscent of Nixon's "last press conference," Dole blasted reporters for exchanging bits of gossip on his campaign plane.

While Mr. Hyde hurled barbs at the press, Dr. Jekyll stood quietly behind the scene, to resurface later as Dole endlessly recounted his mistakes in New Hampshire. For years, according to published reports, he would wake up wondering why he had failed to sign the anti-tax pledge during the television debate that February 14. Perhaps he lost because, in the last analysis, he really did not want to win.

15

BUSH'S SPEAR-CARRIER

In his Senate role, Dole has performed quite well as a loyal trooper, often voting more than 90 percent of the time to support a Republican president's bills. Even in the case of Bush, whom Dole has personally detested since 1972, Dole has loyally shepherded his bills through Congress, supported presidential vetoes, and the like. It is as if the presence of a Republican high priest in the White House brings out the altar boy in the senator. In this role, Dole has flourished in the Senate, his natural battlefield. The institution's inherent chaos, its unpredictability, disorganization, filibuster, and gridlock are all congenial to him.

A voting study by the *Congressional Quarterly* revealed that in 1992 Senator Dole supported Bush's position on bills in the Senate 88 percent of the time; in 1991, 96 percent of the time; in 1990, 80 percent; in 1989, 94 percent. But under Reagan, his record was a little lower. He supported Reagan's proposals 68 percent in 1988; 71 percent in 1987; 92 percent in 1986 and 1985; 90 percent in 1984; 78 percent in 1983; 86 percent in 1982; and 85 percent in 1981.

With Bush as his master, Dole slavishly towed the administration's line on everything from raising taxes in 1990 to opposing the Civil Rights Act, the Family Medical Leave Act, and numerous other progressive bills. Bush's positions were often unpopular with the public, but Ensign Dole went down with his captain. This is all the more bewildering since George Bush's political fortunes have had an inverse relationship to Bob Dole's: The more popular the president became, the bigger was the shadow he cast over the senator.

Perhaps Bob Dole's self-destructive streak can explain his devotion to his hated rival, just as it can his behavior in permitting Bush to defeat him in the 1988 presidential primaries.

One of the major bills that came up during Bush's term was Senate bill S.5, the Family and Medical Leave Act of 1992, which required employers to give employees leave for family medical emergencies. Congress passed the bill but George Bush vetoed it. Dole, in a Senate floor speech on September 24, 1992, defended Bush's veto: "We are not voting on whether family and medical leave is a good idea, what we are really voting on is the best way to bring socially desirable programs and benefits to the American people." The bottom line, he indicated, "is that the money to find these benefits comes out of employers' pockets."

Dole also criticized the bill as being a "one-size-fits-all mandate. Everyone gets continuation of existing health insurance benefits. That is it. No more, no less." Dole also called this bill a "hidden tax for businesses" and urged that such family leave policies should be granted only through collective bargaining agreements rather than through congressional mandate. The family leave bill would have applied only to businesses with fifty or more employees. In such companies, employees who had worked an average of twenty-five hours a week for at least a year would be entitled to receive up to twelve weeks of unpaid leave.

Dole cosponsored an alternative bill, the Family Leave Tax Credit Act of 1992, proposed by Senator Larry Craig of Idaho, which provided the basis for flexible leave programs by means of a refundable tax credit to help employers provide these benefits. This "voluntary" scheme had no teeth, and little support.

If Senator Dole's opposition to the Family and Medical Leave Act was unpopular with women, it *was* popular with businesses. Equally popular was Dole's opposition to federal funding of public broadcasting.

In 1992, he led a Senate Republican effort to freeze federal funding for public broadcasting, decrying "liberal elitism on the airwaves." The Dole amendment was defeated by a vote of 75 to 22, and the Senate went on to authorize $1.1 billion in federal money to the Corporation for Public Broadcasting (CPB). Senator Jesse Helms claimed that the federal outlays to CPB amounted to an "upper middle-class entitlement program," while Dole himself painted a portrait of public television executives living high off the hog, bloated bureaucracies, and PBS programming that spread "left-wing and anti-American propaganda." He ridiculed children's programs like "Sesame Street," claiming they were a waste of taxpayer money. Once, after eating eggs, he sardonically told a group of public broadcast supporters, "I just ate Big Bird for breakfast."

The 1990 Civil Rights Bill would have overturned a series of 1989 Supreme Court decisions that had limited the impact of the federal laws against job discrimination. Dole's filibuster against the bill was beaten by a 62 to 38 cloture vote. He became incensed. "If we are going to shove it down the throats of the minority [Republicans]," Dole said, "things are going to get tough around here. It's totally unfair to force a vote that would put our party on record against civil rights. This senator had never voted against a civil rights bill, but he's never had one shoved down his throat before."

After many Republican senators abandoned Dole on the filibuster cloture vote, he told the Republican Caucus: "Maybe we should get together and elect another leader."

Twice during the Bush administration, Dole threatened to quit his position as Senate Minority Leader and hinted loudly that he would not seek reelection to the Senate in 1992. As late as November 1991, he publicly mused about leaving the Senate, and said he was depressed about the idea of "leading a dwindling and unruly minority." Twice during the 101st Congress he sardonically suggested that Republicans get a new leader. At one point he said, "Party discipline is not a problem on this side of the aisle. We never had it. We are all free spirits. We are [all] leaders on this side." With his voice quivering in anger, Dole accused Democrats of treating Republicans "like a bunch of bums." He then blew up at his own flock.

But he never abandoned Bush, even over the most unpopular act of his former rival's administration: the decision to break the infamous 1988 campaign pledge of "read my lips: no new taxes."

As Dole should have learned from his own bitter defeat in the 1988 New Hampshire primary, the American people suffer from an acute case of tax phobia. "Down with taxes" was *the* battle cry of the times. But in mid-1990, George Bush was locked in another political Gordian knot: the massive federal budget deficit that he and his predecessor Reagan had stacked up over ten years in office.

With midterm elections coming up in 1990, the country was mired in a recession, and Bush felt vulnerable on "the deficit thing," so he decided to break his no-tax-hike pledge. During the tedious, protracted budget debate in summer 1990, Dole supported Bush's position, claiming that he was just trying to get Democrats to "bargain seriously." Dole was instrumental in cutting a deal with Senate Democrats to raise taxes by $137 billion, an amount exceeding even his own previous 1982 record hike of $98 billion. (This was part of a budget bill that was supposed to reduce the deficit by $500 billion over the next five years, but which failed to make even a dent.)

Dole's role as chief tax collector for the Bush corporate welfare state tarnished his claim that he was a tax-buster, and his indecisiveness on this issue would haunt him later. In 1992, consistently supporting Bush, Dole voted yes on the bill to approve a school choice pilot program, no on shifting defense funds to domestic programs, and yes on opposing deeper cuts in spending for Star Wars. In 1991, he voted yes on the bill to approve the waiting period for handgun purchases. He voted to approve the senators' pay raise and ban honoraria, to authorize the use of force in the Persian Gulf, and to confirm Clarence Thomas to the Supreme Court.

Dole reaped kudos from corporate America for his role as Bush's spear-carrier, and was feted by the RJR Nabisco Corporation, Southwestern Bell Telephone, Chicago Mercantile Exchange, U.S. Telephone Association, the American Association of Retired Persons, and the American Bankers Association, as well as other organizations.

"Get ready to meet the real comeback kid," Dole told the cheering delegates to the most conservative Republican convention in twenty-eight years, which took place in Houston in August 1992. Dole introduced George Bush as the party's nominee for a second term as president, and supported a platform that denied any kind of civil rights protection to gays—saying that AIDS should not be compared to cancer or heart disease—banned women from military combat duty, and called for an amendment denying the constitutional right to an abortion.

Mocking Democratic nominee Bill Clinton as a lightweight, Dole thundered: "Michael Dukakis knows better. The Butcher of Baghdad, Saddam Hussein, knows better, and come November, the Liberal from Little Rock will know better, too." Bob Dole campaigned aggressively for the Bush-Quayle ticket in the fall campaign, trying to defend the administration's dismal record of recession, higher taxes, and corporate welfare policies. But when Bush lost, Dole became the titular head of the Republican Party.

IV

A SENATOR IN ACTION: CASE STUDIES IN CORPORATE WELFARE VIA "MADE-TO-ORDER" LAWS

Don't tax you, don't tax me, tax that fellow behind the tree. . . .

A tax loophole is something that benefits the other guy. If it benefits you, it is a "tax reform."

—Senator Russell Long, former Chairman
of the Senate Finance Committee

16

HOW HE IS RANKED

Having examined Dole's massive money machine, we are now ready to examine the senator in action where he is at his best, the halls of the U.S. Senate.

It is illustrative to begin by examining how certain special interest groups have ranked Dole in terms of his voting record. Giving him a rank of zero at least once between 1990 and 1994 were:

- National Abortion Rights Action League
- League of Conservation Voters
- Vietnam Veterans of America
- National Association of Retired Federal Employees
- Communications Workers of America
- the Teamsters
- American Federation of Teachers
- Justlife Education Fund (Economic Policy)
- Professional Coalition for Nuclear Arms Control
- American Federation of Government Employees
- Machinist Non-Partisan Political League
- National Gay and Lesbian Task Force
- Competitive Enterprise Institute (Environment)
- U.S. Student Association (Education Funding)
- the National Council of Senior Citizens
- the AFL-CIO.

In the years between 1990 and 1994, many other groups ranked him very low:

- Congress Watch, 13 percent
- American Civil Liberties Union, 26 percent
- National Women's Political Caucus, 5 percent
- National Education Association, 14 percent
- Bread for the World, 14 percent
- National Farmers Union, 20 percent
- National Committee to Preserve Social Security and MediCare, 20 percent
- National Association of Social Workers, 20 percent
- Campaign for U.N. Reform, 27 percent
- Just Life (Arms Reduction), 20 percent
- Handgun Control, 14 percent
- the Woman Activist, 20 percent
- Americans for Democratic Action, 5 percent
- Council for a Livable World, 11 percent
- American Public Health Association, 20 percent
- American Postal Workers Union, 20 percent
- Liberty Lobby, 20 percent
- Libertarian Economic Freedom, 10 percent
- U.S. Student Association (General), 29 percent.

Virtually none of the organizations listed above gave Dole any campaign contributions, and he has consistently voted against their interests in the Senate.

On the other hand, in 1994 the American Conservative Union, American Farm Bureau Federation, American Security Council, and Justlife Education Fund all ranked him at 100 percent. Competitive Enterprise Institute on Trade rated him at 88 percent in 1993. The U.S. Chamber of Commerce in 1991 put him at 80 percent, and the Christian Voice at 93 percent.

Thus, in general, business and right-wing groups ranked Dole at nearly 100 percent while civil liberties or pro-choice organizations ranked him at nearly zero. (See the tables on pages 205 and 206.)

Table 16.1

SPECIAL INTEREST GROUPS THAT RATED DOLE'S PERFORMANCE

SPECIAL INTEREST GROUP	RANKING (%)	YEARS RATED
American Conservative Union	100	1994
American Farm Bureau Federation	100	1993–94
American Security Council	100	1993–94
Business-Industry PAC	100	1994
Justlife Education Fund (anti-abortion)	100	1991
American Civil Liberties Union	26	1993–94
American Fed. of Government Employees	8	1993
American Public Health Association	7	1993
Campaign for U.N. Reform	27	1991–92
Christian Voice	93	1991–92
Competitive Enterprise Institute	88	1993
Congress Watch	13	1990
Consumer Federation of America	10	1993
Handgun Control	14	1985–93
Leadership Conference on Civil Rights	7	1993–94
NAACP	10	1993–94
National Association of Retired Fed. Employees	80	1993–94
National Farmers Organization	30	1991–92
National Federation of Government Employees	50	1990
National Federation of Independent Business	94	1994
National Taxpayers Union	74	1993
National Women's Political Caucus	5	1990
The Teamsters	30	1991–92
U.S. Student Association	29	1993–94

SOURCE: Voter Research Hotline (Reprinted courtesy of Project Vote Smart)

Table 16.2
SPECIAL INTEREST GROUPS THAT GAVE A ZERO RATING ON DOLE'S PERFORMANCE

SPECIAL INTEREST GROUP	RANKING (%)	YEARS RANKED
AFL-CIO	0	1994
American Association of University Women	0	1993–94
American Federation of Governmental Employees	0	1992
American Federation of State, County & Municipal Employees	0	1993
American Federation of Teachers	0	1993–94
Americans for Democratic Action	0	1994
Communications Workers of America	0	1991–92
Competitive Enterprise Institute (Environment)	0	1991
Justlife Education Fund (Economic Policy)	0	1991
League of Conservation Voters	0	1992
Machinist Non-Partisan Political League	0	1990
National Abortion Rights Action League	0	1994
National Association of Retired Federal Employees	0	1991–92
National Council of Senior Citizens	0	1993
National Gay and Lesbian Task Force	0	1991
Professional Coalition for Nuclear Arms Control	0	1991
The Teamsters	0	1990
United Food & Commercial Workers	0	1993
U.S. Student Association (Education Funding)	0	1991
Vietnam Veterans of America	0	1990

SOURCE: Voter Research Hotline (Reprinted courtesy of Project Vote Smart)

In his book, *Open Secrets: The Encyclopedia of Congressional Money and Politics*, Joshua Goldstein of the Center for Responsive Politics details Dole's record as follows: between 1987 and 1992, the senator received a total of $3,143,115 for his 1992 Senate reelection campaign. At the end of 1992, his cash on hand was $1,756,483. Dole served on four Senate committees: Agriculture, Nutrition and Forestry; Finance; Rules and Administration; and Joint Committee on Taxation. Leading business contributors to Dole during recent years break down as follows: The agriculture industry contributed $430,350; the communications electronics business interests $229,600; the construction industry $100,250; energy and natural resources $319,187; finance, insurance and real estate industries $795,271; the health industry $186,100; lawyers and lobbyists $267,617; miscellaneous business $358,728; transportation $245,786; ideological single-issue PACs $91,168; and others $38,990.

If we look at the actual contributions of special interest groups to Dole's Campaign America, we see that they gave $400,000 in 1992 in addition to contributing more to his Senate campaign. Dole also sat on the Agriculture, Nutrition and Forestry Senate Committee, and it is interesting to note that agriculture companies contributed $262,381 to Dole in the 1991–92 campaign cycle. As to the Senate Finance Committee, where he is also a ranking member, Dole received $1,949,015 in total PAC and large individual contributions from entities with a stake in tax, health, and other legislation written by the Finance Committee.

In addition, scores of wealthy individuals and corporate officials with a vested financial interest in Dole's legislation have showered millions of dollars on Campaign America and Dole's other committees. Why would anyone be so generous toward a politician?

To grasp the true picture, we shall study several specific case studies that illustrate what Dole has done for special interest groups in the Senate.

17

CASE STUDIES IN CORPORATE WELFARE

B ob Dole is the most dramatic practitioner of corporate welfare Washington has ever known. One of the most salient distinguishing characteristics of Dole's tenure as U.S. Senator over the past 26 years has been his crafting, supporting, and persuading the Senate to adopt a large number of obscure laws that benefit many of his prime campaign contributors. Most of these laws involve arcane tax law, federal regulations or government subsidies that are so complicated and obscure few people have ever heard of them. Unfortunately for the American taxpayer, Dole's corporate welfare giveaways have deprived the U.S. Treasury of much-needed revenue, have exacerbated the federal deficit, and contributed to the quadrupling of the national debt. His unabashed alacrity in providing federal "Aid to Dependent Corporations," and to the dependent tycoons who fund his campaigns, is striking for its sheer boldness. A few case studies will suffice to give the reader a flavor for how such custom-made Dolean laws get enacted.

Commodity Traders and "Senator Straddle"

In 1984, Senator Dole helped to engineer a major raid on the Treasury, this time involving commodity traders based mainly in Chicago. Home to the Chicago Mercantile Exchange and the Chicago Board of Trade, the Windy City is the nation's center for trading commodities.

For years many professional commodity traders had been avoiding taxes by engaging in a clever transaction involving "straddling" of commodity futures contracts. Typically, the traders would purchase both a buy and a sell futures contract or position, thereby offsetting positions and hedging their bets as to an increase or decrease of futures contracts' prices. If they lost money on the buy future contract, because the futures market went the other way, the traders would close out their buy contract and take this "loss" as a write-off on their taxes for that year. But they would *not* close out their sell contract (which had produced a gain), and thus would roll over the gains year after year, and avoid paying taxes on the gains by not closing out the transaction on paper. Similarly, if they lost on their sell position, they would close it out and keep their buy position open and roll it over into the future. For tax purposes, their income would be deferred indefinitely.

Not surprisingly, this scheme, permitted until 1981, attracted the interest of the IRS, which investigated this practice. In 1981, when Congress passed the Economic Recovery Tax Act (ERTA), it amended the tax code to outlaw the practice, specifying that gains had to be recognized at year end, regardless of whether a futures contract was closed out. But there was a debate as to whether this law was retroactive and covered straddling prior to 1981. The wording was ambiguous. The traders claimed that the 1981 tax bill granted them "amnesty" for prior tax avoidance. The IRS said the law *was* retroactive, issued regulations to that effect, and insisted there was "no amnesty."

Dole initially sided with the IRS. In a major speech on the Senate floor on July 23, 1981, he attacked the commodity traders for getting "corporate welfare" and for "not paying any taxes on a million-dollar gain." Blasting the commodity traders, many of whom had seats on the Mercantile Exchange or the Board of Trade, he sounded like a populist:

> I just believe . . . that if you are out there making a million dollars, I do not care if you are a trader or not a trader, you ought to pay some taxes. It just seems to me that is what we are going to try to make certain happens. . . . I regard it as an abuse for any American to earn $1 million and pay no taxes. . . . This Senator believes that any American earning $1 million must pay taxes . . .*

In 1981, Senator Dole was instrumental in blocking a proposal to give the commodity traders special treatment. On the Senate floor, he blasted the commodity traders for having contributed money to Democratic incumbents in Congress. "They haven't missed a fund-raiser," Dole said of them. "If you do not pay any taxes, you can afford to go to the fund-raisers. . . . They [the traders] are great contributors."

Dole personally wrote to the IRS and urged it to go after the commodity traders for taxes owed. The IRS did, and by 1984, a huge backlog of cases, involving hundreds of millions of tax dollars in dispute, was pending in U.S. Tax Court as the traders fought the IRS interpretation. But then an unusual thing happened: between 1983 and 1984, the commodity traders gave Dole's Campaign America PAC $70,500, which was six times more than they had given in 1981 and 1982. In 1984, the commodity traders gave $10,500 to Campaign America and another $3,600 to a fund-raiser co-hosted by Campaign America. Only three months later, Dole changed his tune and supported a proposal that gave the traders amnesty for all straddles prior to 1982, and cost the Treasury $300 million. When the Tax Reform Act of 1984 became law with Dole's support, it included Section 108(b), which

---

*Dole is quoted from the *Congressional Record*, July 23, 1981, p. 17107.

provided amnesty for pre-1982 straddles and also specified that losses for pre-1982 straddles were deductible only by professional commodity traders, and *not* by ordinary citizens who straddled. (See Section 108 of the Tax Reform Act of 1984, as corrected by Public Law, P.L. 99-514, and the Internal Revenue Code, Section 1256, where "commodity dealer" is defined.)

The 333 commodity traders affected by Dole's flip-flop each saved an average of more than $866,000 in taxes, an excellent return on their "investment" in Campaign America.

Single Premium Life Insurance and AmVestors Insurance Company

One of the most striking case studies of custom-made corporate welfare laws crafted by Dole for his supporters concerns an obscure provision in the 1986 Tax Reform Act. In a nutshell, the "single premium life insurance" tax loophole deprived the U.S. Treasury of millions of dollars of tax revenue, and greatly benefited the AmVestors Finance Corporation, based coincidentally in Topeka, Kansas. AmVestors is the parent company of American Investors Life Insurance Company. (Insurance industry executives and PACs have been among the most generous contributors to all arms of Dole's money machine.)

In 1986, the Senate considered the all-important Tax Reform Act, which began its legislative journey in the Senate Finance Committee. Dole had been chairman of this committee from 1981 to 1984, when he gave up his chair to become Senate majority leader, while remaining a member of the committee. As the committee's key Republican member, Dole had considerable influence over the content of the tax reform bill, and as majority leader he had the power to determine which bills came to the Senate floor.

The bill provided a huge tax loophole for the sale of

single-premium life insurance (a life insurance product that also serves as an investment vehicle). Buyers of single-premium policies earn a return on their investment and can borrow from those earnings. Income taxes on this income would be deferred under the terms of the Tax Act crafted by Dole.

As a result of this legislation, single-premium life insurance became one of the major lucrative tax shelters available to investors after 1986.

After the act passed, American Investors Life Insurance Company marketed its new insurance product aggressively, and the company's assets skyrocketed from $128.5 million in 1985 to $633.8 million in 1987. Fletcher Bell, commissioner of the Kansas Insurance Department, admitted that "the product responsible for their tremendous growth is a result of the Federal Tax Reform Act of 1986."

AmVestors was headed by Chairman T. M. Murrell, who became one of several national cochairmen of Senator Dole's 1988 presidential campaign. In 1986, while the Senate was working on the tax reform package, the AmVestors board also included Dole's longtime financial whiz kid and political guru, Dave Owen. Owen had been Republican state chairman in Kansas (1982–84), and had served as lieutenant governor of Kansas (1972–74). Early in 1986, Owen was vice-chairman of the AmVestors board. When he resigned from the board that year, he was paid $7,650 for his brief tenure, according to records on file at the Kansas Insurance Department. Owen then started his own new company, affiliated with AmVestors, to market single-premium life insurance. Owen was also the "investment adviser" to Elizabeth Dole's blind trust, which was worth about $1.67 million at that time. (According to federal law, in a blind trust, the assets of a federal public official are supposed to be administered by a trustee without the knowledge of the beneficiary in order to avoid conflicts of interest.)

AmVestors, with its extremely close ties to the Dole blind trust and to Dole's political fortunes, benefited inordinately from the 1986 Tax Reform Act. With an aggressive marketing strategy for promoting single-premium life insurance, AmVestors was a pioneer in peddling this product as a clever investment vehicle to avoid taxes, and soon became the top insurance enterprise in the country selling this product.

Was single-premium life insurance more analogous to an investment than to an actual insurance policy? It was a hybrid, which found a gold-mine niche in the go-go 1980s.

The essential idea of single-premium life insurance is that the insured pays only one large premium when he buys the policy, not a continual series of installment payments. The amount of the single premium ranged from several thousand dollars to several million dollars, depending on the value of the policy—and on the assets of the policyholder.

AmVestors then invested the huge single premium, paid annual "annuity" returns to the policyholder, and sought to make a killing on its investment.

What made single-premium life insurance so attractive to policyholder investors was that under the terms of the 1986 Tax Reform Act, the federal taxes on all earnings from the policy were deferred indefinitely and could be borrowed against by the policyholder, without having to pay taxes.

It is not difficult to see why an investor playing the "beat the tax man" game would choose to invest in single-premium life insurance rather than an alternative investment vehicle, such as an annuity, stocks, bonds, or a savings account, for in the latter investments the interest and/or dividends are taxed upon receipt.

By contrast, under single-premium life insurance, all of the earnings from the policy remain tax-free and can be bequeathed tax-free to the survivors of the policyholder.

As Elliot Kaplan, the attorney for AmVestors and David Owen, would later testify under oath, AmVestors became a top firm in the country marketing single-premium life insurance when the 1986 tax bill became law. Dole's cronies thus stood to make a killing as their hitherto obscure pet project acquired the glamour and glow of easy money.

On August 28, 1986, Dole's Senate Finance Committee put the finishing touches on the tax bill. The very next day, AmVestors borrowed $10 million from the Merchants Bank of Kansas City, according to SEC records.

The $10 million was used by AmVestors to market its new single-premium life insurance product aggressively all across the country.

The marketing campaign paid off handsomely. In 1987, the first year the new tax law was in effect, AmVestors reported a whopping increase of 57 percent in its net earnings, over its earnings in 1986.

In 1986, before the new tax law went into effect, AmVestors paid out dividends of only 13 cents per share to its shareholders, as seen in the 1986 federal income tax returns for Liddy Dole's blind trust, which received $1,438 in dividend income while holding 11,061 shares of AmVestors stock.

But in 1987, the blind trust appears to have sold off all its shares of stock, thus cashing in its chips on the Life Insurance Deal of the Decade.

How did the AmVestors tax loophole originate? To comprehend the full magnitude of the intersection of politics and money—Kansas style—we must zero in on Dole's home base of Topeka, the capital of Kansas.

In 1986, while the U.S. Congress debated the tax bill in Washington, forces were at work 1500 miles away in Topeka. AmVestors corporate headquarters, a renovated brick building, was just a stone's throw from the state capitol and the Kansas Department of Insurance. In the politically incestuous world of Topeka politics, where Dole reigned supreme as the Kingfish of Kansas, the proximity of these buildings is more than coincidental.

This is a state where the state insurance commissioner has been a Republican for the past hundred years, and where the Dole machine carved up political patronage like so many slices of salami.

Dole's Golden Boy, Mike Hayden, who served as governor of Kansas from 1987 to 1991, proudly displayed a photograph on the wall in his governor's office, depicting a smiling Hayden flanked by Kansas insurance commissioner Fletcher Bell and AmVestors chairman T. M. Murrell.

Murrell had been an enthusiastic contributor to Hayden's 1986 gubernatorial campaign, a campaign during which Dole pressured Owen, Kaplan, and others in his inner circle to raise money for Hayden. Hayden, himself a former insurance agent in Kansas, was certainly no stranger to the political climate surrounding regulation of insurance in the Sunflower State. Murrell and Owen were destined to become national cochairmen of Dole's 1988 presidential campaign, a campaign for which Dole had been accumulating political IOUs long before 1986.

Dole's close ties to AmVestors extended to Liddy Dole. In 1986, her blind trust wanted to purchase the College Park II office building in Overland Park, Kansas. Owen, who was serving as adviser to the trust, eventually set up corporate offices in that building, as did John Palmer, the former Dole aide who used Owen and Dole's help to obtain from the Small Business Administration a controversial $26 million minority set-aside contract with the Army.

In order to buy the College Park II building, Liddy Dole's blind trust needed a $1 million mortgage loan, which it obtained from AmVestors. In addition, the blind trust borrowed yet another $150,000 from AmVestors to purchase rental real estate in Washington.

In 1987, Bob Dole's former chief counsel, John Petersen, left Washington and went to work for Governor Hayden in Topeka. Petersen also set up a private law practice in Kansas City. One of his key clients was none other than AmVestors.

So AmVestors was off to the races, easily leaping over several nominal obstacles in its way. As a bona fide insurance company, AmVestors was required by law to obtain the approval of the Kansas Insurance Department to operate its business in the Sunflower State. To clear this hurdle, AmVestors hired Bill Sneed, a former chief counsel to Insurance Commissioner Bell and counsel to the Kansas Republican Party.

Did Bell have any direct or indirect ties to AmVestors figures? Bell himself in 1982 had personally invested over $5,000 in a company in Lawrence called Exitec, a medical product manufacturer. One of Exitec's founders was Bob Billings, who also happened to be on the AmVestors board of directors.

Bell claimed he was an owner of Exitec, even though he was allegedly losing money in the company. He explained that he had invested in this enterprise as a favor to an old dentist friend who lived in Lawrence.

Bell's relationship with AmVestors extended to chairman T. M. Murrell. In 1983, Murrell traded in his Lincoln Continental to a Topeka car dealer, who then sold the vehicle to Bell at a bargain price of $4,700, explaining that Murrell was a "good customer." Five months afterwards, Bell traded the Lincoln in for a Buick and received $8,000 as a trade-in value for the car.

In commenting on Commissioner Bell's business relationships with AmVestors officials, Kansas Democratic State Representative Larry Turnquist noted dryly, "I would think it would be highly unusual for the Commissioner to be in business on the side with a board member of one of the insurance companies he regulates."

What is it that Bell's Kansas State Insurance Department is supposed to do? Theoretically, it is supposed to regulate and investigate all insurance companies operating in the state, to be sure there are no irregularities or risks posed to policyholders and investors. How well has this task been carried out?

In 1987, American Investors Life raked in $76 million due largely to its major product, single-premium life insurance. Was anything awry with the manner in which AmVestors sold and financed its new product?

A Bell spokesman explained that "any time a company puts a lot of new business on the books, it is a concern you follow at the Insurance Department.'' The department had the power to require upstart companies to post larger "reserves" to safeguard their assets and protect policyholders. State law required all insurance companies to post reserve securities of equal value to the policies they wrote.

This safeguard is all the more important when a company is selling a new product in a politically or financially unstable market.

In 1987, some Democrats in the U.S. House of Representatives, such as House Ways and Means Committee Chairman Dan Rostenkowski of Illinois, urged that Congress repeal or reduce the tax loophole advantages of the single-premium life insurance policy in light of the skyrocketing federal deficits. This looming threat put AmVestors' shaky financial base in jeopardy.

One of AmVestors' competitors, the Kansas Farm Bureau, based in Manhattan, Kansas, was concerned that if the tax giveaway was repealed and AmVestors failed, under state law AmVestors policies would have to be funded by other companies in the state. The Farm Bureau was also worried about the extent to which AmVestors was backing up its insurance policies with junk bonds. (Junk bonds are securities that, because they are deemed riskier, generally pay higher returns than top-rated investment-grade bonds. During the 1980s, Wall Street was rocked by several major scandals because junk bonds were used to fund shaky financial empires and savings and loans throughout the country, including the Madison Guaranty Loan in Arkansas, which involved Bill Clinton in the Whitewater scandal.)

It appears from the records that AmVestors invested heavily in junk bonds and went on a junk bond buying binge to get higher yields and use those yields to pay higher returns to its single-premium life insurance policyholders, during the go-go late 1980s. According to records at the Kansas State Insurance Department, AmVestors placed only 60 percent of its investment portfolio in

investment-grade securities in 1986 and only 69 percent
in 1987, the rest being junk bonds.

By comparison, the Kansas Farm Bureau placed 92
percent of its portfolio in investment-grade bonds in 1987.

While the insurance commissioner was supposed to
regulate and investigate insurance companies for sol-
vency, the junk bond feast seemed to be playing haywire
in Kansas during the late 1980s. The Farm Bureau also
offered a single-premium life insurance policy but, unlike
AmVestors, did not aggressively market this product and
such policies represented only a small portion of the
Farm Bureau's business.

The head of the Kansas Farm Bureau's life insurance
division said that "We are trying to provide tax-free
life insurance benefits. Other companies, while calling
themselves life insurance companies in name, are really
more of a pseudo-investment company." AmVestors had
extremely close ties to Owen and Dole. Owen's attorney,
Elliot Kaplan, said that he had agreed to contribute
$6,000 to Republican gubernatorial candidate Mike Hay-
den in 1986, on Owen's and Dole's request, on condition
that he be paid "legal fees for work in connection with
AmVestors," which was then owned by Richard Halford
and managed by Owen. Kaplan insists he was paid $6,000
from AmVestors, and after depositing the check, Kaplan
and his wife each donated $3,000 to the Hayden cam-
paign.

In a 1989 Kansas state criminal case brought against
Owen, Palmer, and Kaplan, the indictment said that the
Halfords (Richard Halford was the owner of AmVestors)
and AmVestors were repaid by Owen. Owen and Kaplan
were accused of making illegal campaign contributions to
Hayden in violation of state law. The charges, however,
were dismissed by a judge. (See chapter 27 for a detailed
description of the Owen case.)

Dole, who repeatedly rails against the deficit, nonetheless saw fit to help his friends get lucrative tax breaks
that in no way benefit the American people in reducing
the federal deficit or in tax fairness.

Another major piece of legislation, the Deficit Reduction Act of 1984, which Dole carried on to the Senate floor as chairman of the Senate Finance Committee, was also extremely beneficial to American Investors Life Insurance Company and to the Topeka-based Security Benefit Life Insurance Company.

American Investors claimed a special benefit of $1.3 million as a result of this act, according to the company's 1984 annual report. The Security Benefit Life Insurance Company did even better. The firm's president at the time, Archie Dykes, was a major contributor to Dole's money machine and later became another national co-chairman of Dole's 1988 presidential campaign. As a result of wording in the statute giving the company an exclusive benefit, Security Benefits lowered the equity base used in determining its annual income tax. This saved the company up to $5 million per year, according to the 1984 *Congressional Record*.

In analyzing these made-to-order laws that directly benefited Dole's political supporters, we must ask: How do these laws benefit the American economy in general?

Saving Ruan's Tax Deduction from Ruin

Let's turn now to an obscure provision that Dole helped write into the Internal Revenue Code in 1986—a tax exemption for a specific trucking company in Des Moines, Iowa: the Ruan Trucking Company, whose chairman, John Ruan, has long been a major contributor to Dole's campaign committees, Campaign America PAC, and the Dole Foundation.

The thirty-six-story Ruan Tower in Des Moines is the tallest building in Iowa. From there John Ruan commands a network of trucking, leasing, real estate, banking, and insurance companies. In 1986, the Ruan empire had been having problems, particularly as the Ruan's Carriers Insurance Company had been ruled insolvent in 1985 by the Iowa Department of Insurance. Policyholders and creditors filed claims amounting to $117 million against Carriers.

The lawsuit sought $63 million in damages to policyholders and creditors. At the same time, Ruan's truck leasing company was embarking on an ambitious expansion plan. Ruan had contracted to purchase a new generation of long-haul vehicles called Mega Trucks, which were supposed to be able to drive up to a million miles with minimum maintenance. These expensive additions were ordered in 1985, but delivery was not expected until 1987. Ruan made his decision to purchase the trucks on the basis of the existing income tax law, which in 1985 allowed a 10 percent investment tax credit for purchases of equipment, including trucks.

When Congress initially wrote the Tax Reform Act of 1986, it repealed the investment tax credit, "retroactive to January 1, 1986." As a result, Ruan was faced with the disaster of a 10 percent increase in his cost of doing business, because he would not be able to take the investment tax credit for the Mega Trucks.* But Ruan was able to persuade Iowa Senator Charles Grassley and Dole to go to bat for him.

In May of 1986, Dole played a key role in crafting the so-called Dole-Grassley Amendment, which granted a specific exemption to Ruan from the investment tax credit repeal and enabled Ruan to keep the investment tax credit even though his trucks would not be delivered until 1987. Grassley and Dole claimed that the Ruan exemption had been "inadvertently left out" of the tax bill, and it was incorporated into the measure that passed the full Senate in June 1986.

After the House passed its version of the Tax Reform Act and a conference committee of Senators and House members met to negotiate and resolve the two versions of the Tax Reform Act, the Ruan tax exemption again

---

*Existing tax law provided that for purposes of claiming the investment tax credit, a transaction would be considered complete *upon delivery* of the trucks—in this case in 1987.

was left out, because the conferees thought it was an outrageous tax giveaway.

Dole and Grassley went to bat again and inserted the Ruan tax exemption into a special Senate resolution intended to correct "bookkeeping mistakes," such as misspelled names, incorrect dates, and misidentified sections in the tax bill itself. This was called an "enrolling resolution." The Senate was appalled and refused to pass the resolution. Exhibiting the never-say-die spirit of the pioneers, Dole and Grassley attempted to graft the Ruan exemption onto another unrelated piece of legislation, namely the Budget Reconciliation Bill, which Congress enacted in September 1986.

In Iowa, newspapers ridiculed the Ruan exemption as "The Tax Break That Would Not Die." But Dole and Grassley finally prevailed, and the Ruan Amendment eventually found its way into an obscure Senate bill that directed the sale of ConRail Railway, reduced government payments for cataract surgery, and increased the federal debt limit. The Ruan paragraph in that bill read as follows: "The amendments made by section 201 [of the Internal Revenue Code, repealing the investment tax credit] shall not apply to trucks, tractor units, and trailers which a privately held truck leasing company headquartered in Des Moines, Iowa contracted to purchase in September, 1985."

This clause, which eventually became law, enabled Ruan's company to escape taxes of approximately $8.5 million. Meanwhile, Dole praised the Tax Reform Act: "We can be proud of this legislation and proud that we voted in favor of it. It is a tax bill that we can honestly describe to the American people as tax reform."

Federal Election Commission records show that in the 1991–93 campaign cycle, John Ruan and the Ruan Corporation contributed $5,000 to Dole's Campaign America PAC, the maximum allowed by law. Ruan companies contributed $2,500 to Campaign America on February 25, 1991, Elizabeth Ruan donated $5,000 on February 19, 1993, and John Ruan contributed another

$5,000 to Campaign America on the same day. In February 1994, Ruan contributed another $10,000 to Campaign America. Additional money was contributed earlier and later. Also, the John Ruan Foundation has showered money on the Dole Foundation.

As a result of such made-to-order tax loopholes, the aggregate level of total corporate income taxes paid to the federal government has trailed even the interest paid on the national debt under Republican presidents. In 1987, for example, the federal government had to pay $138.6 billion in interest while corporate income taxes paid to the government amounted to only $83.9 billion, which was slightly more than half. By contrast, in 1980, and in all previous years in American history, corporate income tax revenue vastly exceeded the interest paid on the national debt. Ruan's individual tax giveaway may seem relatively small, but the cumulative effect of such giveaways shows up in the burgeoning national debt and chronic federal deficits. Between 1981 and 1993, under Presidents Bush and Reagan and Dole's Senate stewardship, the national debt quadrupled to $4.3 trillion, and the annual federal deficits nearly quadrupled from $78 billion to $290 billion per year. The legacy of such policies is thus a massive debt burden for Joe Six-Pack and his heirs.

18

"MADE-TO-ORDER" LAWS

ADM: Supermarket to Bob Dole

While the commodity traders, Ruan Trucking, and AmVestors Insurance may have received enormous tax breaks from Bob Dole, their made-to-order laws look like mere tips when compared to the massive amount of corporate welfare given by Congress to Dole's favorite campaign contributors, Archer-Daniels-Midland Corporation (ADM) and its chairman, Dwayne Andreas.

ADM is a giant food-processing firm in Decatur, Illinois, whose motto is "Supermarket to the World." Dole's grocery list of special tax breaks, federal subsidies, and other prizes for ADM constitutes a cornucopia truly fit for a king—King Dwayne Andreas.*

Dole's relationship with Andreas and ADM goes back twenty years, when Bob was still "small time," and when he was begging for support from friendly farm state agribusiness giants, because he too was a "farm state senator." The relationship has blossomed into a fruitful, multimillion-dollar relationship. John Ford, who was

---

*Andreas himself has been the subject of several investigations by the Federal Election Commission for making illegal contributions to various candidates. He and ADM's PAC have contributed lavishly to both Republicans and Democrats, clearly hedging their bets. But Dole has been a special recipient of ADM largesse.

Deputy Secretary of Agriculture under Reagan and helped write the 1985 Farm Bill, called Dole "Dwayne Andreas's gofer on Capitol Hill," and accused the senator of "shameless" pandering for Andreas.*

Behind closed doors in the Senate, Dole has argued fanatically in favor of extending tax incentives to prop up the marginal and dubious ethanol, or "gasohol," fuel industry. Approximately 70 percent of the nation's ethanol is produced by Archer-Daniels-Midland. Ethanol, a corn-distilled alcohol, is mixed with gasoline in order to make gasohol, which environmental studies by the U.S. Environmental Protection Agency (EPA) have designated a serious air pollutant. Initiated in 1978, the tax credits were scheduled to expire at the end of 1992, but Dole has succeeded in extending them indefinitely.

The massive tax credits, one for excise taxes and another for income taxes, amount in effect to a 60 cents per gallon federal subsidy on any ethanol alcohol that is used for fuel. The credits go to companies that mix ethanol with gasoline, and thereby provide a boon to ADM by creating a market and government subsidy for ethanol. Dole has argued that ethanol production is important because it provides a market for American corn, which is in chronic oversupply, and helps expand U.S.–produced fuels.

But Congressman Bill Frendzel, the senior Republican on the House Budget Committee and a high-level budget negotiator, is one of many critics. "It shouldn't be in there," says Frendzel. "I assume it is in there because Bob Dole wants it. He has always wanted tax breaks for ethanol. It is not worthwhile in the context of deficit reduction. We have probably oversubsidized that industry [ethanol] particularly since that industry is largely one company [ADM]."

*Ford, disgusted with Andreas's policies, went on in 1987 to become president of the American Corn Growers Association, a renegade lobbying group at odds with Andreas's National Corn Growers Association.

The Sierra Club, an environmental lobbyist group, has expressed great doubts about the ethanol tax credits, and the American Corn Growers Association has denounced Dole for this policy.

Dole's action in pressing for the ethanol tax credit extension was not limited to debate on the budget bill of 1990. Over the years he has delayed at least two trade bills in the Senate in order to gain leverage for extension of the ethanol tax credits.

The gasohol program has severely hurt the wheat and soybean farmers because some gasohol byproducts compete against soybeans in the market and have significantly depressed their prices. American tariffs on Brazilian grain alcohol, which Dole has supported in order to suppress competition with ADM, have discouraged Brazil from opening its huge market to American wheat farmers. Moreover, ADM and other gasohol producers have received great government favors at the expense of corn farmers. The federal government has given ADM huge donations of federally owned corn surpluses, thus weakening corn market prices.

In 1980, Dole introduced as an amendment to a complicated revenue bill a tariff that aided ADM gasohol production. He rammed it through the Senate Finance Committee and the full Senate without a serious debate. The original tariff phased in a 40 cents per gallon import charge over three years, which has been raised to 3 percent of value. Dole's tariff was attacked by Congressman Charles Vanik as "the birth of new monopoly and a steal for the benefit of one company"—ADM. Since 1978, Dole has sponsored more than fifty Senate bills designed to promote gasohol. Between 1981 and 1985, he helped ADM by cosponsoring or sponsoring five bills maintaining or setting sugar price supports.

In 1984, Dole successfully lobbied the U.S. Customs Service to tighten some loopholes through which certain blends of Brazilian grain alcohol had been seeping into the United States. ADM supported this move. In response to a question by *Washington Post* reporter Michael Isikoff, Dole said "Our primary goal was not to help one company. I'm a farm state senator, and our interest was in finding an outlet for some farm commodities. . . . I don't know anything about ADM."

In the state of Kansas, the biggest state crop is wheat, which is worth nearly five times as much to the state as is corn. Brazil is the world's fifth-largest importer of wheat. If Dole were truly looking out for the interests of his Kansas constituents, he would not have brought about an anti-Brazil tariff, which had the effect of reducing U.S. exports of wheat into Brazil. In 1984, when Dole urged that loopholes for Brazilian gasohol be closed, Brazil threatened to retaliate against the United States with higher trade barriers against wheat. In 1985, the Brazilian Minister of Industry and Commerce, Roberto Guzmal, said that if the United States wanted to relax import restrictions against Brazilian grain alcohol, Brazil would make corresponding trade concessions, including increasing its allocation for receiving wheat exported to Brazil from the United States. He also said Brazil would buy corn from the United States for an increased grain alcohol production plant in Brazil. But this proposed deal fell through. The U.S. ambassador to Brazil, Diego Asencio, later explained why: "Because it ran afoul of the objectives of ADM." The minister returned home crestfallen.

The ethanol issue must be seen in the larger context of Senator Dole's purported support for the American farmer. The American Corn Growers Association, which supports the small and independent farmer and is protectionist, has long argued that federal government policy and loan rates should discourage corn production in order to keep prices relatively high so the independent farmer can survive. By contrast, huge agribusiness conglomerates such as ADM and its lobbying arm (the National Corn Growers Association) have long argued for the opposite policies and are "pro-free trade." In the long run, it may be argued that undermining the independent American farmer is not good for the American economy.

Among other things, many agribusiness companies tend to be controlled by foreign interests, and they tend to support trade policies such as NAFTA that further weaken America's agricultural base.

Another issue concerns foreign trade. Dole, by supporting foreign trade rivals and eliminating U.S. tariffs and by his support for NAFTA in 1993, has repeatedly sabotaged the efforts of the small independent American farmer to compete in the international market. Dole has advocated policies opening up American markets to cheap imports of foreign agricultural products, while doing nothing to persuade foreign nations to open their markets to U.S. agricultural products. Dole's former top Senate Finance Committee aide, Bob Lighthizer, went on to work for the U.S. Trade Representative under the Reagan administration. The U.S. Trade Representative has often been accused by critics of yielding to Japanese and other foreign lobbyists on trade issues. Ross Perot made a big issue out of this in 1992.

The conflict between large agribusiness conglomerates such as ADM and the small independent farmer is quite extensive and complicated. Dwayne Andreas, chairman of ADM, has been called the "Armand Hammer of Agriculture." As early as 1967, *Fortune* magazine called Andreas "a fascinating executive type, a shrewd, tough-minded trader with the attitudes of a questioning intellectual, persuasive talents of a master salesman and the zeal of a missionary." Greg Potvin, a Washington lawyer and one-time adversary of Andreas, says, "I have seen him on Capitol Hill and he is so effective it is scary." ADM's annual sales exceed $7 billion, its products including soybean, sunflower, cottonseed, and corn oil. ADM refines corn, mills wheat, merchandises grain and sells pasta. It is also the nation's largest producer of ethanol and high-fructose corn syrup (HFCS), two products that would be nonexistent in this country without massive government subsidies shepherded through Congress by Dole.

Gasohol was conceived in the late 1970s as a kind of

homespun American fuel source to replace petroleum-based fuel. Typically, gasohol consists of a 9-to-1 mixture of gasoline and grain alcohol distilled from corn. The problem is that, like other synthetic fuels, gasohol is so expensive to produce that the "free market" would never support it unless oil gets much more expensive or unless the government subsidized gasohol. Grain alcohol production grew from almost nothing in 1978 to 120 million gallons by 1982. In 1985, in the middle of an oil glut, more than 625 million gallons of grain alcohol were produced and blended with some 6 billion gallons of gasoline, accounting for 7.2 percent of total gasoline sales.

Only the massive federal government subsidies urged by Dole explain why ethanol was produced at all. Jim McCarthy, of the Federal Highway Administration, said that the ethanol subsidy has cost the federal government's Highway Trust Fund roughly about $225 million in 1984 and $480 million in 1986. Between July 1985 and July 1986, ADM made an estimated gross profit of $483 million, of which 7.5 percent or $36 million came from its ethanol division.

But gasohol is only part of the ADM-Dole story. Massive federal subsidies for gasohol helped ADM to create yet another industry, which now makes more than seven times as much money for the company as gasohol itself. This is high-fructose corn syrup (HFCS). Like other corn-based sweeteners, HFCS has been around for a long time, but it took the boom of the gasohol industry to enable HFCS to become important, because the "wet milling" grain alcohol plants, whose construction was subsidized by the federal government at Dole's urging, are also used to produce HFCS.

In 1985 and 1986, ADM made $267 million from corn sweeteners. HFCS and grain alcohol provided ADM with profit margins of respectively 21.5 percent and 8 percent compared to only 6 percent for flour milling. A U.S. Department of Agriculture study concluded that the combined cost of gasohol subsidies and increased food prices cost consumers several billion dollars more than corn farmers ever received as a result of the gasohol subsidies.*

Carl King, currently president of the American Corn Growers Association, told me that more than half a million independent farms have been lost between 1980 and 1993 due to Republican administration policies (supported by Dole), which have favored large agribusiness.

Although Senator Dole likes to speak about the "farmer" as a monolithic entity and claims that he represents him in Washington, the truth is that the American farm industry is split up into two camps: giant agribusiness versus the small, independent family farm owner. Dole has generally pursued policies supportive of the interests of agribusiness and against the interests of the small, independent operator. Dole has generally favored "free trade" policies that make it difficult for small American farmers to compete with Japanese cooperatives and other foreign agribusinesses. As a result, according to a *New York Times* story in November 1994, the number of farms in the United States is now at its lowest level since 1850, ten years before the Civil War.

Why has Dole become ADM's "gofer"? According to FEC records, between 1980 and 1990 alone, Andreas and his family and ADM's PAC contributed more than $80,000 to Dole's campaigns. In the 1970s and 1980s, Andreas, his family, and ADM's PAC contributed $2.7 million to Republican candidates and "soft money" donations to the GOP, and ADM jets frequently fly Dole across the country. In addition, the ADM Foundation has given $185,000 to the Dole Foundation.

The Andreas-Dole relationship culminated in a sweetheart deal on a cooperative apartment in the posh Sea View Hotel in Bal Harbour, Florida, in 1982. Robert Strauss, the former Democratic National Chairman and ambassador to Russia, who has sat on the ADM board and also owns a unit in the Sea View Hotel, said that

---

*See the *National Review*, March 13, 1987, "Some Dare Call Them Robber Barons" by Michael Fumento.

Dole inquired personally about the "availability of an apartment" in the early 1980s and shortly thereafter Dole and his wife acquired 75 shares (3.4 percent of the total number of shares), which had belonged to Dwayne Andreas. The price quoted to the Doles for the three-room unit was $150,000. Andreas gave preferential treatment to the Doles for this unit, not only as to the purchase price but also as to making his own seventy-five shares in the co-op available to them. The Sea View Hotel is a very exclusive building. An average citizen walking into Bal Harbour and wanting to buy a co-op there would not get to first base. One has to have special clout to get in the door.

The three-room unit was sold to the Doles for $150,000, which amounts to $50,000 per room. But an equivalent three-room unit in an even less desirable location in the same building was sold for $190,000 to someone else just three months before the Doles purchased their apartment, according to Sea View officials. An independent appraisal prepared by a managing partner of the Miami office of Kenneth Leventhal and Company, a leading accounting firm specializing in real estate, estimated that the actual market value of the Doles' unit was about $190,000 in 1982, thus indicating that the Doles received about a 25 percent discount on that purchase price.

James Brock, a member of the Sea View Hotel board of directors, said that "Dwayne Andreas seems to have complete control of everything that goes on here." He indicated that if Sea View units had been openly available on the market, there would have been no shortage of persons willing to bid. Another former Sea View official who handled the transaction insisted that the sale was "basically consummated as a personal thing by Dwayne Andreas."

The ownership of the Doles' seventy-five co-op shares is somewhat obscured by conflicting paperwork. A stockholders' list and the minutes for the hotel's 1982 board meetings state that "Bob Dole and Mrs. Dole" were both joint owners of the unit. The original deed signed between the hotel and the Doles, which was dated March 19, 1982, named Elizabeth Dole as the sole owner of the unit. A subsequent deed, which was actually executed several months later but then backdated to March 19, 1982, lists Elizabeth Dole and her brother, John Hanford, as joint owners. Elizabeth Dole claims that she and her brother bought the apartment and split the cost because they wanted "a place we could use as a little family retreat," as if Bob didn't even exist.

Although Bob Dole denies personal knowledge of the details of the Sea View transaction, and insists that his wife bought it, he has regularly used the unit for weekends, vacations, and the like, and he hobnobs with Andreas there.

In early 1994, Dole even appeared, from the co-op at Bal Harbour, on "This Week with David Brinkley," one of whose sponsors is ADM. Appropriately, after the senator invited Brinkley to visit him in Florida, an ADM commercial filled the screen.

The Gallo Vintage

Like Dwayne Andreas, Ernest and Julio Gallo preside over a vast agribusiness empire. Multimillionaires in their seventies in 1985, the Gallos had a problem: How to avoid massive federal estate and generation-skipping taxes? The Gallos brought in Bob Dole. He said he didn't like the generation-skipping tax (GST), didn't like it one bit. This federal tax was intended to prevent wealthy families from avoiding an entire generation's worth of estate taxes by transferring much of their assets to grandchildren.

Ernest and Julio Gallo preside over a wine-making empire in Modesto, California, including four wineries, a bottle-making plant, vineyards, and other assets that bottle one-quarter of all the wine produced in the United States. The Gallo operation, which is controlled through a Delaware firm named Dry Creek Corporation, is entirely owned by the Gallo family members and does not publish financial reports. However, wine industry consultant Louis Gomberg estimated the Gallo brothers' combined net worth at about $600 million as of 1985.

In the 1985–86 campaign cycle, Ernest and Julio Gallo and their wives each contributed $5,000 to Dole's Campaign America PAC. In 1989–90, the Gallos contributed $65,000 to Campaign America and another $18,000 to Dole's Senate campaign. The Gallo clan's many in-laws and relatives are all targeted for campaign money. In a three-year period, the clan gave a total of $97,000 to Dole's Senate reelection committee and Campaign America, and they have continued to be steady contributors.

In 1985, Senate majority leader Dole supported a "special" exemption to the "generation-skipping estate tax," of $2 million per grandchild, which in effect benefits prolific families like the Gallos, because the more grandchildren one has, the more money he can pass on tax free. This exemption to the tax law was derisively dubbed the "Gallo Amendment" because it allowed Ernest and Julio Gallo to pass on an estimated $80 million to their grandchildren without incurring a special 33 percent tax. It stands as one of the most blatant of the made-to-order laws Congress has passed.*

The Gallo amendment technically would benefit any prolific family that had a large inheritance to leave to their grandchildren. But the number of families in the United States who fit this description is very small. The U.S. Treasury and congressional staff sources estimate that there are only about seven thousand estates every year that incur any estate tax at all and that fewer than 5 percent of those would benefit from the Gallo amendment; namely, very wealthy families with many grandchildren.† The more grandchildren a rich person has,

*See *The Wall Street Journal*, October 31, 1985.
†The generation-skipping tax (GST) is discussed in Section 2611 of the Internal Revenue Code. In general, generation-skipping

the greater number of $2 million tax exemptions he can harness.

The Gallo amendment was approved as part of the "tax overhaul" bill that was supposed to make the income tax system "simpler and fairer." According to several politicians, including Democratic Congressman Frank Guarini of New Jersey, who voted against the measure, "the Gallo Amendment means more benefits for rich people at the expense of the working man, Joe Six-Pack." As Guarini and other opponents of the measure pointed out, "the Gallo Amendment serves no purpose in tax reform."

The Gallo amendment was not the end of the story, however. French and American champagne companies soon found themselves opposing the Gallos' efforts to change tough federal policies.

Between 1989 and 1992, ten members of the Gallo family contributed $12,000 to Dole's Senate '92 Committee and $85,000 to Dole's Campaign America PAC. The Gallos were pressing the Treasury Department to abolish a fifty-six-year-old regulation requiring U.S. wineries that, like the Gallos', fermented champagne in huge steel tanks, to print the words "bulk process" on their labels.

The Gallos wanted the regulation abolished to avoid the stigma of an inferior product, which the term "bulk process" implied. Their demand was opposed by French and American champagne companies that used the superior *champenoise* method to ferment champagne in individual bottles. Many Baptists also opposed the bulk process method because it led to higher alcohol content in the champagne, but Dole seemed untroubled by their objections. On February 7, 1992, Dole, together with Senator John Seymour, a Republican from California, wrote a letter to Deputy Treasury Secretary John E. Robson, supporting the Gallos' position and insisting that

---

transfers are taxed at a flat rate derived from the maximum estate tax rate. See Code Sections 2631 and 2632 on the generation-skipping transfer exemption.

"champagne is champagne, regardless of the production." Seymour and Dole had received $112,000 in campaign contributions from the Gallo clan in recent years.

Dole's efforts on behalf of Gallo were successful. The Treasury Department's Bureau of Alcohol, Tobacco, and Firearms (BATF) amended its regulation on labeling requirements. As of July 1993, the new regulations allowed the Gallos and other wineries to use alternative label phrases, such as "not bottle fermented," to describe the bulk process.

The Gallos now dominate the U.S. champagne market, and their gratitude and support for Dole continues. In one month alone, February 1994, the Gallo clan and Gallo executives contributed $45,000 to Dole's Campaign America.

The Cable Television Industry

The preceding case studies show Dole's *offensive* actions on behalf of his contributors. But offense is just half the story. Dole campaign contributors may also expect the best "defense" in the "National Financial League"—the Senate's NFL. Dole can be devastatingly effective as a defensive tackle, targeting bills opposed by his contributors. Dramatic evidence of his obstructionist tactics against President Clinton's health-care reform bill and campaign finance reform bill will be discussed in part VII.

During Bush's administration, Dole was the only member of the Kansas delegation to Congress who opposed the Cable Television Consumer Protection and Competition Act of 1992, which aided consumers. Senator Nancy Kassebaum was one of its twenty-five Republican supporters. But not Bob Dole.

FEC records reveal that between 1990 and 1992, Dole received about $30,000 from special interest PACs in the cable television industry. The largest contributor, National Cable Television Association, gave Dole a total of $10,000 in two $5,000 checks. By contrast, he received only $3,000 from the National Association of Broadcasters, the main proponent of the Cable Television Consumer Protection and Competition Act.

This new cable TV bill called for the promulgation of new Federal Communications Commission Rules to guarantee *reasonable rates* for basic cable service (under existing law, cable companies were allowed to set their own rates without limits). The bill also required cable companies to meet minimum standards for consumer service, to negotiate for the rights to carry television station signals previously gotten for free, and to give satellite broadcasters and other cable rivals access to cable programming.

The cable television industry and Hollywood movie studios waged a fierce campaign against this consumer protection bill. Cable rates increased more than three times the rate of inflation between 1984 and 1992. The bill passed Congress, but was vetoed by Bush. Congress overrode Bush's veto, and the cable bill became law in October 1992.

19

SUMMER SOLDIER FOR ISRAEL: FROM STAUNCH SUPPORTER TO ANGRY CRITIC TO SEEMING SUPPORTER

Dole resents it when wealthy special interest PACs and individuals "boycott" him. Once a staunch supporter of Israel, he has proven to be a mercurial friend. He feels that Jonathan Pollard, an American Jew arrested for "spying for Israel" and sentenced to life imprisonment in a U.S. federal prison in the 1980s, should "stay in jail for life," and winces when a pardon for Pollard is suggested, most recently on "Meet the Press" in 1994.*

Like his hero Richard Nixon and many other traditional WASP Republicans, Dole has sometimes been critical of Jews, their politics, and their financial power.† While careful to avoid any direct attack on Jews as an ethnic or religious group, Dole sometimes privately expressed envy and resentment at Jews for having an

*In a bizarre case, Jonathan Pollard, an American Jew who worked in U.S. Naval Intelligence, was arrested in November 1985 for turning over classified military documents to Israel. He pleaded guilty, and in March 1987 was sentenced to life in prison. Many in the Jewish community have urged a commutation of his sentence.

†In his book, *The Haldeman Diaries: Inside the Nixon White House*, published posthumously in 1994, former Nixon Chief of Staff H. R. Haldeman revealed that Nixon had been anti-Semitic, a fact carefully concealed from the public for twenty-five years.

unduly large amount of money, power and influence in the United States, and for bankrolling liberal Democrats' campaigns. Some he called Communists.

In the dust bowl days of Depression Kansas, populist politicians often sprinkled anti-Semitic comments into their anti–Wall Street harangues. Dole was undoubtedly exposed to the classic attitude of poor Midwestern WASP farmers about a fabulously wealthy group of wire-pullers in the great cities of the East, manipulating the stock exchange and the economy. They were sometimes identified by populist WASP demagogues as Jews.

Still hoping to attracting Jewish money, Dole claimed to be a card-carrying friend of Israel in his early days as a politician. When he emerged on the national scene in the 1970s, he paid the traditional homage to the Jewish State. But he always harbored a deep dislike of such Jewish politicians as Congressman Dan Glickman, a bitter rival from Kansas, and Henry Kissinger.

In July 1977, before the national convention of the Zionist Organization of America, which was held in Israel, Dole lavished praise on the Jewish State. One eyewitness observer on the scene, John Rothmann, commented that "Dole was given the full VIP treatment. He was given a helicopter tour of critical areas in Israel. The state of Israel thought he was a true friend. In his speech he made Menachem Begin, who was on the platform with him, sound like a dove."

Dole frequently solicited the support of wealthy Republican Jews in his bitter primary fight against George Bush for the 1988 GOP presidential nomination. However, much to Dole's chagrin, GOP Jews overwhelmingly supported Bush and, to a lesser extent, Jack Kemp. Pro-Israel PACs gave Dole only $5,000 in 1988.

Many Jews tended to distrust Dole because of his reputation for flip-flopping on issues, his personality traits, his "dark side," and his close identification with Richard Nixon. Dole's slashing, ruthless campaign tactics also disturbed some Jews, who saw him as a demagogue. Rumors of his vindictive streak led many to feel alarmed by the prospect of such a person having his finger on the nuclear button and his hand on the lever for aid to Israel.

In 1980 Dole received $8,500 from pro-Israel PACs; in 1984, $3,000, and in 1986, $9,500, for a total of $21,000. Yet in 1986, Alan Cranston took in $241,232, and in 1984, Senator Tom Harkin of Iowa got $109,830, and Senator William Cohen of Maine received $42,930. In 1988 he got only $5,000. In comparison, 1988 Democratic presidential candidate Michael Dukakis received $24,713; Al Gore, $18,250; Paul Simon, $12,694; and Republican Jack Kemp, $13,250.

Dole dramatically changed his position toward Israel in 1988.

On March 13, he refused to join twenty-one other senators in signing a letter from Senators Dennis De Concini (D-AZ) and Pete Wilson (R-CA) to Secretary of State George Shultz stating that the Palestinian Liberation Organization was a terrorist organization and that Shultz's planned meeting with members of a Palestinian group set a dangerous precedent. Such senators' letters to top administration officials are generally signed and cosponsored by both Republican and Democratic senators to demonstrate bipartisan support for Israel.

Dole also refused to sign a letter on April 13, 1988, sponsored by Senators Rudy Boschwitz (R-MN), Howard Metzenbaum (D-OH), Robert Packwood (R-OR), and Arlen Specter (R-PA), and signed by fifty-four other senators to Secretary of State Shultz, urging the Reagan administration to reconsider any new arms sales to Saudi Arabia until the Chinese CSS-2 intermediate-range ballistic missiles were removed from Saudi Arabian soil.

On June 21, 1988, Dole again refused to sign a letter from Senator De Concini to Secretary of State Shultz urging the Reagan administration to halt consideration of a $1.9 billion arms sale to Kuwait. The senators expressed concern as to the basing of the planes and Maverick missiles within range of Israel. Twenty senators signed the letter.

On July 7, 1988, in the Senate, Dole voted against a key foreign aid bill, H.R. 4637, the Fiscal Year 1989 Foreign Aid Appropriations Bill, which included $3 billion in "All-Grant Aid" for Israel and numerous pro-Israel provisions. The bill passed the Senate by a vote of 76 to 15 and passed the House by a vote of 328 to 90, on May 25, 1988.

Dole refused to sign a letter dated April 13, 1989, by Senators Patrick Leahy (D-VT) and Bob Kasten (R-WI) to Secretary of State James Baker urging that the United States oppose any move by the PLO to seek "member state status" in the World Health Organization and other United Nations–affiliated agencies.

In August 1989, Dole began to alarm pro-Israel PACs and American Jews. Israeli commandos had seized a Shiite leader, Sheik Obeid, in southern Lebanon. In retaliation, Shiite Hezbollah extremists in Lebanon claimed that they had killed an American hostage, Marine Colonel William Higgins, and threatened to kill more hostages unless Sheik Obeid was released. Dole said, "We cannot apologize for Israeli actions in this country when it endangers the lives of Americans in some far-off country. Perhaps a little responsibility on the part of the Israelis would be refreshing."

On September 26, 1989, Dole refused to sign a letter by Senators Connie Mack (R-FL) and Joseph Lieberman (D-CT) to Secretary of State Baker urging Baker to deny a visa to PLO chairman Yasir Arafat, who was coming to the United Nations in New York to speak. (Sixty-eight senators signed the letter.)

Then Dole wrote and published a bitter Op-Ed piece in *The New York Times* on January 19, 1990. Shocking many Jews and supporters of Israel, Dole proposed a 5 percent cut in American aid to Israel, along with Egypt, the Philippines, and Turkey. He also blasted "those pressure groups that have turned some of our foreign aid programs virtually into 'entitlement programs.' Perhaps an even larger across-the-board cut and reallocation would be warranted," Dole suggested. "That would represent a better balancing of our limited resources with our changing priorities."

In April 1990, Dole gave an interview to the *Jerusalem Post*, Israel's leading English-language newspaper, in which he again criticized certain Jewish "groups" in the United States for being "too selfish." His rambling interview, published in the *Post* on April 13, 1990, is laced with ethnic stereotypes that hint at anti-Semitism. Abe Foxman, head of B'nai B'rith ADL, was appalled and said so publicly. Malcolm Hoenlein, another Jewish leader, also criticized Dole for ethnically stereotyping Jews.

Hyman Bookbinder, a representative of the American Jewish Committee and veteran lobbyist in Washington, said of Dole, "His recent actions and words I find tragic. . . . By his comments he has become the darling of the anti-Israeli forces."

In February of 1990, seventy-three senators signed another major letter to President Bush, sponsored by Senators Carl Levin (D-MI) and Pete Wilson (R-CA) opposing Dole's proposal to cut aid to Israel, Egypt, the Philippines, and Turkey. Dole saw this as a personal affront.

On March 22, 1990, Dole voted for Senate Concurrent Resolution 106, the so-called Moynihan Resolution, which had eighty-four Senate cosponsors and expressed the view that Jerusalem should be recognized as the capital of Israel.

Then on April 12, 1990, Dole met with Iraqi President Saddam Hussein in Mosul, Iraq, unconcerned by Hussein's vow to turn Israel into a "sea of fire" and to "burn Israel with chemical weapons." Moshe Arens, Israeli defense minister in 1990, said he was "astounded" when Dole, who met with him in Israel two days after meeting Saddam, assured him that Saddam posed no threat to Israel. Arens was also dismayed that Dole rejected his dinner invitation, put Israel last on his list of countries to visit, and told everyone that President Bush and he strongly supported Saddam's regime. (Dole became one of the chief Senate apologists for Hussein, and when Iraq invaded Kuwait in August 1990, Dole counseled Bush not to go to war.) Just seven days after the meeting with Hussein, Dole returned to the Senate and urged his colleagues to repeal the vote on Senate Concurrent Resolution 106. Dole claimed that the resolution had been submitted to the Senate on March 20, and that in two days it had eighty-four cosponsors. Dole said:

> The resolution had come to the floor in what was "wrap-up" at the end of the day on March 22. There was no debate. In my recollection, the text of the resolution was not even read into the record. We had a voice vote. And I doubt that half the sponsors even knew what they had signed or what had been adopted. Now you see it, now you don't.

Dole stressed that on his visit to Syria, Egypt, Jordan, Iraq, and Israel, he had learned that the issue of the status of Jerusalem was one of the most sensitive and emotional ones in the Middle East, and that the Israeli government's position that Jerusalem is the capital of Israel is "a position one hundred eighty degrees contrary to the views of the Arab States and the Palestinians." He claimed that "everywhere we went, Senate Concurrent Resolution 106 was on the agenda." He said he had met with about two hundred anti-Resolution demonstrators in Jordan and "they felt pretty strongly about it." He mentioned Syria's President Assad and Iraqi's Hussein, who also condemned the resolution.* Dole claimed that the resolution had "sailed through the Senate in about fifteen seconds."

Even as Dole was addressing the Senate, a group of four Republican congressmen led by Newt Gingrich (R-GA) held a conference down the hall on the U.S. Capitol, to denounce Dole for his remarks. Dole went

*See the *Congressional Record*, Senate, April 19, 1990, pages S-4456 through S-4458.

ballistic at being criticized, blasting the Congressmen for going behind his back to sabotage his speech. Meanwhile, he continued to boycott most pro-Israel legislation and symbolic policy letters.

On June 11, 1990, Dole refused to cosponsor Senate Resolution 138, which recommended a suspension of the U.S.–PLO dialogue following the failed attack on the Israeli coast. Cosponsored by fifty-eight senators, the measure passed, and the Bush administration terminated the dialogue.

Dole's bitterness was matched by an increasing support for Saddam Hussein and Iraq. Dole said Hussein could be trusted. Dole urged Bush to sell wheat to Iraq. Dole said Hussein was a good leader, "a leader to whom the United States can talk."

The senator was accused in 1992, by the Democratic vice-presidential candidate, Al Gore, of "cozying up to Saddam" and of being an "apologist for Saddam."

After Saddam Hussein invaded Kuwait in August 1990, and Bush began rattling swords for war, Dole was conspicuously critical of Bush. "I don't think the American people want war," Dole said on national television. On October 29, 1990, Dole again refused to sign another major letter (fifty-three senators did) to President Bush, sponsored by Senators Charles Grassley (R-IA) and Frank Lautenberg (D-NJ), which opposed any linkage between Iraq's withdrawal from Kuwait and Israel's withdrawal from the West Bank and the Gaza Strip. (Hussein had refused to withdraw from Kuwait, claiming that Israel's occupation of the West Bank and the Gaza Strip since 1967 was "morally equivalent" to Iraq's invasion of Kuwait. He said that Iraq would withdraw from Kuwait only if Israel withdrew from the West Bank and the Gaza Strip.)

On July 24, 1991, Dole voted for Senator Jesse Helms's (R-NC) amendment to the Fiscal Year 1992–93 Foreign Aid Authorization Bill, which called for a 10 percent cut in all foreign aid, including aid to Israel.* The Helms amendment was defeated by a vote of 87 to 12 in the Senate, and was strongly opposed by the pro-Israel lobby. Two days later, on July 26, Dole voted against H.R. 2508, the Fiscal Year 1992–93 Foreign Aid Authorization Bill, which included $3 billion in All-Grant Aid to Israel as well as numerous other pro-Israeli positions. The bill passed the Senate by a vote of 74 to 18.

On October 8, 1991, Dole voted against H.R. 2508, the Fiscal Year 1992–93 Foreign Aid Authorization Conference Report Bill, which included $3 billion in All-Grant Aid to Israel and numerous other pro-Israel provisions. The bill passed the Senate by a vote of 61 to 38.

In October and November of 1991, Dole was again conspicuous for not cosponsoring Senators Kasten-Inouye's Amendment to the Fiscal Year 1992 Foreign Aid Appropriations Bill, which would have provided $10 billion in loan guarantees to Israel for the absorption of Soviet and Ethiopian Jews in Israel. Seventy-two other Senators cosponsored the Kasten-Inouye Amendment as of December 1, 1991.

On November 22, 1991, Dole refused to sign the Metzenbaum-Packwood "Dear Colleague" senators' letter to President Bush expressing opposition to the reported Saudi Arabian interest in purchasing seventy-two new F-15 jet fighter aircraft from the United States (sixty-seven other senators signed the letter). That same month he refused to cosponsor the Mack-Robb Resolution in the Senate urging Arab states to recognize Israel (there were eighty-three other senators who cosponsored the bill as of December 1, 1991), and he declined to sign a senators' letter sponsored by Senators Grassley and Lautenberg to Secretary of State Baker urging him not to remove Syria

---

*Helms has been one of the harshest critics of Israel in the Senate. In 1995 he became Chairman of the Senate Foreign Relations Committee, and urged Congress to terminate all foreign aid. Israel is the top recipient of U.S. foreign aid.

from the government's official "terrorist list" (fifty-five senators signed the letter).

On April 26, 1991, Dole refused to sign the Senator Lautenberg-Packwood letter to King Faud of Saudi Arabia expressing disappointment with the Saudi's refusal to join the peace process with Israel (sixty-eight senators signed the letter).

On June 10, 1992, Dole declined to cosponsor Senate Resolution No. 113 commemorating the 25th Anniversary of the reunification of Jerusalem and declaring it the undivided capitol of Israel. This resolution was cosponsored by seventy-four senators and commemorated the twenty-fifth anniversary since June 10, 1967, when Israeli forces reunified Jerusalem in the Six-Day War.

In September 1992, Dole again did not sign Senate letters urging Bush to reconsider selling seventy-two F-15 aircraft to Saudi Arabia.

On January 26, 1993, Dole did not sign Senators Connie Mack (R-FL) and Daniel Moynihan's (D-NY) letter to Secretary of State Christopher urging the Clinton Administration to veto possible United Nations sanctions against Israel following the temporary removal of nearly 400 Palestinian HAMAS activists. (Seventy-two senators did sign.)

On February 8, 1993, Dole refused to sign the Grassley-Lautenberg letter to Secretary of State Christopher supporting the State Department's decision to include the activities of Hamas, a Palestinian terrorist group, in its annual report on terrorist organizations. (Fifty-five senators signed the letter.)

On July 9, 1993, Dole did not sign Senators Mitch McConnell (R-KY) and Frank Lautenberg's (D-NJ) letter to President Clinton praising his commitment to the Middle East peace process and expressing the senators' support for maintaining current levels of aid to Israel. (Seventy-five senators signed the letter.)*

*This information was furnished to the author by John Rothmann from his personal library.

The pattern is clear.

In 1990, Dole even sponsored a Senate Resolution commemorating the genocide of 1.5 million Armenians in 1915–23 in the Ottoman Empire. This resolution offended Turkey, one of the few Muslim nations that recognized Israel, and was also opposed by Israel, which felt it demeaned the unique historical significance of the Holocaust. A filibuster killed Dole's resolution.

As Dole revved up his presidential campaign in early 1995, he resolved this time to secure Republican Jewish money, and once again flip-flopped on issues pertaining to Israel.

With his front-runner status clear by early 1995 (polls in March showed him with the support of 52 percent of Republicans), Dole reached out to secure the backing of wealthy Jewish contributors who had shunned him in the past. On February 3, 1995, he signed a letter to Secretary of State Warren Christopher urging the transfer of the U.S. Embassy in Israel from Tel Aviv to Jerusalem—the exact opposite of his position in the bitter days of 1990. On May 8, 1995, Dole addressed a convention of the influential American Israel Public Affairs Committee (AIPAC) and promised to offer legislation in the Senate to move the U.S. embassy in Israel from Tel Aviv to Jerusalem. The next day, he made good on his promise, introducing a bill to force the U.S. government to move the embassy to Jerusalem, over the objections of the Clinton administration and the Arab world.

Dole's sudden metamorphosis into a seemingly fanatical supporter of Israel's interests is striking, and must be seen as one of the most dramatic flip-flops of his career. The status of Jerusalem is one of the most sensitive issues in the Arab-Israeli dispute, and has yet to be officially settled via peace negotiations. The question is: Should Dole's about-face be seen as just presidential politicking, or is the man sincere?

In early 1995, as Dole announced his presidential bid, a stampede of Jewish moneymen signed up to support his campaign for president. The most prominent of these was the dean of Jewish Republican fundraisers, octogenarian Michigan mogul Max Fisher, who became Dole's "honorary national finance chairman" in March 1995. Other major Jewish backers of Dole's presidential bid include financier Henry Kravis, Revlon's chairman Howard Gittis, and real estate tycoon George Klein.

It appears that many of these Jewish supporters are willing to disregard Dole's record of flip-flops on Israel in light of his status as the likely Republican presidential nominee.

It would be interesting to see what happens if Dole becomes president and Arab moneymen hostile to Israel decide to give Dole more money than his current Jewish supporters.

20

"THE BUTCHER OF BAGHDAD"

Dole's pro-Iraq position is the other side of the anti-Israel coin and was also influenced by the advice of his former mentor, Richard Nixon.

Bob Dole's friendly relationship with Saddam Hussein and Iraq goes back a long way. In 1980, a year after the Ayatollah Khomeini overthrew the Shah of Iran, Iraq attacked a weakened Iran. This act led to the Iran-Iraq War, which lasted from 1980 to 1989, in which millions were killed and great damage was incurred by both sides. During the conflict, Congress declared a total embargo on U.S. arms to both of the belligerent forces, an embargo that was broken surreptitiously by the Reagan administration in selling arms to Iran in the notorious Iran-Contra scandal.

Rarely presented for public view is the extent to which certain elements of the U.S. foreign policy elite secretly supplied arms and support to Saddam Hussein's Iraq. Dole was one of Iraq's key supporters and an apologist for Saddam Hussein.

Richard Nixon, who had been a staunch supporter of the corrupt Shah of Iran during his presidency, and who worried about his ouster in 1979, continued to exert enormous influence over U.S. foreign policy long after his resignation from the presidency. Nixon regularly spoke with Dole and other top Republican officials and foreign policy operatives and urged Republican presidents Reagan and Bush to prop up the Saddam Regime in Iraq as a "bulwark against extremist Muslim fundamentalism," which was represented by Khomeini's fanatical theocracy in Iran. Nixon's goal was to "maintain a balance of power" in the Middle East. Dole, who had never had much of an interest or expertise in foreign policy and had never served on any foreign relations Senate committees, soaked up Nixon's geopolitical theories like a sponge.

Dole consistently influenced the Senate, Reagan, and Bush to sell American wheat and grain to Iraq, via generous loans subsidized by the American taxpayer. Dole generally supported Iraq and Saddam Hussein right up to his invasion of Kuwait in August 1990, and Dole seemed undisturbed by Saddam's increasing belligerence. For instance, in February 1990, Saddam began to talk menacingly about the U.S. presence in the Persian Gulf. In March 1990, Saddam executed a British journalist for "spying for Israel." (This journalist had been gathering evidence that Iraq was trying to build nuclear and chemical weapons.) On April 2, 1990, just ten days before Dole's meeting with Saddam, he threatened to "burn half of Israel with chemical weapons if Israel attacks Iraq." Yet on April 12, Dole told Saddam, "We want to improve our relations with your country and your government."

After the meeting between Dole and Hussein, as well as four other senators, in Iraq, the Senate in July 1990 debated the 1990 Farm Bill and U.S. commodities credits to the Saddam regime. At this time, there were disturbing reports of up to 30,000 Iraqi troops massing on the Kuwaiti border. Senator Alfonse D'Amato (R-NY) offered an amendment to the Farm Bill to impose sanctions against "countries using chemical weapons," specifically aimed at Iraq. The D'Amato amendment passed the Senate by a vote of 83–12. Although Dole did vote in support of this amendment, he first tried to weaken the sanctions by pushing the so-called Gramm amendment, which would have permitted the Bush administration to waive the provision at will. The Gramm amendment was not approved by the Senate.

D'Amato also presented another amendment that would have cut off all aid to Iraq unless Iraq opened its weapons site for inspection by the West and the United Nations. This amendment was strongly opposed by Dole. During the Senate floor debate on another D'Amato amendment, Dole referred to his meeting on April 12th with Saddam and said publicly that the D'Amato amendment would "kill efforts to draw Iraq into a reasonable peace settlement." Dole said Saddam was a rational person who could be bargained with. Based on Dole's opposition, D'Amato withdrew his amendment.

Additional sources cited Dole's and other senators' desires to tap the lucrative Iraqi markets for rice, wheat, computer technology, and construction projects as justification for Dole's support of Saddam. Iraq was, in 1990, a major importer of U.S. grain, albeit grain subsidized by the U.S. taxpayer. By 1990, the United States had extended more than a billion dollars a year in agricultural loan guarantees to Iraq, with Dole's active support. Most of these loan agreements signed by Iraq were not worth the paper they were printed on and would never be paid back, especially after relations between Iraq and the United States broke off with the invasion of Kuwait. Many of Dole's favorite agribusiness contributors, such as Archer-Daniels-Midland, ConAgra, and Cargill, however, stood to gain millions of dollars by selling their "surplus" wheat to the Butcher of Baghdad.

There is yet another connection between Dole and Iraq. Prior to the invasion of Kuwait in August 1990, Coastal Corporation, a Texas oil firm, was negotiating with Saddam to sell Iraq 50 percent of Coastal's refining operations. Over the years, Coastal has contributed lavishly to Dole's campaigns and has allowed Dole to use its corporate jet fleet as a frequent flyer. Following the Kuwaiti invasion, Dole counseled Bush to be patient and to wait for economic sanctions to work and to negotiate an Iraqi withdrawal from Kuwait.

But as public opinion seemed to support Bush, Dole finally jumped on the bandwagon. In January 1991, at the president's request he offered a resolution in the Senate supporting Bush's prerogative to start war. Yet even here he counseled patience: "What we are attempting to do is strengthen [Bush's] hand for peace, not to give him a license to see how fast we can become engaged in armed conflict," Dole said. The resolution passed narrowly, 52–47.

But war came in January 1991 when Bush unleashed a mighty air and ground assault. Saddam withdrew from Kuwait, but only after firing 31 Scud missiles into Israel, which killed 14 people, wounded 241 others, and damaged nearly 7,000 buildings. His goal had been to lure the Israelis into the war, and thereby galvanize all the other Arab states to join the war on his side, but the "Holy War" he envisioned never materialized. After Saddam fled from Kuwait, Bush and the American media painted him as a demon. Even Dole began to call him "the Bully of Baghdad," and when asked what he had thought of Saddam before the Kuwaiti invasion, Dole replied, "I had no opinion."

V

PAC-MAN IN AN
ELECTORAL SYSTEM OF
"ONE DOLLAR, ONE VOTE"

The law, in its majestic equality, forbids the rich as well as the poor to sleep under bridges, to beg in the streets, and to steal bread.

—Anatole France

A latter-day Anatole France might well state, after observing American election campaigns, "The law, in its majestic equality, allows the poor as well as rich to form political action committees, to purchase the most sophisticated mailing, media and direct mail techniques and to drown out each other's voices by overwhelming expenditures in political campaigns."

Financial inequities pose a pervasive and growing threat to the principle of "one person, one vote" and undermine the political proposition to which this nation is dedicated—that all men are created equal.

—Federal Judge Skelly-Wright

21

DOLE'S FUND-RAISING FLEET: CAMPAIGN AMERICA, THE DOLE FOUNDATION, AND BETTER AMERICA FOUNDATION

B ob Dole raises more money every *two days* (over $500,000 per week) than he earns in an *entire year* as an elected senator.

When I worked for him, Dole was just a minor player on the PAC stage and used to groan about how his rivals for the presidency "storm into town with a vacuum cleaner, sucking up all the money, and then I come along with a whisk broom." That was in 1979, and just the year before Dole had created Campaign America, his own "leadership or multicandidate PAC." (A "leadership PAC," or "multicandidate PAC," is a political action committee controlled by a senator or congressman that raises money all over the country and dispenses it to favored candidates at every level of government, thus gaining the recipients' loyalty.) He had hoped to build Campaign America up into a political "corporation," as he liked to say, a corporation that raises and brokers money for "the interests." Campaign America PAC had a slow start and raised only $43,405 in 1979–80. But Dole became Senate majority leader in 1984, and in 1985 and 1986 alone, individuals gave $2.5 million and PACs chipped in $500,000 to Campaign America. And that was just the start.

Ten years later, Campaign America PAC is the largest

leadership PAC operated by any member of Congress. FEC records reveal that in 1994 Dole's Campaign America PAC vastly surpassed its closest rival, Newt Gingrich's GOPAC in campaign contributions received. Dole's leadership PAC has a sister organization, Campaign America—Kansas PAC, which is equally successful in the Sunflower State, where Dole reigns supreme.

Unlike Dole's special campaign committees, which sprout up every few years to raise money for specific Senate and presidential campaigns, Campaign America PAC has a permanent life in Washington, D.C. It pays for most of Dole's fund-raising travels across the country, and donates money to favored candidates loyal to Dole.

The role of Campaign America, Dole's own personal "multi-candidate PAC," cannot be underestimated. Preparing for upcoming election battles from January to June 1993, Campaign America raised $1.5 million, which was five times more than Dole had raised during the same period of time in 1992 and nearly three times greater than during the first half of 1991. During the first five months of 1994 alone, Campaign America raised $2.56 million, with much more on the way for this election year.

During a cameo campaign for reelection in Kansas in 1992, Dole spent most of his time during the fall outside of Kansas, campaigning for and bankrolling other candidates in more than twenty other states. His Campaign America PAC had contributed about $242,000 to fifty-five Republican House and Senate candidates from 1991 through the end of July 1992, according to FEC reports. Campaign America gave the maximum amount allowed by law, $10,000, to eleven Senate candidates.

In addition, Campaign America contributed $85,000 to state Republican organizations and state office candidates across the country, $60,000 of this going to state legislative candidates and Republican groups in Kansas.

During a previous campaign cycle, 1989 to 1990, Campaign America contributed more money to federal office candidates than any other leadership PAC, $30,000.

During the 1991–92 campaign cycle, Campaign

America again raised and contributed more money to federal office candidates than any other leadership PAC operated by any other member of Congress. It raised $1.4 million and gave $377,000 of that to federal candidates across the country. In 1993, Campaign America again led the fund-raising race.

During the 1994 campaign, Dole's flagship gave vastly more money to candidates than ever before and raised more than $5 million to help produce Republican majorities in the House and Senate.

Dole has unabashedly used Campaign America PAC as a cash cow to build loyalty, which he hoped would generate important endorsements for his presidential bid. To see exactly how he has done this, let us consider the example of South Dakota, a crucial state in the 1996 presidential primaries.

In 1994, Dole's Campaign America gave $13,000 to the reelection campaign of South Dakota Governor Bill Janklow. Campaign America was the largest single donor to Janklow's campaign, which raised over $1.2 million for the governor's successful bid for a third term.

In April 1995, just about six months after receiving Dole's $13,000, Janklow publicly endorsed Dole for the 1996 GOP presidential nomination. Janklow's support is critical to Dole's chances because South Dakota will have one of the earliest presidential primaries in the country, in February 1996.

This example is typical of Dole's use of Campaign America to help his presidential bids. In 1994, according to a Campaign America spokesperson, Campaign America gave more than $1 million to 402 candidates across the country. Though Dole denies any link between campaign cash and endorsements, human nature suggests otherwise.

Nelson Warfield, a Dole campaign spokesman, said that Janklow's endorsement was "a tremendous boost" to Dole's campaign, and admitted that "we've focused much of the campaign on winning the support of governors because they have a strong network of support within each of their states and they're very in touch with local concerns."

In February 1994, in a single fund-raiser gala at Washington's posh Willard Hotel, Campaign America PAC raised half a million dollars in *one night*, as each fat cat paid $1,000 for a drink and $5,000 for dinner.

According to Ellen Miller, Executive Director for The Center for Responsive Politics, an independent Washington-based think tank that researches campaign finance laws, "It just makes it easier for the special interests to buy influence when you use leadership PACs as a fund-raising device. You get more money, bigger chunks, more access." By law, individuals are allowed to contribute up to a limit of $5,000 per year to a "leadership PAC" such as Campaign America, and this limit is far higher than the $1,000 per year limit on individual contributions to a congressional or Senate campaign committee for a primary and general election.

The contributors to Dole's Campaign America literally read like a *Who's Who of Corporate America* and the Forbes 400 list. Among Dole's biggest financial supporters are California wine-makers Ernest and Julio Gallo. Ten Gallo family members each contributed $5,000 to Dole's Campaign America in January and February of 1993 alone, while another Gallo executive and his wife contributed $10,000 more.

In April 1993 alone, Dwayne Andreas, chairman of Archer-Daniels-Midland Corporation, and his staff and family gave Campaign America a total of $6,000. Dole has been Andreas's chief water carrier on Capitol Hill for twenty years, and has promoted the ethanol tax subsidy and other "made-to-order" legislation.

More than 85 percent of Campaign America's money is drawn from wealthy individuals, not from corporate PACs, which are more limited in the amount of money they can contribute to leadership PACs than are individuals. The limitation is meaningless, however, because corporate executives can legally circumvent the law by having their families contribute money to a favored PAC.

On the 1993 list of Campaign America contributors are such other beneficiaries of Dole's legislation and favoritism as John Ruan, John Palmer, commodity traders, and countless other wealthy corporate figures who have benefited from Dole-crafted legislation and his intervention with federal regulatory agencies.

Former U.S. Senator Russell Long, the son of "Kingfish" Huey Long, used to say that giving a campaign contribution to a senator was akin to "casting your bread upon the waters and getting it multiplied back manyfold." This biblical allusion, from the Book of Ecclesiastes, is quite accurate. If a contribution amounts to an "investment" in a "political bank" represented by an elected official, and that investment comes back "manyfold," is this wrong?

Bob Dole and corporate America would say "No," because they feel that "the business of America is business," and they subscribe to the trickle-down theory of economics, whereby a tax break (or other form of corporate welfare) for a company executive will inevitably lead to jobs for even the lowliest American.

Others of a more liberal persuasion say that this system is a sham. Professor James David Barber of Duke University feels that democracy is supposed to be a government of "laws," but is in danger of becoming a government "manipulated by the rich."

Each American must ask himself whether this practice is right or wrong. If the list of contributors to Bob Dole's campaign committees and Campaign America reads like a *Who's Who of Corporate America*, the same can be said of the list of contributors to the Dole Foundation for Employment of People with Disabilities, Bob's nonprofit, humanitarian fund-raising conglomerate. But while more than 80 percent of Campaign America's contributors are individuals, more than 90 percent of the Dole Foundation's contributors are corporations, corporate "foundations," and other similar entities.

Would it be accurate to describe the Dole Foundation as another branch of the Dole political-financing empire?

The answer depends on one's perspective. But the sheer genius of the man in crafting so many ways to raise money from the same sources, over and over again, is amazing.

Based in Washington, the foundation was created by Bob Dole in 1984, with the official goal of bringing together business and people with disabilities so that disabled and handicapped people could get a job and be trained properly. Grants of up to $100,000 are available from the Dole Foundation to help the handicapped. Since 1985, more than $5 million has been awarded to more than 200 projects nationwide, which expanded opportunities for citizens with disabilities. Priorities are services to rural areas, small employers, minorities, women, and older workers. A typical example would be fifty job seekers with visual impairments being teamed with fifty visually impaired volunteer mentors in a Lighthouse for the Blind.

In 1992, the Dole Foundation gave typical grants of $25,000 to Goodwill Industries of Southern California; $25,000 to the World Institute of Disability; $35,000 to Columbia Lighthouse for the Blind; $60,000 to the Partnership for People with Disabilities; $87,000 to the Career Services for the Disabled in New Mexico, $50,000 to the Multi-Tasking System of New York; and $30,000 to the National Center for Disability Services. In 1993, the total in grants was $1,091,936.

In 1992, the Dole Foundation raised $1,222,657 in contributions and revenue; in 1993 the figure increased to $1,275,460. In 1993, its "endowment fund" had $463,981 in the bank.

Some of the major funding partners have been AT&T Foundation; Chase Manhattan Bank; The William Randolph Hearst Foundation; The American Express Philanthropic Program; and New York Telephone. The Dole Foundation's list of major contributors in 1992 and 1993 include: Archer-Daniels-Midland; ConAgra; Exxon Corporation; The Gallo Foundation; American Express Foundation; American Stock Exchange; The Bircher Life

Insurance Company; Anheuser-Busch Companies; Cessna Foundation; Cargill Inc.; Chemical Bank; The Dun and Bradstreet Corporation; The Forbes Foundation; ITT Corporation; IBM; The Grocery Manufacturers of America, Inc.; The Guardian Life Insurance Company of America; H. J. Heinz Company Foundation; The Massachusetts Mutual Life Insurance Company; McDonalds Corporation; MCI Communications; Mercedes Benz of North America; Merrill Lynch and Company; Metropolitan Life Foundation; The New York Stock Exchange; Pacific Telesis Foundation; Pitney Bowes; Philip Morris Companies, Inc.; United Airlines; TRW Foundation; Southwestern Bell Corporation; RJR Nabisco Corporation; Ralston Purina Company; Proctor and Gamble; Texaco; Time Warner Inc.; The Tobacco Institute; Torchmark Corporation; Sears Roebuck Company; Shell Oil; Smokeless Tobacco Council Inc.; The John Ruan Foundation Trust; Safeway Inc.; David Rockefeller; and Henry Kissinger—200 major corporations in all.

Many of the same companies have donated money to Dole's campaigns.

The 1992 annual report released by the Dole Foundation indicates that as of the end of 1991, the foundation had $761,000 in current funds plus another $655,000 in endowment funds. The 1993 annual report reveals $526,471 in current funds plus $463,981 in endowment funds. Bob Dole, who serves as the Chairman of the Board of Trustees, also has placed many of his corporate friends on the foundation's board. Many vice-chairmen are on the list of his campaign contributors.

The Dole Foundation helps many disabled and handicapped individuals get training and find jobs, and it is to be commended for that. It is unfair to view the Dole Foundation as just another arm in the Dole political money machine. But corporations and wealthy individuals seeking Dole's support on legislation in Congress can certainly try to build up credit and increase access to Dole by contributing money to the foundation. Also, whereas all corporations have been banned by federal law since 1907 from contributing directly to any political candidate for any election, they are not prohibited from contributing unlimited amounts of money to a non-political entity like the Dole Foundation. There is a serious question as to whether it is appropriate for Dole himself to serve as chairman of the Dole Foundation and take unlimited amounts of money from corporations directly. As an elected official, it might be more appropriate if Dole stepped down.

It should also be pointed out that when the Dole Foundation contributes large "grants" to specific corporations to employ and train handicapped individuals, those companies have more money freed up to contribute (via their PACs and executive officers) to Dole's many campaign committees. This exemplifies Dole's skill as a broker of special interests. Meanwhile, Dole scores public relations points as the media showers him with kudos for his "humanitarian" activity. The Dole Foundation is substantial P.R.

Cigarettes kill and disable more than 500,000 Americans every year, and Senator Dole has privately said he believes cigarette smoking killed his brother Kenny, yet he has resisted congressional attempts to declare nicotine a drug and to have it regulated by the FDA, and he has supported tobacco subsidies. He has embraced the tobacco lobby with open arms. At numerous Dole Foundation galas, he has been mobbed by dozens of tobacco executives (and generous contributors), who patted him on the back and congratulated him for supporting the tobacco lobby in the Senate.*

The Dole Foundation spawned yet another nonprofit entity, the Better America Foundation (BAF), which

---

*Dole is personally a non-smoker. He became a tobacco bat boy in 1985, in exchange for Jesse Helms's support in his bid to become Senate GOP leader. See chapter 12. At least one tobacco company, U.S. Tobacco, frequently shuttles Dole around the country on its corporate jets, as will be discussed in chapter 23.

Dole created on February 4, 1993. As a nonprofit organization, BAF was able to raise unlimited amounts of money from corporate America, PACs, and individuals, tax free, without being subject to any limits of campaign finance laws or scrutiny by the FEC.

The Better America Foundation said that its official purpose was to: "Promote and advocate values and principles espoused by the Republican Party. . . . Research and develop innovative answers to public policy issues for the benefit of the American public, with a focus on reducing the size and cost of the federal government. . . ."

BAF, with Dole as the "honorary chairman," was an obscure organization that promoted the senator's political interests and raised massive contributions from corporations and persons whose identities were not publicly disclosed. In 1994, its first full year in operation, BAF raised well over $1 million.

BAF was run by Dole's political aides. Jim Wittinghill, Dole's former Senate deputy chief of staff, became BAF chief in 1994. According to BAF's 1993 Tax Return, Jo-Anne Coe (who is the executive director of Campaign America) was listed as BAF's president, and BAF's return address was identical to that of Campaign America. For 1993, BAF's tax return revealed $235,000 in donations. In its application to the IRS for tax-exempt status, the foundation projected that it would raise $2.75 million in 1994.

On October 31, 1994, just eight days before the national elections, Better America Foundation began running a thirty-second television commercial across the nation on CNN and some local stations. This ad, which cost a million dollars, began with a picture of Reagan addressing Congress, and then showed Dole with Newt Gingrich and finally Dole alone in a presidential pose, in front of a billowing American flag, while voices proclaimed Reagan's clichés about reducing government and balancing the budget. The ad glorified Dole, blasted Congress, and concluded: "A plan for a better America. Call and help turn Congress around."

It is interesting that federal campaign laws are so loose that groups such as BAF can avoid federal election regulations and requirements that they disclose their donors.*

Dole has explained that he created BAF as a "think tank in exile" for Republican theorists who had been thrown out of government jobs after Bush's defeat in 1992. But it is also a de facto Dole for President Committee. In the spring of 1993, Wayne Angell, a Dole crony from Wall Street, publicly said that he was being considered to head BAF, and that it would "help clarify Senator Dole's visions for a better America," although Angell ultimately did not get the job. Those visions need cash and ideas. BAF had an "800" toll-free telephone number to solicit both.

In June 1995, Dole abruptly shut down the Better America Foundation after being subjected to media criticism for failure to reveal the identities of BAF donors. But he can always reopen BAF's doors, once the media dust settles. Or, he can create another similar "foundation" and raise money without limit, behind closed doors.

BAF, like the Dole Foundation, is a monument to Dole's unique creativity in legally circumventing campaign laws. Using tax-exempt nonprofit foundations to promote one's presidential ambitions is an act of political genius.

---

*Internal Revenue Code section 501(c)(4) has often been used by advocacy groups such as Common Cause and the Sierra Club. Since BAF technically did not directly engage in lobbying or political campaign activity, it was in a gray area of the law and seemed to be in compliance with the law in what it was doing. In its application for tax-exempt status with the IRS, BAF asserted that it would conduct various "public policy programs," including those on deficit reduction and health-care reform, winning the war against crime and drugs, and insuring the survival of democracy.

In theory, Dole can create an unlimited number of such nonpolitical and nonprofit foundations, use them to rake in millions of dollars, and then turn around and use the money for political activities furthering his presidential candidacy.

22

THE DOLE CAMPAIGN COMMITTEES AND NATIONAL REPUBLICAN PARTY COMMITTEES

While Campaign America PAC is a permanent institution that raises campaign contributions year-round, Dole's financial machine has many short-term, special interest committees. These include the Dole for Senate '92 Committee, the Dole for President '80 and '88 and '96 committees, and committees for each election in which Dole himself has been a candidate.

The newest "Dole for Senate '92 Committee" raised a total of $3,115,690, far outstripping his Democratic opponent, Gloria O'Dell. The vast majority raised came from PACs and individuals outside of Kansas.

Spending only about $1.4 million on this campaign, Dole easily won reelection with 63 percent of the vote, and accomplished this largely by running an "absentee campaign" in which he made a few cameo appearances in Kansas and looked good on television. His campaign surplus leaves a $1.7 million cash reserve on hand. Though raised for a specific election, the money can be used for any other purpose Dole chooses.

In 1986, Dole's Senate Committee collected nearly $2 million to run against a token candidate who raised only $4,000, spent nothing, and didn't even campaign.

In effect, contributions to Dole's Senate campaign committees amount to a contribution to his overall political interests. He brokers the money and gives it to candidates personally loyal to him. Dole is a truly "na-

THE DOLE FUND-RAISING OCTOPUS

tional'' politician who happens to be an absentee Kansas Senator, and whose main priority is servicing his national business constituents and running for president. In effect, Dole's Senate '92 Committee, like his upcoming ''Dole for President '96 Committee,'' is the rubric for his national campaign for president. Contributors know they are really supporting his future presidential campaign in 1996. Dole has legally transferred money left over from his Dole for Senate '92 Committee to his Dole for President '96 Committee.

Table 22.1 shows a breakdown of the PAC contributors to the Dole for Senate '92 Committee, broken down by special interest groups. Most of his PAC contributors are business PACs. Looking at table 22.1, we see that agriculture, finance, insurance, and real estate industries are especially well represented. Not coincidentally, Dole is a key player on the Senate Finance and Agriculture Committees.

The single-issue PACs are broken down by issue in table 22.2 and table 22.3 shows the contribution limits

Table 22.1

INDUSTRY (SECTOR) PACS AND LARGE INDIVIDUAL CONTRIBUTIONS ($200 OR MORE) TO DOLE'S SENATE '92 CAMPAIGN COMMITTEE

INDUSTRY (SECTOR)	AMOUNT CONTRIBUTED
Agriculture	$430,350
Construction	$100,250
Communications/Electronics	$229,600
Defense	$66,104
Energy and Natural Resources	$319,187
Finance, Insurance and Real Estate	$795,271
Miscellaneous Business	$358,728
Health	$186,100
Lawyers and Lobbyists	$267,617
Transportation	$245,786
Labor	$9,500
Ideological (Single Issue)	$91,168*
Other	$38,990
TOTAL	$3,138,651

SOURCE: Center for Responsive Politics. Reprinted by permission.
*Note: The ideological (single issue) contributors are broken down in detail in Table 22.2.

imposed by federal election law on contributions in general. (These rules are routinely circumvented by bundling and soft money.)

Note that the figures in Tables 22.1 and 22.2 do not include additional sums raised by the National Republican Senate Campaign Committee (NRSC), and Republican National Committee (RNC), for whom Dole constantly solicits via mass mailings to individual Republican voters throughout the country. Routinely signed by Dole as "Republican Leader," the solicitation literature is couched in glowing patriotic terms, typically attacks the Democratic Party and the Clinton Administration as a "leftist" mob that is ruining the country, and exhorts the Republican voters to send in money to "help us take back our country."

In effect, this serves as another arm of the Dole financial machine. Individuals who have already given the maximum contribution to Campaign America and to Dole's Senate '92 Committee can now donate through the NRSC and RNC.

The National Republican Committees typically raise far more money than Dole's own personal committees, and they often raise great amounts of soft money. Between January 1993 and March 1994, the National Republican Senate Campaign Committee raised $38,408,701 and the Republican National Committee raised $46,718,000, while the National Republican Congressional Campaign Committee (NRCCC) raised $13 million in 1993–94 for House candidates.

Much of the money raised is "soft money," which is untraceable and used to support whole slates of party candidates. In the 1991–92 campaign cycle, for example, the Republican National Committee raised $42.9 million and the Republican Senatorial Committee raised $40.5 million.

It would not be accurate to describe Dole as the boss of all these committees, but he is their most influential single solicitor, and he plays a large role in deciding which candidates across the country receive funding.

Table 22.2

IDEOLOGICAL-SINGLE ISSUE PAC CONTRIBUTIONS TO DOLE FOR SENATE '92 CAMPAIGN COMMITTEE (DETAIL)

IDEOLOGY/ISSUE	PAC NAME	AMOUNT	YEAR GIVEN	TOTAL
Republican/Conservative	American Citizens for Political Action	$5,000 $1,000	1988 1990	
	Conservatives Acting Together	$5,000	1988	
	Committee for the Presidency	$5,000	1992	$16,000
Leadership PACs	American Space Frontier Committee	$1,000	1988	
	Campaign America	$250 $5,000	1988 1992	
	Fund for America's Future (G. Bush)	$8,216	1988	
	Senate Victory Fund	$5,000	1992	$19,466
Foreign and Defense Policy	American Security Council	$1,000	1988	
	Free Cuba PAC	$5,000	1988	
	American Task Force for Lebanon Policy	$2,000	1992	
	National Association of Arab-Americans	$1,000	1992	$9,000

Category	Name	Amount	Year	Total
Pro-Israel	National PAC	$5,000	1988	$5,000
Anti-Abortion Policy	National Right to Life PAC	$1,000	1992	$1,000
Gun Rights/Gun Control	National Rifle Association	$4,950	1992	$4,950
Human Rights	Asian Indian	$1,000	1988	
	Health Care Concerns PAC	$250	1988	
	India Association	$1,302	1988	
	Korean American National PAC	$1,000	1988	
		$2,000	1990	
		$4,000	1992	
	National Albanian American PAC	$1,000	1988	
		$9,000	1992	
	Kids PAC	$5,000	1992	$24,552
Miscellaneous Issues	Public Service Research Council	$1,000	1992	
	Right to Work PAC	$1,000	1992	$2,000
				$81,968

SOURCE: Center for Responsive Politics. Reprinted by permission.

Table 22.3
CONTRIBUTION LIMITS

DONOR	RECIPIENT					SPECIAL LIMITS
	CANDIDATE COMMITTEE	PAC[1]	LOCAL PARTY COMMITTEE[2]	STATE PARTY COMMITTEE[2]	NATIONAL PARTY COMMITTEE[3]	
Individual or Partnership	$1,000 per election[4]	$5,000 per year	$5,000 per year combined limit		$20,000 per year	$25,000 per year overall limit[5]
Local Party Committee[2]	$5,000 per election[4] combined limit	$5,000 per year combined limit	unlimited transfers to other party committees			
State Party Committee[2] (multicandidate)[6]	$5,000 per election[4] combined limit		unlimited transfers to other party committees			
National Party Committee[3] (multicandidate)[6]	$5,000 per election[4]	$5,000 per year	unlimited transfers to other party committees			$17,500 to Senate candidate per campaign[7]
PAC[1] (multicandidate)[6]	$5,000 per election[4]	$5,000 per year combined limit			$15,000 per year	
PAC[1] (not multicandidate)[6]	$1,000 per election[4]	$5,000 per year combined limit			$20,000 per year	

1. These limits apply to nonconnected committees and to separate segregated funds. Affiliated committees share the same set of limits on contributions received and made.

2. A state party committee shares its limits with local party committees in the same state, unless a local committee's independence can be demonstrated.

3. A party's national committee, Senate campaign committee and House campaign committee each have separate limits, except with respect to Senate candidates. See Special Limits column.

4. Each of the following is considered a separate election with a separate limit: primary election, caucus or convention with authority to nominate, general election and special election.

5. A contribution to a party committee or a PAC counts against the annual limit for the year in which the contribution is made. A contribution to a candidate counts against the limit for the year of the election for which the contribution is made.

6. A multicandidate committee is a political committee that has been registered for at least 6 months, has received contributions from more than 50 contributors and—with the exception of a state party committee—has made contributions to at least 5 federal candidates.

7. This limit is shared by the party's national committee and Senate campaign committee.

SOURCE: Federal Election Commission.

The relationship between the RNC, NRSC, and Dole's own Senate reelection and presidential committees and Campaign America PAC cannot be overlooked, either. Mailing lists are interchanged and anyone contributing to Dole's Senate Committee or Campaign America is likely to be showered with further solicitation letters signed by Dole on behalf of the RNC and NRSC.

In addition to the authorized and acknowledged fund-raising committees, a more controversial organization sprouted up in 1987. It was called Americans for Dole. This shadowy group claimed to be raising money for his 1988 presidential campaign, and solicited money from people all around the country. However, Dole later accused Americans for Dole as being "a classic scam" and totally unauthorized by him. He claimed it was a "con game through the mail" after the media exposed its activities publicly.

Americans for Dole was perfectly legal, however, until November 1992, when new federal rules went into effect that limited unauthorized political fund-raising. And the organization allegedly raised about $3.9 million in the name of Bob's ill-fated 1988 presidential campaign. Where did all this money go?

Americans for Dole still remains shrouded in mystery. The group seemed to prey on elderly and naive Republicans, such as a ninety-two-year-old widow living in Washington County, Kansas, who was persuaded to pony up $1,200. After news stories broke out, Dole said he wanted to "punch him [the man behind the operation] in the nose." The man's name is Robert Dolan.

Bob Dole claimed that "practically none" of the money raised by Americans for Dole actually went into his own campaign. But Dolan said that $5,000 actually went into Dole's 1988 presidential race and $1,000 went into his Senate race. Dolan also ran a group called American Citizens for Political Action, which, according to FEC records, raised $3.9 million during the 1988 election season, hardly a small operation.

In 1991, after being stung by media reports of Americans for Dole's activities, Bob Dole introduced legislation in the Senate to halt the unauthorized use of any candidate's name in fund-raising.

Other apparently unauthorized fund-raising groups have been used to raise money in a Republican candidate's name and then run demagogic commercials that support a candidate but enable him or her to maintain a hands-off image. For example, in 1988, a group named Americans for Bush headed by Floyd Brown (who was once Bob Dole's Midwest presidential campaign coordinator), raised millions of dollars and then used the money to prepare the infamous Willie Horton television commercial, which employed racism and fear of crime to blast Michael Dukakis. The ad showed Dukakis as a "soft on crime" governor who had allowed Horton, a black convict in Massachusetts, to escape while on furlough and rape a white woman in Maryland and knife her boyfriend. The ad was devastating.

The Americans for Dole operation bears some similarity to the shadowy anti-abortion groups that supported Dole in his critical 1974 Senate campaign in Kansas by plastering the state with last-minute grisly photos and leaflets depicting dead fetuses and branding Dole's opponent, Dr. Bill Roy, as an abortionist. In 1974, too, Dole claimed that group was unauthorized by him, although Roy's campaign manager, Bob Brock, claims Dole's campaign money paid for some of the grisly leaflets. Here, however, there is no evidence that Dole supported the group's activities.

While Dole may not have had knowledge of such unauthorized activities, he has benefited directly or indirectly from many of them, while maintaining the luxury of standing at a distance and denying any involvement in their controversial activities.

23

THE PAC-MAN GOBBLETH

Senator Dole's voting record on behalf of those interests and individuals that have supported him financially over the years is only one side of the coin. The other is the extent to which Dole has retaliated against those who have *not* supported him.

Should a senator like Dole act like neutral Solomon or should he be entitled to give different weight to constituents' needs based upon the extent of their financial contribution?

Is he required by law to do so? An elected senator is not a judge. However, an elected senator makes the laws that judges eventually enforce, and laws are supposed to be neutral and fair to all.

Bob Dole has denied being for sale, but his primary job is that of a professional fund-raiser. Consider the side benefits he derives from the funds raised.

Dole's lifestyle can be described as a "lifestyle of the rich and famous."

One week after the November 1992 elections, he gleefully hosted a banquet for lame duck President George Bush in Washington. For that one evening, Dole's bills included $43,645 for "banquet services" at the Columbus Club, an opulent banquet room at Washington's refurbished Union Station; $7,940 for the caterer, Ridgewells, a top-flight Washington catering company; $1,590 for flowers and $1,133 for engraving and printing. The

$54,308 spent for one night's entertainment is half of Dole's entire yearly Senate salary! Such spending is not atypical.

Bob Dole's campaign and PAC reports on file at the FEC reveal that his campaign committees have spent money in more unusual ways. For example, in late 1992, in one night $432 was used for calendars, $922 went for a "limousine service" in New York, and $171 was spent on candy from Mrs. Burden's Gourmet Candy. "The candy was made in Kansas and used for Christmas gifts," Dole's spokesman explained. Meanwhile, the $922 limousine was used in New York for a fund-raising night by Dole.

While this may not seem too high a price, the figures do add up when we consider how much money is showered on the senator by those groups sponsoring his fundraisers. Sometimes corporate sponsors pay for fundraisers, and sometimes Dole does.

The fact that Dole's campaign can use the money raised for almost anything personal remotely related to "campaigning," such as the airplane fares and candy and limousine services, shows that in effect politicians' real salary comes from campaign contributions, not the Senate payroll. If Dole can use money *after* the elections are over, and if the amount of "campaign" money dwarfs his Senate salary, why should he care about serving the lowly taxpayers who pay him only a "tip" of $143,000 per year?* Once elected, politicians can live on the basis of gifts from those who have a vested interest in legislation they pass, which creates an inherent conflict of interest.

While Bob Dole has placed no limits on the amount of PAC contributions he accepts, his colleague Senator

---

*Dole also stands to collect a hefty federal pension if he ever retires. According to *Money* magazine (August 1992), the National Taxpayers Union has estimated a $4 million federal pension for Dole and his wife when they both retire, courtesy of the U.S. taxpayer.

Nancy Kassebaum of Kansas, and many other elected officials, have a policy of accepting no more than $1,000 per PAC as a campaign contribution, and routinely return any amount more than $1,000. The result is that Dole has raised far more money than any other senator over the past fifteen years.

Some of the major agribusiness PACs that have showered Dole with money have been Archer-Daniels-Midland (ADM); Farmland Industries; Philip Morris Tobacco Company; Dow Chemical Company; John Deere; Kellogg's; and General Mills. Among the chief finance industry PACs that have given Dole money have been Equitable Life; Goldman Sachs; American Express; Glendale Federal Savings & Loan; Paine Webber; First Boston; Mutual of Omaha; Chemical Bank; New York Mercantile Exchange; The Chicago Board of Trade; Prudential Insurance; and Salomon Brothers.

In addition, AT&T and other telephone, utilities, defense, aerospace, oil and gas, real estate, manufacturing, pharmaceutical, automotive and air transport PACs and interest groups have produced an avalanche of money. Records show that between 1985 and 1990, 94 percent of the PAC dollars collected by Dole were from business interests.

In addition, many of the individual campaign contributions for Dole's 1992 Senate race, totaling $1,172,588, were from business executives of industries associated with his favorite PACs and 87 percent of the contributions came from outside the state of Kansas.

How does he actually raise money?

Dole has aggressively participated in soliciting contributions from business interests and individuals with great stakes in his legislative role in the Senate. Peter Lauer, executive director of AMPAC (the PAC of the American Medical Association), has expressed distress. "I got a letter from Dole asking for money for his PAC," said Lauer. "I also got a telegram from him two weeks out from the election saying, 'I see you have not supported [a Dole-backed candidate from Kansas]. Deeply disappointed. Signed, Bob Dole, Chairman, Senate Finance Committee.' What kind of sledgehammer is that? I find those things deeply disturbing," says Lauer.

During the 1992 Republican National Convention in the Four Seasons Hotel in Houston, several large corporations hosted a lavish brunch bash for Dole in his honor in the elegant ballroom. The huge tab was picked up by RJR Nabisco Corporation, the giant tobacco and food products company for whose tobacco interests Dole had done so much in the Senate. RJR Nabisco had already contributed $25,000 to the Dole Foundation. In addition, AT&T, another major Dole cash cow, had given the Dole Foundation $100,000, and contributed to regaling Dole in Houston.

As if this were not enough, he raked in more money via honoraria. Before the practice was halted in Congress and the Senate in 1991, Dole was year after year the top senatorial recipient of speaker's honoraria from 1981 to 1991, collecting more than $1.1 million for speaking engagements and writing op-ed pieces.* Many of the groups he addressed were those that have funded his campaigns. Up to 1986, he had accepted honoraria from seventy-eight groups whose PACs had also contributed to his reelection efforts, Campaign America and/or the Dole Foundation.

"Money is the mother's milk of politics," Dole has boasted. "Money buys access to the politician," former Senator Alan Cranston has said. Both statements are correct.

Dole's attitude has been to accept any contribution from anyone with a stake in Senate legislation, regardless of the nature of the source. Even when sources are alleged to have violated laws, Bob Dole has not had any qualms about taking their money.

---

*The 1989 Ethics Reform Act banned federal officials from accepting honoraria effective 1991. However, a lawsuit challenging the constitutionality of this law is pending before the U.S. Supreme Court as of November 1994.

Consider the investment banking finance industry. Dole sits on the Senate Finance Committee, and as such and in his role as Senate Minority and majority leader, powerfully affects the banking industry. He received $30,000 in campaign contributions at a fund-raiser held in New York in May, 1991. The money came from managing partners and the political action committee of Salomon Brothers. At the time of the fund-raiser and contributions, Salomon Brothers was under federal investigation for allegedly illegally bidding for the U.S. Treasury securities. A major scandal erupted, and several Salomon executives resigned under fire.

The Salomon Brothers' contribution shows the "revolving door" nature of how big money and big politics work hand-in-hand with the Washington political aristocracy. The May 1991 fund-raiser for Dole in New York was organized by Steve Bell, who had known Dole when Bell was a former staffer on the Senate Budget Committee, and who now worked for Salomon Brothers. Dole claimed that he knew nothing about the federal investigation at the time he took in the money.

"I don't think he should have taken it in the first place, but since he has, he obviously should give it back," said Kansas Republican state party chairman, John Bird. FEC records show that among those who gave Dole money from Salomon Brothers were Chairman of the Board John H. Gutfreund, Thomas Straus, Paul Mozer, and others who resigned during the scandal. "The appearance of impropriety is clear," Bird told reporters. "Dole's contributions were received just prior to one of the largest scandals in recent years in U.S. financial markets." The Senator refused to return the money to Salomon Brothers, ignoring the scandal that rocked Wall Street.

Dole's attitude extends to a realpolitik indifference about the money's eventual recipients, as is shown in his supporting Oliver North for a U.S. Senate seat, despite his conviction for perjury, and Kay Bailey Hutchison, a GOP candidate in Texas for the U.S. Senate, despite her indictment for using state office for campaign purposes. (The district attorney of Travis County dropped his charges against Hutchison.) North lost, but Hutchison won and feels personally indebted to Dole.

There's another conflict of interest that merits attention. Chartering a Lear Jet or a Cessna Jet costs the average person about *$1,600 per hour* for a pilot, and thousands of dollars more for a crew, drinks, and food. For example, in June 1994, a first-class commercial airline round-trip ticket from San Francisco to New York costs $2,375, but a full frills private charter jet round-trip costs $46,585, twenty times higher, and a no-frills ride $21,000. But Bob Dole regularly rides on corporate jets for less than 10 percent of the actual market price, because federal election law only requires Dole to reimburse the corporation for the price of "first-class commercial airline travel."

Dole, in effect, gets a $44,000 campaign contribution from a corporate jet-owning company and is not limited as to how many rides he can take from any corporation. But the $44,000 gift is "invisible" and not reported as such on his FEC disclosure reports. It is just as real as a campaign contribution of cash, because the senator would otherwise have to pay for his flights with campaign money from Campaign America or his other committees, if he had to buy a ticket like an ordinary mortal.

Jim McGhee, a lobbyist for Common Cause, has stated that "If you are going to fly on these corporate jets, it should be done at the same price as if you are going to charter a private jet. Corporations end up providing special treatment and special favors for politicians, and it opens up the door for special access." Candice Nelson, Professor of Government at American University, adds: "If you have got members of the corporation there in the jet, it is a chance to chat [with Dole in flight]. It is another way for the corporation to interact with the senator."

Financial disclosure documents reveal a staggering schedule of corporate jet rides by Dole to fund-raising galas, speeches, and campaign appearances. He paid corporations more than $27,000 for flying in their private jets in 1992 alone. Archer-Daniels-Midland Corporation was reimbursed $2,904 for two trips Dole took in December 1992. Coastal Corporation, a Houston energy firm, was reimbursed $10,836 for three trips that he took from November 1992 to early 1993. Torchmark, an Alabama-based financial corporation, was reimbursed $9,785 for two trips in November 1992. Food Lion, a North Carolina–based grocery retailer, was paid $740 for a trip in December 1992 and NTC Group, a New York firm, was paid $500 for a December 1992 trip. This money was paid by Dole's Campaign America. Scott Moxley, an FEC spokesman, said that all this spending was legal and that federal campaign law "gives campaigns extremely broad discretion in how they spend campaign funds."

Between January 1991 and September 1992, Dole crisscrossed the country on corporate jets more than forty-four times. In June 1992 alone, he flew once aboard jets of ConAgra, three times on the Archer-Daniels-Midland fleet, twice on U.S. Tobacco's aircraft, once on a Growth Industries of Grandview (Missouri) airplane and once on the corporate jet of Torchmark Corporation. Dole's campaign committees reimbursed the corporations for a total of $119,000 for these flights according to the FEC, or 5 percent of true market value.

From January 1991 to September 1992, Dole took at least fourteen flights on jets owned by Archer-Daniels-Midland Corporation (ADM), which cost him $33,000. ADM officials repeatedly refused comment on why their plane fleet is basically at Dole's beck and call. In 1991, ADM's PAC contributed $5,000 to Dole's Campaign America, and much money to the Dole Foundation. ADM officials gave another $16,000 to Dole's Senate reelection campaign between 1985 and 1990. ADM Chairman Dwayne Andreas has also been a generous contributor to the Senator for more than twenty years.

In the summer of 1992 there was great debate in the Senate over the extent of support for renewing government ethanol subsidies and allocating tax breaks for this industry. Credible scientific studies show that ethanol, made from corn, actually worsened the smog conditions in the ozone layer of the air. The Environmental Protection Agency (EPA), in writing the Clean Air Act regulations, prohibited the use of a 10 percent blend of ethanol gas. ADM and its CEO, Andreas, said this was a "severe blow to the ethanol industry." When President Bush hesitated to provide more federal money and tax breaks for ethanol, Dole told him he could lose farm state voters unless he did so. Bush then put pressure on the EPA to change its regulations to boost ethanol production. "We don't think the EPA is telling the truth," Dole insisted, claiming that the EPA had "no evidence" that ethanol would hurt the earth's ozone layer or worsen smog in the air.

What is interesting is that Kansas itself is not a large ethanol producer. The Sunflower State has just four ethanol companies, employing 110 workers, and is able to produce only 27.8 million gallons of ethanol per year, which is 3 percent of the country's capacity.

The ethanol example illustrates the symbiotic relationship between Dole and his jet joyride benefactor, ADM, but corporate jet rides are not provided on an equal access basis to all candidates. During Dole's 1992 Senate reelection campaign, his Democratic opponent, Gloria O'Dell, telephoned ADM and other corporations that routinely gave Dole jet rides, and asked if she could charter a jet, too. The companies told her they were "not in the jet chartering business."

Corporate jet taxis offer many other benefits: convenience, point-to-point quick travel, and the comfort and luxury of a "magic carpet" not available to most of us.

In 1990, Congress imposed a 10 percent "luxury tax" on light airplanes (private airplanes weighing 5,000 pounds or less), luxury cars, and other items. Originally all new private airplanes were included. But Senator Dole loyally went to bat and managed to get all corporate jets with a market value of less than $250,000 stricken from the list.

Is there anything wrong with Bob's frequent flying on the private air fleets of corporate America? Common Cause President Fred Wertheimer said in 1991 that "politicians who fly on corporate jets are in effect receiving significant financial benefits from corporations and other private interests that would otherwise constitute illegal gifts or illegal campaign contributions." It is a common enough practice, perhaps because so few citizens know it even exists.

Dole's corporate jet joyrides have continued unabated. Between 1993 and April 1995, according to campaign records filed with the FEC, Dole flew 187 times on corporate jets owned by his corporate clientele, most of whom had a vested interest in legislation pending before the Senate at the time of the flights. The most generous of the Dole jet benefactors has been Archer-Daniels-Midland, which has flown him 29 times. But other corporate beneficiaries of Dolean corporate welfare and tax giveaways have not lagged far behind.

In the same period, Dole flew 26 times on aircraft belonging to UST Inc., the country's largest smokeless tobacco manufacturer. UST Inc. contributed $40,000 to Dole's political committees between 1987 and 1995, and its senior vice president is a fund-raiser and board member of the Dole Foundation. While raking in UST's cash, Dole has toiled on behalf of this corporate giant by keeping down taxes on smokeless tobacco in the Senate. In 1985, a Dole amendment sharply limited the federal tax on smokeless tobacco to only one fifth the tax rate on regular tobacco. Dole has been unequivocal in his support for this product despite a 1992 report by Bush's Department of Health and Human Services, which ominously predicted "an impending oral cancer epidemic" caused by sale of smokeless tobacco products, including UST's cherry-flavored Skoal.

Another favorite Dole Corporate Airline benefactor has been the American Financial Corporation (AFC), which flew the senator three times in the past two years. AFC's chairman, Carl Lindner, gave $20,000 to Dole's

Campaign America PAC in 1994, and his firm gave an additional $200,000 to the Republican National Committee, for which Dole has solicited money via mass mailings.

And what has the senator done to help out this corporate benefactor? In November 1994, Dole successfully pressured the Clinton administration to challenge European quotas on banana imports. This move helped Lindner's company, Chiquita Banana, which grows bananas in Latin America and exports them to Europe.

Regarding Dole's unabashed use of corporate jet aircraft, *Newsweek* concluded in a study that while other politicians also accept corporate jet rides, Dole "seeks them out more than anybody else," and opined that "as a Senate power and Finance Committee member, he [Dole] has helped his corporate fliers in a variety of ways."

Having a ready fleet of corporate jets at his command is proving most useful to Dole as he seeks to operate both as Senate majority leader and presidential candidate in 1995 and 1996. To fulfill both roles, the indefatigable Bob must be able to fly at a moment's notice from Washington to points all across the country. For this, he needs a private airline, and he has found more than one among the recipients of his Senate legislative largess.

Dole's policy of "Aid to Dependent Corporations" has created a symbiotic relationship between a powerful politician and his financial supporters.

At a time when the Republican Congress says it has no money left for people's welfare, it seems ironic that money can be found for corporate welfare.

VI

LAWBREAKERS AND LAWMAKERS

Being Bob Dole means never having to say you're sorry.

—*The Wichita Eagle*

I can't imagine anyone who gets a check from Bob Dole assuming it's not OK to take it.

—Tim Shallenburger, Republican
Kansas State Representative

24

"THE BIGGEST CAMPAIGN FINANCING VIOLATION IN FEC HISTORY"

B ob Dole was a member of the Congress that enacted the Federal Election Campaign Act (FECA) in the early 1970s. He swore to uphold the law. Yet he hired and associated with an odd assortment of characters who, often acting in his name, willfully broke that law. And during his ill-fated 1988 presidential campaign, he sought desperately to reel in money from any source available.

Dole found himself in deep trouble after a serious complaint was filed against him with the Federal Election Commission for violating the campaign financing laws.

The Federal Election Commission (FEC), a notoriously weak federal agency headquartered in Washington, was created in 1974 to administer and enforce the FECA and numerous federal election campaign laws and rules relating to campaign financing, the reporting of campaign contributors, imposing limits on individual contributions, and imposing spending limits and other restrictions on federal candidates for office. The FEC accepts complaints that are filed against any candidate's campaign, maintains enormous computer databases on candidates, political action committees and the like, and investigates suspected violations. The law creating the FEC and imposing strict campaign financing rules was first passed in 1974, as a reaction to the Watergate scandal, in which wholesale campaign abuses had been perpetrated by Dole's hero, Richard Nixon.

Whenever an investigation is carried out, the FEC creates a file that is called a MUR ("Matter Under Review"). Each case is given a MUR number and the entire file is kept confidential until the case is resolved, either by a legal determination of violation or innocence or by some kind of "conciliation" agreement.

The FEC has a general counsel, a staff of lawyers, and investigators. The penalties that can be imposed on individuals, candidates, and others who violate the law can range from monetary fines to possible criminal sanctions. If a violation merits criminal penalties, however, the FEC may refer the matter to the Department of Justice.

Dole knew he needed a strong showing in the early primary states of Iowa and New Hampshire in order to have any serious chance of defeating Bush in 1988. Most of the Republican Establishment saw Bush as the heir apparent to Reagan, and viewed Dole as an insurgent without a rationale to his candidacy.

Dole's campaign treasury toward the end of 1987 stood considerably below that of Bush, primarily because Dole's own staff had squandered his money. However, polls showed Dole ahead of Bush in Iowa, a farm state in the Midwest contiguous to Kansas. Dole knew that if he could make a strong showing in Iowa, he would have a serious chance of beating Bush in New Hampshire one week later.

In 1987 and early 1988, Dole's campaign broke federal election laws so extensively that the conduct sparked a record five-year investigation by the FEC. The investigation finally ended in the summer of 1993, when the FEC general counsel issued a report finding that Dole's campaign had engaged in many wholesale violations of the law. This led to the imposition of a record monetary fine of $100,000 against Dole's committee, higher than anything previously imposed on any other candidate. In addition, Dole was forced to return illegal contributions. The senator's reaction was one of angry denial.

When I worked for Dole during his 1980 presidential campaign, he showed few qualms about using his Senate office for political campaigning activities, even though the law technically forbids this. In December 1979, for example, Jo-Anne Coe, then Dole's top secretary (now the chair at Campaign America PAC), used Senate stationery to communicate with David Owen on a matter relating to using Elizabeth Dole's blind trust in obtaining a $50,000 loan to Dole's campaign from Owen's Bank of Stanley. The FEC investigated that loan for two years, but dropped its investigation in 1981 with no action.

But on his 1988 violations, he was so not lucky. The official FEC investigative file on Dole's 1988 campaign was called "In the Matter of Dole for President Committee and James L. Hagen as Treasurer, MUR 3309."

The Dole for President Committee admitted violating the federal laws and entered into a "conciliation agreement" with the FEC—in effect a settlement agreement—on July 13, 1993. The FEC found that the Dole for President Committee was a political committee (2 U.S. Code, Section 431); that it was the "principal campaign committee of Dole during the 1988 presidential primary election campaign"; that during the 1987–88 election cycle Dole's Campaign America PAC was a "a multicandidate political committee" (2 U.S. Code, Sections 434 and 441); and that Dole himself served as "honorary chairman" of Campaign America PAC in 1986 and in 1987.

Under federal law, "a contribution" included any gift, subscription, loan, advance, deposit of money, or anything of value made for purposes of influencing a federal election. "Anything of value" includes in-kind contributions. The law is clear that no multicandidate PAC (such as Campaign America) is allowed to make contributions to any candidate or his or her authorized committee for a federal election that in the aggregate exceeds $5,000 (2

U.S. Code, Title 2, Section 441a). Also, no PACs may accept contributions in excess of statutory limitations.

The FEC revealed that in Iowa in 1986 and 1987 Campaign America had made expenditures on behalf of Dole's candidacy totaling $41,887, which became in-kind contributions when he became a candidate for president in November 1987. The commission also discovered that in 1986 and 1987 Campaign America spent $5,359 and made a total expenditure of $47,247.24 on behalf of the Dole for President Committee, which exceeded the $5,000 statutory limit on contributions.

In addition, federal law is explicit that no candidate for the presidency who is eligible to receive federal matching funds from the Treasury may make any expenditures in any one primary state aggregating in excess of $200,000 or 16 cents multiplied by the voting age population, whichever is greater. (2 U.S. Code, Section 441, and 26 U.S. Code, Section 9035). The rationale behind the limit is that in order for a candidate to qualify for taxpayer funds, he or she must be willing to limit the amount of his own money that he spends in each primary state.

The breach of public trust is staggering. Dole's campaign received $7 million in federal matching funds, by way of taxpayers who checked the $1 box on their income tax returns. To be eligible, he had to make promises about limiting his spending in the primary states of Iowa and New Hampshire. It is clear that the senator did not.

The commission stated that for the 1988 primary elections in Iowa, the expenditure limit according to federal law was $775,217.60 for each presidential candidate. The commission also found that Dole's campaign committee exceeded this spending limit by $304,065.44. Dole's campaign for the 1988 Iowa presidential primary election made total expenditures of $1,079,283 in Iowa, which exceeded the campaign limits by 39 percent.

In New Hampshire, the expenditure limit per candidate was $461,000. The FEC found that Dole's campaign had spent a grand total of $745,084.46 there, which exceeded the spending limits by $284,084.46, or 62 percent.

Since 1907, it has been illegal for a candidate to accept campaign contributions from any corporation or "corporate entity." In its investigation the FEC found that for the 1988 campaign, Dole's committee "knowingly accepted direct and in-kind contributions totaling $64,043 from corporate entities." These contributions included two uses of corporate aircraft for which Dole's committee made reimbursements, which were found to be $3,750 less than the usual charges for the services provided. Of the $64,043 illegally obtained from corporations, only $7,201 was refunded by Dole's committee, and $56,842 remained unrefunded as of the date of the FEC conciliation agreement, July 13, 1993.

Federal law also provides that a candidate or candidate's agent who flies in a corporate jet must reimburse the corporation *in advance* for the cost of such transportation. (11 C.F.R. Section 114.9). The FEC found that during the 1988 campaign Dole used the corporate aircraft of fifteen corporations for which he made twenty-six payments totaling $54,264.85. Since these payments were not made in advance, the travel was illegal. Included in this figure was an in-kind contribution from a corporation that had accepted reimbursement from Dole that was $2,475.00 less than the amount billed.

Federal law imposes a $1,000 limit per election for any "individual, partnership or political committee which is not a multicandidate committee, as money which can be contributed to a candidate or its committee." (2 U.S. Code, Section 441a). The FEC found this individual limitation law was violated by Dole in 1988 because he knowingly accepted a total of $239,131.81 in contributions from a total of 418 individuals, each of whom exceeded his respective $1,000 limitation. In addition, Dole knowingly accepted a total of $4,000 from three partnerships, which each exceeded their $1,000 limitations. Of the $4,000, only $2,000 had been refunded by Dole as of the date of the FEC conciliation agreement, five years after the violations had occurred.

In addition to the above breaches, the FEC found

that Dole knowingly accepted a total of $8,375.00 in contributions from seven political action committees that exceeded the committees' own respective $1,000 limitation. Of these, $1,000 remained unrefunded as of the conciliation agreement.

The FEC's laundry list continues. Under the law, presidential candidates are permitted to accept contributions to a "legal and accounting compliance fund" prior to nomination, for use *if and only if* the candidate becomes his party's nominee for president in the general election. Otherwise, contributions must be refunded, redesignated, or reattributed within sixty days from the date of the party's nomination (11 C.F.R., Section 9003.3).

Dole sought redesignation for, and transfer to, a legal and accounting compliance fund of $102,662.55 in "otherwise excessive contributions received for the primary election." He also received $16,292 in direct contributions to the fund. Dole withdrew as a presidential candidate in late March 1988 and conceded the nomination to Bush at that time. The Republican Party officially nominated George Bush on August 17, 1988. However, as of October 16, 1988, $48,598.55 in the legal and accounting compliance fund had not yet been refunded or redesignated by Dole.

Federal law requires that each treasurer of a political committee regularly file "reports of receipts and disbursements, including a consolidation of the reports submitted by any of its authorized state committees" (2 U.S. Code, Section 434). The FEC found that the Dole for President Committee had eighteen authorized delegate committees in 1988, three in Maryland and fifteen in Illinois. As the principal campaign group, the Dole for President Committee was responsible for obtaining information on the receipts and expenditures of all these delegate committees and for consolidating that information in its reports to the FEC. The FEC found that Dole's Committee had failed to report the receipts and disbursements of the eighteen delegate committees and failed to consolidate the reports. We have no idea how much money was received or disbursed by any of these eighteen committees in Maryland or Illinois.*

The FEC built up a strong case against Dole and also found that his committee had knowingly accepted excessive contributions totaling $8,375 from seven other political committees in violation of the law. One thousand dollars remained unrefunded as of the date of the conciliation agreement.

As part of the "conciliation agreement" the Federal Election Commission reached with Dole in July 1993, the FEC insisted that the Dole campaign committee refund all outstanding excessive and prohibited contributions, for a total of $104,564.30. These were supposed to be refunded directly to the original contributors or to the U.S. Treasury. In addition, pursuant to 2 U.S. Code, Section 437g, the FEC imposed a civil penalty payable to the FEC itself, in the amount of $100,000. This vastly exceeds any prior penalty leveled against any presidential candidate.†

The conciliation agreement was entered into in July 1993 and was signed by FEC General Counsel Lawrence Noble and by Scott E. Morgan, counsel for the Dole for President Committee. The commission retained jurisdiction to investigate compliance with the conciliation agreement and to sue Dole in a civil action in a U.S. District Court for relief if the agreement was violated.

Most significant of all is Dole's cavalier reaction to the news. When quizzed by several Kansas news reporters in August 1993, when the conciliation agreement was made public, Dole acted as if he were totally unaware of

---

*Illinois held a critical presidential primary in March 1988, and would have been a crucial primary state if Dole had remained a viable candidate against Bush for the presidential nomination.
†The previous record high civil penalty for violation of federal campaign law had been paid by Walter Mondale's 1984 Democratic presidential campaign, which paid $68,000 as a civil penalty.

what had been done in his name by his own assistants and employees. He also lashed out at the FEC as a government bureaucracy, and whined about the five years the investigation had taken.

Senator Dole denied that he was responsible for any of the violations. He grumbled about the bureaucratic process and brazenly cited the FEC investigation as an example of why "we don't need public financing of congressional campaigns." Dole insisted that if there were public financing of campaigns and auditing by the FEC, that would make the FEC "bigger than the Pentagon" and "the only winners are the government lawyers."

Also noteworthy is the fact that Dole actually came out way ahead financially. He admitted breaking the federal spending limits by more than $600,000. Subtracting the $100,000 penalty and the approximately $250,000 he had to repay, he still wound up with $250,000 more in contributions than he was legally entitled to.

When *Wichita Eagle* reporter Bob Norman was assigned to cover the first day of Dole's annual summer tour of Kansas in August 1993, he asked him what he thought about the FEC matter and the penalty meted out by the agency. "The only people interested in this issue are just the *Wichita Eagle,* and they're not really constituents," hissed Dole.

Dan Clements, a veteran editorial writer for the *Wichita Eagle,* wrote an editorial on August 13, 1993, which blasted Dole for "disowning" him and all of the other journalists who worked for the *Eagle.* Clements, who for seventeen years had been a Republican voter, had supported Dole repeatedly for reelection to the Senate, and had actually participated in the drafting of the *Eagle*'s "first in the nation" editorial endorsement of Dole for president in 1986, was appalled by this reaction to the FEC violations.

As Clements editorialized,

Politicians, especially big-time politicians such as Mr. Dole, are supposed to be thick-skinned. Even if it's hard for them to own up to their sins, they should understand that those sins are news and are going to be reported and commented upon. If the ensuing questions and criticisms hack you off, by all means it's OK to lash out at your perceived tormentor as long as you understand that your reactions are going to be reported in the paper. Journalists, who make a living by dishing it out, have to be able to take it. But to disown them as your constituents, even though they live, work, and vote in your bailiwick, is more than outrageous. It's ridiculous.

Clements, reduced by Dole to the status of a "nonconstituent," asked rhetorically in his editorial, "Does it mean that the Senator would try to deny me federal disaster money if a flood swept away my house, even though my neighbors were getting aid? Does he order his staff to throw my letters and postcards into the trash unopened?"

Letters to the Editor of the *Wichita Eagle* and other newspapers show the outrage of many ordinary Kansans who, in the words of letter writers Robert D. Simson and Charles M. Curtis, felt that:

There are real Kansans who are concerned and embarrassed over Bob Dole's unrepentant attitude toward the gross violations of the law and morality perpetrated by him and his presidential election committee. We are too. One of the reasons some are endeavoring to limit the terms of office of elected officials is Mr. Dole's kind of arrogance toward the various laws the officials swear to uphold and protect.

Dan Glickman, Democratic congressman from Wichita, said he was "intrigued by how uninterested Dole was in the seriousness of the [FEC] offense." Glickman said that "In my judgment, the FEC doesn't go after you unless you are involved in repetitive, continuous violations of campaign law." Glickman pointed out that "no one else has been hit with these kinds of violations."

On August 12, 1993, Dole wrote a letter to the editor of the *Wichita Eagle,* in which he accused the *Eagle* of putting a negative spin on a "non-story that few Kansans care about." The *Wichita Eagle* wrote:

> He broke the law. He paid a diddly-squat fine. And then he has the gall to grumble about federal bureaucrats and public financing. His response should have been to apologize to the Kansans who sent him to the Senate and to the Americans who had supported him for President. Clearly, Mr. Dole, can't you at least say you're sorry?

The *Eagle* also noted that it was "perplexing" that Dole "comes out way ahead even with the hefty fine."

Dole remained unrepentant, arrogant, and bitter. He also claimed that a sharp distinction should be made between the Dole for President Committee and himself. He pointed out that the FEC fine was levied against the Dole for President Committee, not against him personally. However, under federal law, Dole is personally liable for all FEC fines imposed, including the $100,000 fine. The federal law imposed this personal liability as part of the requirements Dole made when he agreed to accept taxpayer matching funds for his campaign. He also conceded that his campaign had "knowingly accepted" the illegal contributions in 1988. But he tried to make a distinction between "knowingly accepted" and "knowingly and willfully accepted" illegal contributions.

What is also interesting about the FEC fiasco is that the public news stories did not tell the whole story. The settlement was disclosed publicly on August 6, 1993, but one has to wade through thousands of documents for details not revealed at the time. I have found a definite pattern of violations of the election financing laws in the 1988 campaign.

For example, the FEC investigators believed that the Dole campaign had violated the state spending limits in Iowa and New Hampshire in 1987–88 by a total of $962,000. However, after negotiations between the FEC and lawyers for Dole's campaign in 1992–93, the two sides arbitrarily compromised on a lower figure of $588,000. The FEC documents also revealed that even in early 1988, while Dole's committee was violating the law, it actually began setting up a special fund "to pay for any fines or penalties that the FEC might levy against Senator Dole and Dole for President." This fund collected more than $50,000 in contributions, expecting a fine of about $50,000. The existence of this fund suggests a possible premeditated intent to violate the law.

Another interesting thing to be found in the FEC documents is that even though Dole had publicly pledged to "permit an audit and examination" of his entire committee files, his committee refused to allow the FEC to review his books after the 1988 election during the investigation. Government auditors had to subpoena these records.

Again and again, hundreds of times, the FEC investigators were struck with incredulity at the preposterous explanations Dole's committee offered as excuses for violating the law.

For example, in adding up all the Dole campaign expenses in each state—a task necessary to determine whether Dole had spent more per state than the law allowed when a candidate was seeking federal matching funds—the FEC auditors were shocked to discover a pattern of exceeding Iowa and New Hampshire state spending limits with impudence.

For instance, FEC investigators discovered that in the latter part of 1986, the Dole committee bought whole lists of voters in New Hampshire, but Dole's men told incredulous FEC auditors that this list was totally unrelated to the upcoming crucial New Hampshire primary in February 1988.

In another case, also in 1986, the FEC learned that the

Dole committee paid for a telephone survey of some 225,000 Iowa voters, but Dole's people claimed this survey was totally unrelated to Dole's presidential campaign effort to predict his strength in the critical Iowa caucuses in February 1988.

In early 1988, shortly before the Iowa caucuses, the FEC verified that Dole's campaign workers made 338,675 telephone calls to voters residing in Iowa. The calls were cleverly made from a phone bank in Nebraska, across the Iowa state borderline. Dole claimed this spending was unrelated to the Iowa caucuses. Incredibly, the FEC gave in on this point after negotiating with Dole to reach a mutually convenient conciliation agreement in 1993. Compromise won the day in the final agreement reached.

But in 1993, the Senator was more interested in his 1996 presidential run by the time the FEC violation was made public. He had already collected $1.5 million in the first six months of 1993. So, with the FEC matter a closed file, Dole has gotten away with violating the law, paid a token fine, and come out smelling like a rose.

25

THE KINGFISH OF KANSAS POLITICS: BOSS BOB AND SOME ILLEGAL CAMPAIGN GIFTS

Known as "Goliath," "Kingfish," and "Boss Bob," Dole is the most powerful single politician to dominate a state since "Kingfish" Huey Long ruled Louisiana in the 1930s.

Kansas is the most Republican state in the union. Though the Democrats have made some inroads in recent years, the GOP still dominates state politics at every level. Only twice in this century have Democratic presidential candidates won Kansas, Franklin Roosevelt in 1936 and Lyndon Johnson in 1964. It is small wonder that Bob Dole reigns supreme.

A striking example of the Senator's iron grip on state politics can be seen in the 1992 elections for the Kansas legislature. Nine Republican state house and senate candidates received illegal campaign contributions from the Dole for Senate '92 Campaign Committee. These contributions ranged from $1,000 to $5,000, and violated the Kansas Campaign Finance Act.

Dole's candidates in Kansas slavishly follow his lead. Typical is Congressman Pat Roberts, who has been given the nickname Little Bob.

Because of a relatively small population and a rudimentary, skeletal party organization, Kansas politics lends itself to control by one man. Using Republican Attorney General Bob Stephan as his eyes and ears in Kansas, Dole closely monitors the political pulse in all Kansas races. He scrutinizes lists of contributors to Democratic candidates, and many Kansans are afraid to contribute money to Democrats for fear of retaliation by Dole.

Kansas has a dreary reputation as a flat, drab, small state in the middle of nowhere, filled with cow towns and hicks. Kansas is the thirty-second largest state in the Union, with a population of about 2.5 million. Ninety percent of the population are white, 5 percent are black, 4 percent are Hispanic, and less than 1 percent are Jewish. Discovered in 1541 by the Spanish explorer Coronado, who described its plains as "full of crooked necked oxen," Kansas has lived on in American folklore as the home of Dodge City and its legendary cowboy lawmen, Wyatt Earp and Bat Masterson. Its largest city is Wichita, with a population of 304,000, and its capital is Topeka, home to 120,000.

From the Civil War until the early 1970s, the Kansas House of Representatives, the State Senate, and governorship were almost always dominated by Republicans. "Even the independent voters tend to vote Republican," Jim Parrish, former Democratic State Senator and State Democratic chairman, notes with dismay, "unless you give them a reason not to." Democrats in Kansas have frequently referred to the "uneven playing field" of Kansas politics. In 1936, Kansas Republican Governor Alf Landon ran for president as a Republican presidential candidate against Franklin Roosevelt. Landon was thoroughly trounced and didn't even carry his home state, but he remained a powerful force in Kansas GOP politics for the next fifty years. His daughter, Nancy Landon Kassebaum, was elected to the U.S. Senate as a Republican in 1978 and remains its junior senator.

The Watergate crisis of 1974 slightly loosened the Republican grip. In 1976 Democrats achieved a majority in the Kansas State House for the first time in history and in the Senate they won eighteen Senate seats out of forty, slightly short of a majority. More important, the Democrats elected a governor, John Carlin, in 1978, who was reelected in 1982. In 1978, the Democrats also elected Dan Glickman, a popular Jewish politician, to Congress from the Wichita area. Glickman has been a small thorn in Dole's side since his election, and has frequently toyed with challenging Dole for the Senate, waiting in the wings for Dole to retire.

But since the mid-1970s, the few minor gains by the Democrats have been short-lived and generally been made according to the "Mack Truck" theory of politics. According to this theory, as explained by Parrish, "the Democrats always want to nominate a candidate for any office, but in order for him to win, the Republican candidate generally has to get hit by a Mack truck. So we nominate token candidates just in case their Republican opponents get run over."

A typical example was Guy MacDonald, who ran against Dole for the Senate in 1986. MacDonald, a total unknown, ran on a vague platform saying he would "raise no new taxes and spend no money" if elected. He didn't campaign at all, raised only $4,000 and didn't spend any money in the fall campaign, yet won 30 percent of the vote against Dole in November. "Even if he had spent money and campaigned," notes Parrish with dismay, "he would have lost. The campaign was a big waste of everybody's time and effort."

Kansas is so Republican that even Bob Stephan, a Republican who was rocked by scandal in a nasty sex harassment suit and a perjury indictment, and who filed for bankruptcy, was nonetheless able to repeatedly win reelection as attorney general, generally with lopsided majorities in 1978, 1982, and 1986, and winning despite scandal in 1990.

Dole's operatives permeate every aspect of Kansas politics. The State Republican Party Chairman, Kim Wells, has been a loyal Dole acolyte and confidant for more than twenty years. Before Wells, Dave Owen and other Dole cronies served in that role, meticulously stacking all 105 county chairmanships with Dole loyalists, and dispensing patronage and campaign contributions. Republican candidates up and down the state and local level look to Dole not only for endorsements but also for financing, polling, and expertise.

Consider the 1992 elections for the state legislature. Groups associated with Dole contributed $160,800 to candidates for local appointments, the legislature, and Congress, and to various Republican groups inside the state. Republican officials in Kansas thanked Dole lavishly in speech after speech during their Kansas Day Ceremony in January 1993. The money appeared to have paid off at the state level, for Republicans secured control of the State House and increased their numbers in the State Senate by five.

Dole's donations to the state and local candidates came from three groups: Campaign America, his own personal leadership PAC; Campaign America–Kansas, an affiliated but legally separate PAC that operates within the state of Kansas; and the Dole for Senate '92 Committee.

Campaign America PAC donated $123,800 to Kansas state candidates. Of this total, $42,000 went to state Senate candidates, another $41,500 went to State House candidates, another $23,300 went to Republicans running for Congress and $7,000 went to other GOP nominees. Campaign America–Kansas donated an additional $23,500. Of that, $5,000 went to the state Republican Party, $15,000 to groups formed to help Republican legislative candidates and another $3,500 went to candidates for other offices. Finally, the Dole for Senate '92 Committee made $8,500 in contributions to various GOP state candidates.

Official Kansas election documents show that of the top twenty political action committee contributors to Kansas state candidates from January 1, 1992, through December 31, 1992, Dole's Campaign America (including his national Campaign America PAC and his Campaign America–Kansas PAC) contributed the largest amount, $147,300. That is more than three times larger than some of the major state contributors such as the Kansas Bankers Association (BANK PAC), Kansas Realtors, Kansas Medical PAC, and others.

In 1992, however, the Dole Senate campaign committee made contributions totaling $7,500, which under Kansas state law the recipients were not permitted to accept. Five legislators and four former legislative candidates were investigated by state authorities for accepting the $7,500. The Kansas State Ethics Commission's staff concluded that the candidates had violated a 1991 Kansas state law prohibiting legislative candidates from accepting any money from any other candidates' campaign committees. This is called the Kansas Campaign Finance Act.

When these charges first surfaced in early February 1993, Dole and his spokesmen, typically contemptuous, referred to them as "patently absurd." Jo-Anne Coe, who was the chairwoman of Dole's Campaign America PAC and who also acted as assistant treasurer of the Dole for Senate '92 Committee, said that she and other campaign officials believed that candidates could legally accept the money. "I acted on the advice of counsel," she claimed.

In 1991, the Kansas legislature amended the Campaign Finance Act by adding the following provisions: "No candidate or candidate committee shall accept from any other candidate or candidate committee for any candidate for local, state or national office, any monies received by such candidate or candidate committee as a campaign contribution."

Kansas law provides that anyone who intentionally violates the Campaign Finance Act is guilty of a "class A misdemeanor," a crime punishable by up to one year in jail and a fine of up to $2,500. In order to be prosecuted criminally, a person who violated this law must be shown to have "intentionally" violated the law, however.

The Kansas State Ethics Commission, a semiautonomous body, investigated the illegal Dole contributions. Earl Williams, Executive Director of the Kansas Commission on Governmental Standards in Conduct, said publicly that it was illegal for candidates to accept such contributions from Dole's Senate '92 Committee. Jerry Karr, the State Senate minority leader, said that the violations were serious. "We are striving to bring confidence to voters and show that campaign monies are handled clearly within the framework of the laws of Kansas," he said. The Kansas law was designed to close a loophole that had allowed contributors to give money to a candidate such as Dole while knowing that that candidate would funnel the money to another candidate in Kansas. The campaign disclosure reports filed in the Kansas Secretary of State's office revealed the names of those who had accepted contributions ranging from $500 to $1,000 from Dole's machines. Walt Riker, Dole's mouthpiece in his U.S. Senate office, branded the Kansas rules "confusing at best and contradictory." He blasted the Democrats' complaints about Dole's actions as "sour grapes because they don't like the fact that Bob Dole takes an active role in state politics."

The Kansas state candidates who accepted the money all claimed that they thought the contributions were legal.

Republican Bud Burke said that "our targeted races got tremendous help from Bob Dole. There is little doubt that we would not have done as well [without Dole's money]. I guess his help was instrumental. I don't know how to quantify that."

Kansas State Representative Tim Shallenburger, not one of the recipients of Dole's contributions, acknowledged that the Dole campaign contributions had violated the law, but said that the candidates who took the money "did not intend to commit illegal acts." "I am sorry that it happened," he said. "Sure enough, there was a violation of the law," admitted Shallenburger. "I don't believe there was intent." Shallenburger's comments came five days after Democratic Senate Minority Leader Jerry Karr had asked the State Ethics Commission to review the matter and to investigate Dole's campaign finance practices. Shallenburger claimed that the candidates who took the money may have assumed that "any donation from Dole was legal. Of course, assumptions can get you in trouble," he added.

Representative Shallenburger, who had actually helped

to draft the final version of the 1991 legislature's package of campaign ethics laws, said he didn't believe his colleagues who took Dole's money had intended to break the law. "It never crossed our minds," he said. "I can't imagine anyone who gets a check from Bob Dole assuming it is not okay to take it." Of the six Senate candidates who received $1,000 from Dole's '92 Senate Campaign Committee, four were elected. Of the three House candidates, one was elected. The Dole contributions were listed on reports filed by the candidates and organizations associated with Dole, and these reports were filed with the Kansas Secretary of State's Office. Though the amount of Dole's contributions may seem small, the cost of Kansas State House and Senate campaigns, in rural areas, is often just a few thousand dollars. The issue of whether or not the candidates had the "intent to violate the law" obscures the more fundamental issue. The purpose of the law was to prevent wealthy individuals, corporations, and entities from bypassing the election campaign limit laws.

An even more serious issue is Dole's effect on candidates who may feel beholden to him. One of the major bills pending in the Kansas Legislature is whether to impose term limits on elected officials in the Sunflower State. As the top elected official in the state, Dole has opposed all term limit bills in general. Furthermore, the Kansas Legislature has long acted as a springboard into higher national office and as the breeding ground for future congressmen and senators. It is impossible to overemphasize the importance of the state legislature as a base for Dole's political power, both in Topeka and Washington.

What does it all mean? Once again, Dole and the campaign committees controlled by him disregarded a law. In a state where the top law enforcement official responsible for criminal prosecutions is Republican Bob Stephan, there was no chance that any Republican would be prosecuted for violating this law.

The other disturbing question raised by Dole's illegal contributions to the nine Republican candidates is that it is difficult to undo the damage after illegal contributions have influenced an election. That is, once somebody wins, as several of these Dole supported candidates did in November 1992, it is not practical to remove them from office, even after determining that the law has been broken.

It also seems meaningless that the State Ethics Commission's rules hold that an action is punishable only if it is "intentional." Intent is extremely difficult to prove in the law.

Dole's contributions in 1992 enraged a few Kansans, mostly the ones who resent him for being an absentee senator who uses Kansas solely as a base for mounting his national campaigns for president, and for strutting across the stage of national politics. Dole's real attitude toward his own state was revealed when he referred to it as "My Little Kansas" during an appearance January 15, 1994, on "This Week with David Brinkley."

According to Jerry Karr, Kansas State Senate minority leader, Dole is the candyman of the Kansas Republican Party. "Every two years, Dole comes into the state and plays a major role in shaping the agenda for the elections and selecting the candidates. But you can count the number of visits on the fingers of your hand."

Nancy Kassebaum is more popular than Dole, and tends to win up to 80 percent of the vote, while Dole usually gets about 63 to 70 percent. She will be back in the state every couple of weeks while Dole makes occasional cameo appearances. Yet both are virtual lifetime officeholders with no possibility of being removed from office, short of scandal or assassination.

The huge shadow cast by Dole over Kansas bore fruit in 1994. In the 1994 Kansas election for state office, Dole's Campaign America contributed massively to every Republican candidate and paid for GOP polling throughout the state. The money paid off handsomely on November 8, 1994. Republican candidates swept the state (as they did nationally), winning the offices of governor and attorney general and gaining lopsided 2-to-1 majorities in the state Senate and House.

26

"GLORIA VS. GOLIATH": THE 1992 SENATE REELECTION CAMPAIGN

Most Kansans are proud to have Senator Dole representing them in Washington, and they are grateful for the pork barrel federal projects, highway funds, military contracts and other goodies he is able to extract from the otherwise wicked federal government. After twenty-six years in the Senate, Dole can command millions of dollars to be sent to Kansas "by just picking up the phone"—as even his opponent Gloria O'Dell admits. When he does show up to meet the folks on rare cameo campaign appearances, "He's ten feet tall," as Kansans typically remark. "He's Goliath."

But in 1992, Goliath was challenged by a female David.

Dole found himself being confronted by an unknown but spunky woman named Gloria O'Dell, as he ran for a fifth Senate term in 1992.

Dubbing her campaign "Gloria vs. Goliath," O'Dell ran a gallant campaign whose theme was that Dole was an arrogant, distant megalomaniac who had lost touch with his Kansas constituents and who practiced the "politics of fear."

O'Dell's long laundry list of complaints included the fact that Dole had voted for a congressional pay raise of $23,000 and a pension increase, had brought about tax breaks for his campaign contributors while opposing tax relief for the middle class, and was responsible for the federal budget deficit because of his role in supporting the Reagan and Bush spending and tax-cutting proposals in Congress.

O'Dell also tried to capitalize on what the media had dubbed "the Year of the Woman." It was a year in which Barbara Boxer (D-CA), Carol Moseley Braun (D-IL), Dianne Feinstein (D-CA), and Patty Murray (D-WA) were elected to the Senate for the first time, joining Barbara Mikulski (D-MD), who had been reelected, and Nancy Kassebaum (R-KS).

O'Dell referred to Dole with phrases such as "attack dog," "wrecking ball," "Nixon's Doberman pinscher" and "Senator Straddle." She tried to personalize her approach by pointing out she had grown up in a single-parent home, lost a brother in the Vietnam War, lost a sister to breast cancer, and worked to raise a son after her divorce.

With degrees in English and Social Work Administration, O'Dell had held many jobs ranging from assistant manager of a halfway house, news reporter, press secretary, campaign manager, high-school English teacher, and television news reporter. In 1990, she was the campaign manager for Sally Thompson, who was running for state treasurer. From January 1991 to May 1992, she served as a special legislative communications director for the state treasurer's office. But nothing had prepared Gloria for taking on Goliath.

"Running against Bob Dole for the Senate is like lying down on the street and waiting for a steamroller to roll over you," said many a Democratic Kansan. "We have difficulty attracting qualified candidates because of the money thing," said another. "Nobody can run against him," said a third. "He's a big money machine," said Democrat legislative aide Bob Martin.

When asked why she ran against Dole and thereby incurred a massive personal debt in 1992, O'Dell responded, "I wanted to make sure that someone forced this man to answer some questions about what he had done. His arrogant refusal to come home and face his record and challengers only show his contempt for democracy. Dole has ducked the issues at home because he has no plan, no vision for the future. He is just ignoring it. It is disgraceful that any public servant would ignore his own state, especially during an election year. I wanted him to be accountable."

Early in 1992, Reverend Fred Phelps, a pastor and disbarred Democratic attorney in Topeka, who had waged a colorful and unsuccessful campaign for governor of Kansas in 1990, challenged O'Dell for the Democratic Senate nomination. Phelps stated that "Dole is beating the war drums like some bloodthirsty Oriental tyrant to whom war is a game of amusement for the ruling class." With his thirteen children (eleven of them lawyers) supporting his candidacy and attending his church, Phelps represented the "Christian Right," Kansas-style.

Phelps, who has called AIDS an appropriate punishment from God against gays, is known for harassing gays across the country. He has often followed the burial processions of those who have died of AIDS, carrying anti-gay placards and shouting slogans. Considered an extremist, who spewed scathing campaign and anti-gay literature via armies of fax machines, Phelps sent out hysterical campaign literature calling O'Dell, who is straight, a "lesbian homosexual." Phelps's press release of August 7, 1992, read: NO BULL DIKE IN U.S. SENATE. In an open letter to Gloria O'Dell, Phelps stated, "The present leadership of the Kansas Democratic Party must be operating from an incestuous opium den if they think the conservative Kansas people will send a bull dike to the U.S. Senate—no matter how senile, physically debilitated, and corrupt Dole is." The mudslinging didn't work, however. O'Dell won the Democratic nomination and went on to give Goliath a run for his money.

O'Dell staged an aggressive ad campaign against Dole in the fall. A one-minute TV spot ad called, "Babies," featured a six-month infant surrounded by $140,000. As the baby listened, an announcer spoke about "Bob Dole's record vs. Bob Dole's rhetoric." The ad chided Dole for his duplicity on economic issues. It pointed out that Dole had first called the federal deficit "Public Enemy Number One" in 1974, and vowed to bring it under control in 1981, then promised to lead the fight against it in 1988, and again called it "Public Enemy Number One" in 1992. But over those eighteen years, Dole got himself a $140,000 annual pension and a $23,000 annual pay increase, and continued to give tax breaks to the wealthiest 2 percent, while the deficit increased by 6,000 percent. The final shot showed O'Dell holding two babies on her lap saying, "It is not about his past, it is about their future."

In July 1992, at the Democratic National Convention's opening night in New York, O'Dell blasted Dole as "Senator Straddle" on national television. "When I ask the question: Can Bob Dole be defeated, the answer is loud and clear," said O'Dell. "We cannot afford to reelect the problem." The three-minute speech was a smash. O'Dell told the convention that a contribution to her campaign would put a pebble in her slingshot to bring down Goliath in November. "Bob Dole's power is a wrecking ball to crush family leave, civil rights, aid to Israel, and women's rights," she said. "When he is not Senator Straddle, he is Senator Stop. Either way, he is not the leadership that Kansas or America needs today."

O'Dell got a lot of calls on her 800 number and a considerable amount of campaign contributions from Democrats all across the country. In particular, she scored well with Jews, women, and liberals. "Dole was furious when he saw me address the convention on television," O'Dell told me. "But people in Kansas were afraid to contribute money to my campaign. They know that Dole reads the lists of contributors, and he's a very vindictive person." O'Dell managed to raise $246,000, but this was far short of the senator's own $3.1 million war chest.

At the start of the campaign, Dole initially refused a challenge to debate. "What's there to debate?" he snapped. But then, as O'Dell began to rise in the polls with her "absentee senator" charges, Dole flip-flopped and agreed to debate her on television, along with two other fringe candidates. These were Libertarian Party candidate Mark Kirk and Independent Christina Campbell-Cline, an accountant. On October 17, 1992, the four candidates participated in a televised debate at KTWU-TV in Topeka. O'Dell accused Dole of "preaching the politics of fear this election year" by saying that a small state like Kansas "would not survive should he not be reelected along with Bush." "It will not rock the halls of Congress should a special interest professional politician as exemplified by Dole be removed," she insisted.

Dole declared, "We have got the best health-care delivery system in the world in America. What I would do is build on what we have, not toss it all out." Dole also claimed that he had not lost touch with the Kansan voters: "I haven't forgotten where I'm from. I know precisely how I got to where I am, and have never forgotten the people that helped put me there," Dole insisted.

During the debate, *USA Today*, in its Snapshots section, performed a study which found that Dole blinked an incredible average of 120 blinks per minute, which was almost four times higher than the average person's rate. He also blinked 132 blinks per minute after hearing the first question from Lou Ferguson of the Associated Press on the federal deficit. Professor Joe Tecce of Boston College concluded: "When a person feels good about what they are saying, they blink less. When they feel bad about what they are saying, they blink more. Bob Dole has always blinked very fast, much like Nixon."

In her campaign, O'Dell pointed out that according to the May 1992 issue of *McCall's* magazine Dole was ranked as one of the ten worst senators on women's issues. He had been hostile to congressional bills on family leave, child care reforms, and the 1990 Civil Rights Act.

But the senator fought back. One of his main themes was that all Kansans benefited because he brought special federal money and projects to Kansas. Typical was a last-minute maneuver in the fall of 1992 to secure a $43 million federal contract so that Wichita's Beech Aircraft Corporation could build twelve modified King airplanes for the Army Reserve in Kansas, although the Army Reserve itself had not even requested the planes in its initial budget. The administration opposed this useless boondoggle, since Bush was trying to trim the Army Reserve, not expand it. Eugene Carroll, a retired rear admiral serving as deputy director of the Center for Defense Information (a military watchdog group in Washington) ridiculed the aircraft contract. "It has absolutely nothing to do with defense," he maintained.

But Dole secured the contract, claiming it would help the Army Reserve to modernize its aging fleet. He also succeeded in getting $16 million from the federal government so that Piaggio Aviation Company (an Italian firm with an office in Wichita) could build four P-180-D aircraft for the National Guard. He secured yet another $35 million in the Department of Defense Appropriations Bill to lease as many as 15 T-47 Cessna airplanes so the military could fight drug runners. (Cessna is a Kansas company.) Interestingly, the Pentagon had not requested any of the programs that Dole pressed for. The projects were clearly pork, though pork wrapped in the American flag.

Not all the senator's military boondoggling involved worthless—except to the Kansas economy—last-minute additions to defense projects. During the years before the 1992 election, Dole fought for two very large military aircraft appropriations, both of which *were* supported by the military. One was the re-engine work for the KC-135 tanker fleet for $526 million, which was to be done at the Boeing Plant in Wichita. The second and newer program, the Air Force's "Jay Hawk" trainer plane, cost a cool $178 million. These training airplanes also were being built at the Beech Aircraft Company in Wichita. A spokesman for The Defense Budget Project (another military watchdog organization) said, "Everyone concedes there is pork in the budget, but one person's pork is another person's critically needed program."

Shortly before the 1992 election, Senator Dole helped steer several other projects of dubious urgency toward Kansas: $3.4 million to help construct a new bus garage and maintenance facility in downtown Wichita; $2.2 million for improvements to the Kellogg Freeway program in Wichita; $2 million for an environmental center at Chisolm Creek Park; $2 million to expand science education programs in the Kansas "Cosmosphere" in Hutchinson; $1.2 million for improvements at Plainview, a low-income area of Wichita; and $960,000 for a fire-training facility at McConnell Air Force Base. Pork meant jobs. Kansas had one of the lowest unemployment rates in the country, 3.8 percent, and Dole took credit for this.

Bob Dole also exercised his clout on Capitol Hill when it came to federal disaster funds. During the winter of 1992, he swiftly channeled $100 million out of a $750 million farm disaster relief fund solely for winter wheat growers.

One of the more controversial aspects of Dole's Senate reelection campaign was a television ad that began airing on television stations in Wichita, Topeka, and Kansas City on October 1, 1992. The ad quoted a column that Senator Lloyd Bentsen (D-TX) had written in 1992, saying he had little doubt that if Dole had been elected president in 1988, the federal budget deficit would now be "under control." It also quoted Paul Tsongas, a former senator from Massachusetts, as having said in September 1992 that "Kansans ought to be proud that Dole represents them." But the senator quickly withdrew the ads after Tsongas and Bentsen complained that he had quoted them out of context.

Another example of Dole's campaign style can be seen in a premature promise of a new jet construction plant in Pratt, Kansas. Just a few weeks before the election, Dole emerged from a Piaggio Avanti corporate plane in Pratt promising the voters that his benefactor—the Italian aircraft manufacturer Piaggio—would build an Avanti jet construction plant creating "two hundred new jobs." In fact, Piaggio representatives had met with Dole and Pratt officials only to discuss moving the plant to Pratt from Lincoln, Nebraska.

In response to Dole's announcement, Piaggio's spokesperson released a press release saying that the company had made "no commitment" to move its plant to Kansas. Larry Collier, vice president of Duncan Aviation Company (Piaggio's partner), said that "Senator Dole requested that Kansas be considered. That request does not affect our agreement with Piaggio." No wonder Dole looked nervous as cameras trailed him emerging from a Piaggio jet in the Kansas heat. As it turned out, Piaggio never built a plant in Pratt.

Refraining from his usual ad hominem attacks on campaign opponents, the senator avoided attacking O'Dell personally. Dole felt sufficiently secure to play the role of elder statesman, he spent most of this campaign campaigning for GOP candidates in other states, and behaved pretty well when making cameo campaign stops in Kansas. As noted earlier, Richard Nixon appeared with Dole at a rally in Wichita on June 26—the twentieth anniversary of Watergate. Nixon, who patted Dole on the back and endorsed him as "the best Senate leader I've seen in my forty-five years of political life—without a doubt," praised Dole for having brought Russian leader Boris Yeltsin to Kansas, and launched into a speech about the need to open America's purse to shower billions of dollars on Russia—"to avoid a return to Communism there."* Afterward, Nixon stood like a department store Santa Claus, smiling and signing autographs.

Dole's "elder statesman" role impressed most Kansas voters and newspapers, but one held out. In a scathing editorial, the *Salina Journal* blasted Dole for funding his reelection campaign for a fifth term in the Senate with

---

*Yeltsin came to Kansas with Dole in tow in early 1992 to "see what real Americans are like." Dole gave him a ten-gallon cowboy hat and a belt buckle made in Kansas.

"millions in political action committee donations and millions more in pork from the federal treasury." The editorial urged Kansas voters to deny Dole a fifth term, said that Gloria O'Dell "has the glow of the future about her," and gave her a warm endorsement. The editorial further stated that:

> Dole is part and parcel of what is wrong with Washington, its gridlock, its worship of the almighty dollar and its total lack of concern for the welfare of the vast American public. Dole is beholden to big business and big agriculture for campaign contributions, speaking fees and cheap rides on fancy corporate jets. He hasn't been bought, just rented . . . Dole wants to preserve the twin fossils of the American economy, the health care system and the defense establishment, by pouring more federal money into each while tinkering around the edges and calling it reform . . . Dole puts his Washington insider status and party loyalty ahead of the interests of the people.

Nonetheless, on November 3, 1992, the senator was reelected with an impressive 63 percent of the vote. As a final gesture of arrogance, Dole spent Election Day in Washington and voted by absentee ballot.

O'Dell wound up deeply in debt. Two months later, she went to Washington for a Kansas inaugural reception hosted by Dole and Kansas's Democratic governor, Joan Finney, in Dole's Senate Minority Leader office overlooking the Capitol Mall. Photographed with O'Dell, Dole was all smiles. He also publicly promised to help her "get a job with the Clinton administration," a high-level job.

"I never heard from him again," O'Dell told me.

27

DAVE OWEN: FELON OR VICTIM?

Bob Dole's prominence as the top elected Republican official in the country has managed to obscure a ghost haunting his past—a ghost who rattles in his chains and threatens to haunt him even as he mounts another quest for the presidency.

This scary specter is Dave Owen, Dole's former banker, campaign manager, state boss, and financial whiz kid. "Dave Owen is Bob Dole, and Bob Dole is Dave Owen." This was a common refrain heard around the Sunflower State for twenty years, from 1968 to 1988.

But in 1994, Owen became inmate number 06369-031 at Leavenworth Federal Prison in Kansas, felt himself "a victim of political harassment," and sat in prison trying to come to grips with how he had fallen so far and so fast.

I spoke to Owen in 1994, after he'd had years to reflect on Bob Dole. The picture he painted is not pretty. He has torn up all photographs depicting himself with the senator, and remains hurt at being "cut loose" by the man he had loyally served.

In 1968, Dole first met Owen, a soft-spoken, bespectacled, scholarly investment banker from Stanley, the upper-middle-class suburb of Kansas City. Dole was then running for the U.S. Senate for the first time and facing stiff opposition from popular former governor Bill Avery in the GOP primary. He badly needed help in Johnson County, a pivotal GOP stronghold, and he turned to

Owen, who was then running for the Kansas State Senate, for assistance. He threw his support to Dole, a true act of political courage, and Dole won the nomination. The men began what was to become a long, terribly close, and personal relationship spanning the next twenty years. Owen became Dole's chief confidant, adviser, intimate assistant, and fund-raiser, served as state senator (1968–72), lieutenant governor of Kansas (1972–74), Kansas Republican chairman (1982–84), and national finance chairman of Dole's presidential campaign (1987–88).

In 1974, when Dole's political career came within 13,000 votes of ending as he fought to retain his Senate seat against Dr. Bill Roy, Owen was called in to salvage his campaign. In 1976, Owen served as the Midwest regional director of Gerald Ford's campaign for the Republican presidential nomination. Owen then personally implored Ford to choose Dole as his vice-presidential running mate, and he managed Dole's vice-presidential campaign that autumn.

In 1979 and 1980, when I was working for Dole, Owen was Dole's alter ego—his closest adviser and the architect of Dole's presidential campaign. An investment banker who was president of the Bank of Stanley in Kansas, Owen was also a financial wizard. "If you wanted money to run for anything as a Republican in Kansas," veteran politicians in Kansas told me, "Owen was the man to see. He could put together more money in a shorter period of time than anyone else. He made contacts, moved in the right circles, and helped Dole rise and raise money." As Dole's chief lieutenant, Owen raised more than $20 million for Dole's various campaigns. He also helped the senator win key endorsements and the support of voters.

In addition, Owen acted as a personal adviser to Dole's wife, Elizabeth, and became the "investment adviser" for her blind trust, which was established in conformity with the federal Ethics in Government Act. In December 1979, the trust borrowed $50,000 at below the prime loan rate from Owen's Bank of Stanley. Elizabeth Dole then contributed this money to the Dole for President Committee. Owen wrote to the Dole for President Committee on December 14, 1979, stating that the loan would be made at a 13.5 percent interest rate, considerably below the prime rate at the time. Dole's secretary, Jo-Anne Coe, who was then on the Senate payroll, wrote back to Owen on December 17, 1979, using U.S. Senate stationery with Bob Dole's name on the letterhead. She said:

> Dear Dave: Enclosed is a promissory note with Elizabeth's [Dole's] signature, as well as an assignment for the CD [Certificate of Deposit]. I will appreciate your making arrangements for a wire transfer of the funds to the campaign's bank account: First American Bank of Virginia, King & Royal Streets, Alexandria, Virginia 22314. Account name: 'Dole for President Committee' Account No. 06164765. As I indicated, these funds are needed at the earliest possible time, and I will therefore appreciate your expediting the bank transfer. Sincerely, Jo-Anne Coe.

It is illegal for a Senate office to be used for campaign purposes, including financing campaigns. Questions were raised about the propriety of the loan, and the FEC investigated.

Under complex rules related to personal and family contributions to candidates for federal office, which limited loans and contributions to $1,000 from any individual, including a candidate's wife, the FEC investigated allegations that the loan was illegal and excessive and threatened legal action against Dole's presidential campaign.*

The FEC initially insisted that because Elizabeth

*Federal law did not place a limit on the amount of money a candidate could borrow from his own accounts.

Dole's blind trust had been created five years prior to her marriage to Dole in 1975, it constituted money that Bob "had no control or access to" when he became a candidate for president in 1979. Therefore it was hers and subject to the $1,000 limit. (See FEC Matter Under Review No. 1257.) But in a brief submitted to the FEC at the time, Dole's lawyers argued that "the money lent to the Dole for President Committee derived from the Senator's personal funds under Kansas law and the applicable FEC regulations," and also argued that under Kansas law Senator Dole was joint owner with Elizabeth of the entire blind trust assets used to acquire the loan. The money, said Dole, was "common property." The FEC dropped the "illegal loan" charges after a two-year investigation.

In 1985, after being named Reagan's Secretary of Transportation and after terminating her first blind trust, Elizabeth created a second one. In early 1988, Dole's new presidential campaign faced complaints from Bush's campaign operatives about alleged insider trading regarding the second trust, so Dole sought to immediately distance himself from the trust. On January 14, 1988, *The Washington Post* reported Dole as saying, "I don't know anything about it. It wasn't my arrangement. I didn't consult with anyone about her [trust]. She is somewhere in Iowa. Why don't you talk to her?" Three weeks later, Dole angrily blamed then-Vice President Bush for spreading vicious rumors about "my wife." Dole buttonholed Bush on the Senate floor and yelled at him about an anti-Dole campaign flyer he had disseminated referring to mishandling of the trust money. Dole shoved the press release in Bush's face and shouted: "I think you owe my wife an apology." Bush refused to apologize and the flyers continued to circulate.

One of the major reasons for Dole's about-face on the issue of ownership of the "blind" trust was that nasty rumors began circulating in late 1987 and early 1988 concerning Dave Owen's actions as investment adviser to the trust.* As the investment adviser of the blind trust, Owen was responsible for investing the money without the knowledge of either Dole. The scandal was dredged up by Lee Atwater, George Bush's political hatchet man and guru, in the face of an increasingly tight race for the GOP presidential nomination. Atwater investigated Dole and Owen and found an obscure $26 million Small Business Administration (SBA) contract on an alleged "sweetheart deal" involving John Palmer, who had worked as a Senate aide for Dole from 1980 to 1982. In 1983, Palmer left Dole to found a new company in the city of Overland Park in Johnson County, Kansas, called EDP Enterprises. Palmer, being black, tried to obtain an SBA "Section 8(a)" minority status loan in order to secure a three-year, $26 million U.S. Army contract under a minority "set aside" program to supply food to an Army base.

Dole himself, his top Senate staffers, and Owen all lobbied the SBA on behalf of Palmer and EDP, the senator personally telephoning the Small Business administrator and urging him to make the loan. Dole's administrative assistant accompanied Palmer and Owen to a meeting at the SBA. Owen lobbied and wrote the SBA on Republican Party stationery, saying, "I know Senator Dole is supportive." In August 1986, Palmer was awarded the largest such SBA loan in history—$26 million.

Palmer's EDP headquarters office was located in the same building as Owen's Eagle Distributors, but in different suites, though EDP and Eagle shared some personnel and legal counsel. On December 30, 1986, EDP bought a "half-interest" in an office building (College Park II) owned by Elizabeth Dole's blind trust, in a deal that provided Dole with a capital gain of between $63,000 and $100,000. The deal was consummated just forty-eight

---

*Owen told the author in 1994 that he had never told Bob or Elizabeth Dole where the blind trust's assets were being invested while he'd acted as its adviser.

hours before a new higher capital gains tax rate was scheduled to take effect on January 1, 1987. Dole, as the most influential Republican on the Senate Finance Committee and as Senate majority leader, had helped to craft that legislation.

The $26 million contract raises many interesting questions: First of all, how much profit, if any, did the Dole blind trust return on the real estate deal? Secondly, why was the building sold to a firm that had just obtained a federal contract, thanks in part to Dole? In addition, Owen, who is white, headed quite a conglomerate of companies including Eagle Distributors, Owen & Associates, and Golfun Productions, Inc. Early in 1988, Bush's operatives raised questions with the news media about the entire EDP–SBA contract, suggesting cronyism in favor of Palmer. While these allegations fizzled after Dole withdrew from the presidential primary race in March of 1988, I believe I have pieced together a fascinating puzzle, involving big money and big politics in Kansas and Washington.

Dole's Senate financial disclosure records indicate that in 1986 the Dole blind trust purchased the College Park II office building in Overland Park, Kansas. This was after Owen had obtained a $1 million loan on behalf of the trust from the American Investors Life Insurance Company, a subsidiary of AmVestors Group.* Another Dole political ally and Dole campaign national finance cochairman, Tim Murrell, was then chairman of the insurance company. American Investors Life put Owen on its board of directors one month later. Owen himself received a $139,000 commission on the sale of the building. Two major questions surface here: What were the actual terms of the loan from American Investors Life Insurance

---

*American Investors Life Insurance Company also profited enormously from a single-premium life insurance policy tax loophole (a made-to-order provision) that Dole shepherded through the Senate in the 1986 Tax Reform Act, as discussed in chapter 17 in this book.

Company to the trust? And was the interest rate considerably below the current prime rate, as it was in the case of the 1979 loan of $50,000 to Elizabeth's first trust, which Owen also had arranged?

The problematic relationship between Owen and the Dole blind trust interested not only the media, but also those Democrats who felt Bob Dole would make a far stronger GOP presidential candidate than Bush. In January 1988, the Democratic-controlled House Small Business Committee launched a full-scale investigation into the Dole-Owen connection. Committee Chairman John J. LaFalce (D-NY) issued damning public statements hinting of a sinister conspiracy by the senator to get federal money to his cronies.

A chronology prepared by the House Committee staff noted a disturbing timing of events: In the summer of 1985, Palmer went after a lucrative Army food service contract at Fort Leonard Wood in Missouri. He sought the contract under a special SBA administration program (Program 8(a)), which was intended by the federal government to assist "disadvantaged minority entrepreneurs."* The SBA staff initially balked because "EDP needed to establish some sort of track record as it was trying to secure 8(a) contracts." EDP, a one-man office with no prior experience in this area, was unqualified financially and had a negative net worth.

The chronology also pointed out that Owen had helped EDP with a loan from his own Bank of Stanley, and became a consultant to EDP for a fee of $5,000 to $7,000 per month. In addition, EDP listed its headquarters in the same building as Owen & Associates, Owen's principal company.

In February 1986, Palmer was awarded the first of what amounted to more than $26 million in federal government contracts for his firm. Owen said that EDP "pays me

---

*This program has often been criticized for allowing established white businessmen to select minority front men to act as conduits in obtaining federal contracts without competitive bidding.

consulting fees and I continue to be an adviser.'' Just one month later, Owen created the Eagle Distributing Company, which sold food service supplies to EDP. Owen said the value of the contract was about $480,000 per year. EDP, he said, was Eagle Distributing's main customer.

On the floor of the House of Representatives in early February 1988, Congressman LaFalce stated that ''criminal laws may have been violated'' in the federal government's award of the contract. But LaFalce also said, ''I have found nothing that suggests that Bob Dole was personally involved in any questionable event or occurrence related to the contract.'' Nonetheless, LaFalce strongly criticized SBA officials, Owen, and Palmer. ''That program (minority set-asides) is intended to help disadvantaged minority business to develop and enter the mainstream of the American economy,'' said LaFalce. ''Instead, the program has been mismanaged, misdirected, and abused—very often.''

The chief investigator for the House panel, Thomas Trimboli, later complained that in the clubby world of Congress, the House panel did not thoroughly investigate Dole because he was so powerful. ''LaFalce was very apprehensive of tying Bob Dole personally into any of this, and we didn't have the opportunity to interview any of his [Dole's] staff,'' said Trimboli. ''As a consequence, we were unfamiliar with the extent of his [Dole's] involvement.''

In all fairness to Palmer, Owen, and Dole, it must be said that EDP, as of this writing, still flourishes, independent of Owen. The real issue is whether EDP was a legitimate minority-owned business at the time the $26 million contract was awarded by the SBA. In any case, no criminal prosecutions resulted, and Owen, Palmer and Dole were cleared of wrongdoing. Palmer is now a loyal campaign contributor to Dole. The legacy of the Palmer-EDP ''quasi-scandal'' was that it permanently severed the ties between Dole and Owen, and revealed how Dole blames others for his own disasters.

On January 14, 1988, while the senator was under intense media scrutiny, Owen resigned as National Finance Chairman of Dole's presidential campaign. Dole told the press that Owen would never return, saying, "It's his problem, not mine."

In a letter by Elizabeth Dole erroneously backdated a whole year to January 15, 1987, but actually written on January 15, 1988, Elizabeth asked the Office of Ethics in Government to de-blind her trust. Her request was granted on the same day, which is a highly unusual occurrence. Elizabeth Dole was *not* legally required to de-blind her trust at this time, and this decision was probably a political error of judgment. De-blinding the trust made public scores of documents relating to the Doles' personal finances. This disclosure added fuel to the flames, and Dole became the subject of countless articles that questioned many financial transactions, and that dominated headlines for the next two months.

A bitter Dole never spoke to Owen again. He also blamed Palmer and Kaplan for the scandals of his devastated ex-friend. Dole declared "Dave Owen will never be in this campaign again, or in anything else that Bob Dole has anything to do with." Owen tried to contact the senator repeatedly for years after resigning. He never got a response.

"Dole always blames others for his own mistakes," Owen says. "So he blamed me for the stories Lee Atwater had planted in the news media."

Owen's shadowy network connecting the Dole trust to numerous deals and enterprises resembles a spider's web, at the center of which was the Dole blind trust. An intricate network of deals preceded the Palmer/SBA scandal.

In February 1984, the Elizabeth Dole blind trust loaned Dave Owen $250,000 to bankroll Golfun Productions, Inc., a company created by Owen to produce a television show about golf. Golfun Productions, Inc., lost money during the 1980s, and several other investors in this company were told that Golfun had become insolvent and that their money had been lost. Nevertheless, Owen put the firm's assets up as collateral for a loan from a bank to which he was connected. Two days later, he paid the Dole blind trust a hefty chunk of interest. Just days before the Doles made their financial records public during the 1988 presidential campaign, Owen repaid the entire loan, thereby making it a seemingly successful investment for the trust. Two questions arise: Why did the Dole trust receive special treatment that allowed it to realize a profit on an investment in which other investors apparently lost money, and how much money, if any, did the trust make as interest on the loan?

Federal 1986 income tax returns show that Liddy's blind trust received interest payments from several sources, including EDP Enterprises Inc., Anderson Blass Mortgage Company, Ronald Clanton Chevrolet, GOW Partnership and Windham, and $5,268 from Owen & Associates. The interest from Owen's company was for a loan by the trust to it of an undisclosed sum.

In 1985, Owen obtained for the Dole blind trust an American Investors Life Insurance mortgage of $110,000 at a 12.5 percent interest rate for the purchase of a $137,000 Capitol Hill townhouse in Washington, D.C.

Finally, Owen sold the trust one hundred acres of his own farmland in Johnson County, Kansas, with a value of $270,000. Some in the media wondered whether it was appropriate for a blind trust to buy land from its investment manager.

In 1986, during his reelection campaign for a fourth Senate term, Dole and his Campaign America PAC received $24,000 in campaign contributions from employees of Birdview Satellite Communications, Inc., and from the spouses of these employees. In 1983, Charles Ross, the president of Birdview, had come up with the idea of developing a nationwide satellite television hookup to raise money for Dole's Campaign America PAC. A stockholder in Birdview, Owen was also paid $3,000 a month as a consultant to the company and $100,000 to advertise Birdview on a television golf program owned by Owen's other company, Golfun Productions, Inc. He also brokered a $250,000 land purchase for Birdview.

In early 1988, when the *Kansas City Star* broke a story of allegedly "illegal contributions" by Birdview, Dole hit the roof. He refused to meet with *Star* reporters. Within a day after the article was published, Dole's campaign treasurer wrote to the FEC actually "requesting" an investigation into the Birdview matter. "Dole for Senate Committee strongly desires to refund any illegal allegations [*sic*]," he wrote. "It is our hope that the FEC will conduct a thorough and prompt investigation."

But the most bizarre and nebulous strand in the Owen web was one that landed him in prison. In 1986, the State of Kansas legalized "parimutuel" betting, specifically, state-sanctioned dog racing tracks that allowed gamblers to pool their bets. Being a Bible Belt state, Kansas had outlawed such racing in the past, but for a variety of reasons, including the need to raise revenue for the state, it was allowed in 1986 in two cities: Kansas City and Wichita.

Paul Bryant, Jr., son of the legendary University of Alabama football coach, "Bear" Bryant, was one of the largest operators in the business, directing a vast network of pari-mutuel tracks throughout the country through his company, AIM, Inc., in Tuscaloosa, Alabama. When Bryant wanted a license to operate two tracks in Kansas, he went to Washington and met with Dole, Owen, and Elliot Kaplan, who was Owen's lawyer and sometimes acted also as a lawyer for Elizabeth's blind trust.

In a widely reported interview in 1986, Bryant said that Senator Dole had recommended Owen to him. Though a Democrat, Bryant attended a private Dole fund-raiser in Washington on September 11, 1986, with Owen, and contributed the $5,000 maximum allowable donation to Dole's political action committee, Campaign America.*

One month later, at the Topeka airport, Bryant gave

*See the *Kansas City Times*, August 23, 1989.

Owen a check for $100,000, made out to Owen & Associates.

In 1986, John Peterson was working half-time as Dole's Kansas Senate office director and half-time as a consultant to the Kansas Republican Party. His activities included fund-raising for Dole's campaign. Peterson was present at the Topeka airport when the $100,000 check was given by Bryant to Owen.

Bryant also signed a contract guaranteeing Owen a 15 percent commission on all profits from the racetracks. Owen says profits would have amounted only to about a million dollars per year at best, but others projected a $55 million profit. Republican Kansas State Representative Kerry Patrick later asked, "Why would Paul Bryant give 15 percent of the profits in a projected $55 million racetrack when Dave Owen was not going to be required to invest any money in the project? That would work out to over a million dollars a year for him for life. Why would any businessman in his right mind do that unless he had been given a guarantee [of contract award]?"

Shortly before Bryant gave Owen $100,000, Dole had pressured Owen to raise money for Mike Hayden, the GOP candidate for Governor of Kansas in 1986. Owen told me he hated Hayden for having promised to support Owen in his 1982 gubernatorial bid, and then in fact backing Owen's opponent, but Owen agreed to help Hayden only because "Bob Dole asked me to, and when Dole asked for something, I always complied."

Regarding the pressure Dole put on Owen to raise money for Hayden's campaign, Kaplan testified at Owen's trial as follows:

There was a committee formed for Dole to run for the presidency. And I attended several meetings in Washington with Dave [Owen] and . . . at least one of the meetings, Dole was talking to Dave about the need to raise money for Hayden. And Dave was resisting. And then I had several conversations with Dave about raising money for Hayden and about

some of his personal feelings towards Hayden and
Hayden towards him apparently. And Dole apparently kept putting on the pressure and they were
reaching a real critical point . . . [Dole]'s a big guy.
And Dave felt that he needed to raise the money.
And he asked me to do it. And frankly, if it was
important to Bob Dole and it was important to
Dave Owen, you know, it was something I'd want
to do.

At about the same time Owen received the $100,000,
employees of Owen's companies contributed money to
Hayden's campaign totaling $32,000, then were allegedly
reimbursed by Owen. Owen would later be accused of
reimbursing his employees and improperly deducting this
as a business expense on his tax return.

The real nature of the $100,000 check remains unclear.
Owen did not report the $100,000 as income on Owen &
Associates' 1986 tax return, claiming it was a loan and an
advance against future income on his contract with Bryant, if Bryant won the licenses.

Owen was not the top lobbyist in Topeka. That honor
belonged to Pete McGill, a former Kansas House Representative. One state license to operate dog racetracks
was ultimately awarded by the Kansas State Racing Commission to a client of McGill's, and another was given to
a competitor. Bryant got nothing.

In 1988, Bryant paid Owen more than $200,000 to
cancel the contract he'd made.

Hayden won the election for governor in 1986, and
remained close to Dole for the next four years. But Owen
did not fare so well. In late 1987 and early 1988, as
discussed earlier, Owen's controversial activities involving Elizabeth Dole's blind trust were reported by the
news media across the country, and Owen was forced to
resign from Dole's presidential campaign.

When Dole declared that "Dave Owen is persona non
grata," Bob Stephan, Republican attorney general of
Kansas and a close political ally of Dole, smelled blood.

So did many others in the closely inbred Kansas Republican political establishment. Owen had stepped on a lot of toes in twenty years as the senator's right arm.

Eighteen criminal counts were filed by Stephan against Owen in a grand jury indictment, *The State of Kansas v. John E. Palmer, Elliot M. Kaplan, and David C. Owen,* on October 31, 1989, in Johnson County State Court.

Owen was charged with making illegal campaign contributions to Hayden's 1986 campaign. He was charged with theft, and conspiracy to commit theft, under the Kansas Campaign Finance Act, K.S.A. 25-4142 et seq. He was also charged with making excessive campaign contributions, criminal solicitation, and other crimes. Kaplan was charged with theft and conspiracy to commit theft, and Palmer was charged only with conspiracy to make excessive campaign contributions.

The trio denied all allegations and claimed that a political vendetta was being waged against them. Owen contacted Dole several times and asked for assistance. Dole refused to respond. Dole's close ties to Stephan make it reasonable to assume that Stephan would not normally prosecute a former top Dole aide without first informing the senator. Stephan hired Professor Michael Barbara of Washburn Law School and his own former lawyer, Tom Haney, as special prosecutors to try the case against Owen.

The statute of limitations for these crimes had evidently expired and the charges were problematical, so Owen, Palmer, and Kaplan were able to get the charges dismissed. But Stephan appealed the dismissal. On April 17, 1991, the Kansas Supreme Court affirmed Kaplan's dismissal, but not Palmer's and not all of Owen's. Their cases were remanded to the trial court for further proceedings.*

On remand, Owen decided to plead guilty to a class C misdemeanor, the equivalent of nailing a campaign leaflet

---

*The Supreme Court decision is reported in *State v. Palmer, et al.*, 248 Kansas Reports 681 (1991), 810 P.2d 734.

to a telephone pole. He was fined $500 and sent on his way, or so he thought.

Owen and Kaplan say one of the state prosecutors ran into Owen and warned him that the case "won't go away" and hinted that Stephan would refer the case to the feds for a tax evasion investigation. "We're not through with you yet," he allegedly said. Owen says that Stephan "passed on" his case to the U.S. Attorney.

Owen's lawyer, Elliot Kaplan, who also was indicted in the state criminal case, was angry at having been criminally prosecuted for what he considered to be "blaming us for loaning money to ourselves from ourselves." In state court Kaplan filed a civil suit for malicious prosecution against Stephan and the special prosecutors. Stephan and his prosecutors then filed a motion to dismiss the case under the doctrine of "sovereign immunity." In American law, the doctrine of sovereign immunity holds that no government official can be sued for malicious prosecution for acts within the ordinary course and scope of his official duties. Just one month before the hearing, in early 1992, Kaplan was served with a subpoena by the U.S. attorney in Kansas City and ordered to testify before a federal grand jury then looking into Dave Owen's alleged evasion of income taxes on the $100,000 he'd received from Bryant in 1986.

Shortly after the federal subpoena was served, the state court dismissed Kaplan's malicious prosecution civil suit on the grounds that Stephan and the prosecutors enjoyed "absolute sovereign immunity for their actions in the Palmer-Kaplan-Owen case." Then, a few days after that dismissal, the federal officials withdrew the subpoena requiring Kaplan to appear before the grand jury.

In an interview in 1994, Kaplan remained bitter. Asked if he believed Dole was somehow involved in prosecuting Owen, the lawyer replied rhetorically, "How could you say he wasn't?" In 1992, Kaplan also claimed he was being harassed by Stephan's agents in the U.S. attorney's office, in order to pressure him to drop his civil suit against Stephan. "I felt frankly that they [Stephan and the Feds] were holding this thing over my head," Kaplan said. "I anguished over the injustice of this whole thing, and how it made me feel like a victim. There are all kinds of government abuses, but using the judicial system for personal purposes is the worst of all."

In his civil lawsuit, Kaplan alleged that Stephan had filed criminal charges against him maliciously, knowing that there was not sufficient evidence to convict him of a crime. Kaplan pled in his civil court complaint that in 1986 Owen had asked him to make contributions to Hayden's campaign and Kaplan had agreed on the condition that he would be paid legal fees for work in connection with AmVestors Inc., which was managed by Owen. Kaplan also asserted that he was paid $6,000 from the AmVestor accounts. The check was recorded on the corporate books as legal fees and Kaplan declared the fees as income for tax purposes. After depositing the check, Kaplan and his wife each made $3,000 contributions to the Hayden campaign. Kaplan insisted this was all legal.

"The state didn't even last a day when they got their day in court," in the criminal case, Kaplan explains. "The IRS didn't ask for my records. They said the U.S. attorney wanted to take some testimony from me. And I said 'I know what this is about. If this is the campaign contribution, I will bring my tax returns. I will fully cooperate.' But they wanted to find out about the conversations between Dave Owen and me."

On November 18, 1992, just two weeks after Dole's successful reelection for a fifth Senate term, a federal grand jury in Kansas City, Kansas, indicted Owen. Arrested, Owen faced a public trial in early February 1993 on two felony counts of filing and subscribing to false tax returns (violating 26 U.S. Code, Section 7206).

"I am totally shocked," said Owen when first informed of his indictment. "I can't believe I am still having to defend myself for this." He claimed he was a victim of "double jeopardy" and political persecution, but the federal judge refused to dismiss the charges.

Owen also complained that he had not even been audited or interviewed by the IRS prior to being indicted, and that he was being hounded for political reasons.

Owen was indicted upon the action of the U.S. Attorney for the District of Kansas, Lee Thompson, a Republican political ally of Dole's, who was nominated to his post by President Bush at Dole's behest.

Thompson was the son-in-law of Ray Morgan, a longtime Dole political supporter and a political writer for the *Kansas City Star*. Morgan's son, Scott Morgan, worked for Dole as a staffer in Bob's Senate office, and later worked for Dole's 1988 presidential campaign. An attorney, Scott Morgan also represented Dole before the Federal Election Commission.

It is striking that people so close to Dole were the ones who prosecuted Owen.

In the trial, which began in February 1993, the government's case was handled by Assistant U.S. Attorney Kurt Shernuk. Shernuk was the son-in-law of Pete McGill, the Republican lobbyist who had vied against Owen and Bryant for the dog track license in 1986 (Shernuk and his wife had worked for Stephan in the attorney general's office a few years earlier). Shernuk's contention now was that in 1986 Owen had persuaded others to make political contributions to Hayden via his own shell companies, illegally reimbursed them, then reported the reimbursements as business expenses on his tax return and claimed those as tax deductions. This violates federal tax law and carries criminal penalties. Shernuk also accused Owen of criminally failing to report the $100,000 from Bryant as income. In effect, the federal indictment charged Owen with subscribing to false tax returns.

Owen has offered contradictory explanations of the $100,000. According to him, the money was a loan to be repaid to Bryant if Bryant got a Kansas racetrack license. Since Bryant never got the license, the money somehow became a fee, which the IRS claims was income.

The trial testimony was complicated. The government subpoenaed Palmer, Kaplan, Bryant, and several others to testify against Owen. Bryant stated under oath he had written in his checkbook register that the $100,000 was a "consulting fee." His testimony and checkbook register (entered six months after the check was issued) were the key evidence against Owen.

The federal charges were based on many of the same underlying transactions as Stephan's state case, but the tax evasion charges were new. Kaplan testified under oath that "Dole put a lot of pressure on him [Owen]" to raise money for Hayden in 1986, because Hayden was strapped for cash.* "Dave was resisting, but Dole kept putting on the pressure," recalled Kaplan. Kaplan also testified that "Bob Dole, he's a big guy," and that one did not buck the wishes of the Kingfish of Kansas politics. Otherwise, Dole's name was conspicuously absent from the rest of the trial testimony. Incredibly, Owen's own counsel failed to subpoena Dole as a witness.

The judge in Owen's federal tax evasion trial in 1993 was Thomas Van Bebber, whom Bush had nominated to the federal bench in 1989 at Dole's recommendation. A former Kansas House of Representative colleague and friend of Peter McGill, Van Bebber had also presided over portions of a second sex harassment lawsuit brought against Attorney General Bob Stephan by Marcia Tomson Stingley in 1985.

Owen's federal trial jury was made up of a blue-collar panel. The foreman was a retired janitor. The jurors seemed confused by the esoterica of tax law jargon hurled

---

*Hayden went on to win the 1986 campaign for governor but was defeated for reelection in 1990 thanks in large part to Owen's switching gears and supporting his opponent, Democratic candidate Joan Finney. Owen raised money and tried to convert as many people as he could to Finney's cause in bitterness for having been "abandoned" by Dole after the 1988 scandal had broken out. Hayden is now a lobbyist for the fish and tackle industry. He has fallen out of favor with Dole, who "doesn't like losers."

at them. Throughout the trial, lurid tales of high-flying wheeling and dealing and "hundreds of thousands of dollars" were used by the prosecutors to paint Owen as a wealthy wheeler-dealer. The jurors were not told that Owen's crime deprived the treasury of only $4,200, a figure arrived at by compromise after the verdict was delivered. One juror allegedly said after the trial, "If we had known that this was just about $4,200, we would have acquitted him."

A principal government expert witness against Owen at the trial was an IRS agent who had not passed a CPA exam. Kaplan and Palmer testified rather favorably about Owen's character, but their testimony on Owen's role in financing Hayden's campaign necessarily bolstered the prosecution's case because it tended to prove the corpus delicti and mens rea of the alleged crimes as far as the jury was concerned.

Owen's supporters felt that Judge Van Bebber ruled very unfairly, permitted prejudicial evidence to come in at least sixteen times, and was hostile to Owen. Yet no effort was made by Owen's lawyers to disqualify this judge for bias. Owen was convicted on two counts of subscribing to false tax returns, sentenced to a year and a day in federal prison, and fined $4,200 for back taxes owed. His appeal to the U.S. Court of Appeals for the Tenth Circuit was denied in early 1994 (the case is reported at 15 F.3d 1528) and on March 23, 1994, Owen stepped out of civilian life and into federal prison at Yankton, South Dakota. Owen failed to appeal his conviction to the U.S. Supreme Court, the last step on the appeal chain. He had vowed "not to go down quietly," but changed his mind because of the massive expense of legal fees in battling the government for five years. On June 2, 1994, a few days after hearing from me, Owen was transferred to Leavenworth Prison in Kansas. No reason was given to him for the transfer. Kaplan told me, in August 1994, that Owen's life was threatened in prison and he was warned to "keep quiet." When Owen asked to be transferred back to Yankton after his parole hearing in July, Leavenworth Prison authorities refused. Then, when he decided to stay at Leavenworth (to be close to his wife), the authorities tried to move him back to Yankton. His wife intervened with the Bureau of Prisons and prevented the transfer at the eleventh hour.

The case gets stranger. Owen was eligible for parole July 23, 1994, after serving one third of his sentence. However, the parole board made a "mistake" and erroneously insisted he owed the IRS $46,000 in back taxes. Owen would not have been eligible for parole if his penalty had been over $40,000, but in fact he owed only $4,200. In addition, the parole authorities mysteriously "lost" numerous letters of reference supporting Owen's parole. These mishaps prevented Owen's parole. Owen says, "They stripped my file of any supporting evidence."

Owen then filed a Petition for Writ of Habeas Corpus, which was finally granted by a federal court in Topeka on October 12, 1994. On October 11, 1994, the day of the court hearing on his habeas corpus petition in Topeka, Owen was supposed to be released by Leavenworth Prison to U.S. marshals to attend the hearing. The marshals showed up with a court order for his release, but prison officials refused to discharge Owen. The hearing took place in absentia, after Owen's wife insisted it proceed. The judge ruled that the federal parole board had totally abused its power in falsifying the amount of Owen's fine and denying him parole.

U.S. District Judge Richard D. Rogers decided to immediately order Owen's release from prison on October 12, 1994, rather than remanding the case to the U.S. Parole Commission as would normally be done. The judge found that the Parole Commission had "abused" its authority in denying Owen parole and declared: "The court will take the unusual step of ordering [Owen's] release without further proceedings before the Parole Commission."

It is interesting to note that the chairman of the U.S. Parole Commission in 1994 was Edward F. Reilly, Jr., a longtime Dole protégé and supporter. Reilly, a staunch Republican and a state senator from Leavenworth, Kansas, was appointed U.S. Parole Commissioner by President Bush in August 1992, and confirmed by the U.S. Senate, upon Dole's recommendation.

The government spent an estimated $2 million to prosecute Owen in the state and federal cases in order to collect a $4,200 fine in the federal and $500 in the state case. A year and a day in prison is a stiff sentence for a white-collar defendant with no prior criminal history.

Completely disillusioned by what happened to Owen, Kaplan now calls politics an "unhealthy environment." His closest tie to politics since then has been a cameo role in the movie *Dave*. He appears as the portly gentleman standing behind "President Mitchell" (played by Kevin Kline) in the scene, near the end of the movie, where the idealistic Kline addresses Congress. One of the villains, the chief of staff (played by Frank Langella), bears some striking similarities to Dole in appearance and demeanor.

Palmer has reconciled with Dole, remained a staunch Republican, and made the maximum allowable contributions to Dole's Campaign America as recently as 1994. Palmer's EDP Enterprises is flourishing and expanding and in 1994 was a $9.2 million food service management company expanding into manufacturing. Kaplan says Palmer is Dole's man now because "anyone who pays Dole, he [Dole] supports."

As for Owen himself, upon his release from prison on October 12, 1994, he resumed his work as an investment banker.

Mike Hayden, the "Golden Boy" governor, proved less popular than Dole had hoped. In 1990, he was defeated in his reelection bid by Democrat Joan Finney. A major factor was an unpopular state property tax that unduly burdened ordinary taxpayers in order to give tax breaks to wealthy businessmen, for which Hayden was pilloried. Another factor was Dave Owen, who raised money and campaigned for Finney, an act that "angered many Republicans," says Owen.

Dave Owen's chilling odyssey through the American criminal injustice system shows the dangers of flying too close to the flame of a powerful politician.

28

BOB'S BALD EAGLE, BOB STEPHAN

The strange case of Dave Owen cannot be fully understood without examining the career of Bob Stephan, the longtime Republican attorney general of Kansas who instigated the first felony criminal charges against Owen in 1989. Why would Stephan go after Owen for raising campaign money for a fellow Republican, Governor Hayden?

Bob Dole has always had extremely close ties to Bob Stephan, who has served as attorney general of Kansas from 1978 to 1994 (more than twice as long as anyone else).

Short, bald, and pudgy, dressed in well-cut suits, vivacious and some would say boorish, Stephan started life as a poor kid from West Wichita, and hitched his wagon to Dole's star from the beginning. As the highest law-enforcement official in the state of Kansas, Stephan has had the power to determine who is prosecuted for violating the state's criminal laws, as well as the power to enforce numerous laws, civil and criminal, throughout the state. Reelected three times, Stephan, now sixty-three, has served as one of the major players in Bob Dole's Kansas Republican machine.

Stephan's mother, Julia, owned a variety store in West Wichita and his father, Taft, operated a grocery store and later a bicycle and lawn mower shop. After graduating from Washburn University Law School in Topeka in

1957, just five years after Dole, Stephan opened his own law practice. He became Sedgwick County's Republican chairman just as Dole began to rise in Kansas politics. In 1965, when Stephan was only thirty-two, he was appointed a judge by Governor Bill Avery. Seven years later, Stephan learned he had cancer, which had spread to his liver, spleen, lymph nodes and bone marrow, and was told he had a month to live. He faced down the grim reaper, eyeball to eyeball.

Even while undergoing chemotherapy, he won the attorney generalship of Kansas in 1978. Known as "the Energizer Bunny" for his indefatigable energy, Stephan brought a gung-ho attitude to his job, firing up his army of prosecutors with his trademark phrase, "Let's go for it."

Stephan modeled his career and style after Dole, received his financial and political backing, and returned the favors manyfold. The senator groomed him for the governorship, but in December 1982, Stephan was sued by a former records clerk, Marcia Tomson (whose married name is now Stingley), who claimed he had pushed her up against a wall, sexually harassed her and made sexual demands. She alleged that Stephan had fired her after she rejected his advances.* Stephan denied sexually harassing Tomson.

In the harassment suit which made banner headlines, Tomson was represented by attorney Marge Phelps, the daughter of Reverend Fred Phelps, and by Phelps himself. Rumors that the sex harassment suit was politically motivated by a desire to embarrass Dole's Bald Eagle were encouraged by Stephan and Dole.

The bizarre case led to six years of controversial and ugly litigation, scuttled Stephan's once promising bid for the governor's chair, and ruined some of his political friendships. But, as in the sex harassment cases of Sena-

---

*Stingley was Marcia Tomson when she filed her suit in 1982. She later married. In this chapter she is referred to by her maiden name.

tor Bob Packwood and Judge Clarence Thomas, Dole turned a blind eye. He steadfastly supported Stephan through the thick and thin of the sex harassment litigation. The lawsuit was settled in March 1985 for the relatively small sum of $24,000.

The settlement agreement contained a "confidentiality clause" according to which none of the parties was allowed to make public its details. Then Stephan pushed his luck. On October 29, 1985, he gave a press conference and revealed the terms of the settlement, and thus exposed himself to a second lawsuit for "breach of settlement agreement" and fraud and libel filed by Tomson. Judge Van Bebber disqualified Marge Phelps as Tomson's attorney, and Tomson hired Fred Dalton Thompson, a famous Senate committee lawyer during the Watergate crisis and part-time Hollywood actor.* Stephan claimed, incredibly, that he did not know the terms of settlement.

The Stephan sex harassment case raised many disturbing questions. To settle the original lawsuit several Kansas Republicans contributed to help Stephan pay his legal bills and settlement and costs. Circumstances surrounding the "out of court" payment were made public at a news conference called by Stephan's lawyer Bob Storey, who had raised half of the $24,000 in eight contributions ranging from $500 to $3,000 each, according to a *Kansas City Times* article on October 30, 1985. It was then used to pay the settlement amount to Marcia Tomson. Stephan and Storey claimed that spending $24,000 in private funds "probably saved the government from spending up to $100,000 in public funds" if the case had gone to trial. In 1990, Stephan's opponent, Bert Cantwell, claimed that Stephan's legal defense fees had cost the state $64,000.

---

*Fred Dalton Thompson starred as a lawyer in *Marie*, a movie about a Tennessee female government employee who was fired for exposing corruption. Thompson has also starred in numerous other movies. In 1994, Thompson, a Republican, was elected U.S. senator from Tennessee. He now joins Bob Dole's GOP legion in the Senate.

Why did Stephan shoot himself in the foot by revealing the terms of the settlement? Because he was planning on running for governor in 1986 with Dole's support, and he was pressured to tell the world that the suit was a frivolous action settled for "nuisance value."

Tomson's second suit, filed in November 1985, asked for $15 million in damages against Stephan. In addition to accusing Stephan of breaching the agreement's confidentiality provision, Tomson claimed that Stephan had defrauded and "defamed" her, had failed to fulfill his promise to have a friend buy her a home for $75,000 and get her a job in California, and had also failed to refrain from attacking her on the merits of her sexual harassment lawsuit. She won the second suit in a jury trial and a verdict for $200,000 in 1988.

Interestingly enough, the presiding magistrate was none other than Thomas Van Bebber of Topeka, who went on to preside over Dave Owen's tax evasion trial in 1993.

Van Bebber is not the only tie between Stephan's sex harassment case and Owen's later criminal cases. The lawyer who represented Stephan in Tomson's first suit, Thomas Haney, was also hired by Stephan as a special prosecutor in 1989 to prosecute the Owen case.

In 1989, despite a salary of over $60,000, Stephan filed for bankruptcy, yet he bought a new car, removed his name from the deed to his mother's house (an action the bankruptcy court approved on the ground that he had no ownership interest in the house), and refused to pay Tomson any portion of the $200,000 verdict. Nevertheless, with Bob Dole's lavish support, he was reelected attorney general in 1990, although by a margin of less than 1 percent of the vote. He accused his opponent, Bert Cantwell, of conspiring with Reverend Phelps to bring him down.

Owen and others say that because Stephan filed for bankruptcy, Haney was unable to collect his $75,000 legal fee for the sex harassment case. It is interesting that

Stephan put him on the state payroll in order to prosecute Owen shortly after Stephan had filed for bankruptcy.

In January 1992, a federal grand jury in Kansas City indicted Stephan on two counts of perjury and one of conspiracy to commit perjury. It also indicted Stephan's lawyer, Bob Storey, on the same counts.

The perjury charges against Stephan involve Fred Phelps, the Topeka Dole detractor, whose daughter, Marge, represented Tomson in her first suit. Fred Phelps filed a complaint against Stephan, claiming he had a telephone recording taped by Stephan himself, proving Stephan had lied under oath regarding the settlement agreement, in a deposition, by falsely claiming he had not been aware of the terms of the agreement.

In the taped phone conversation, taped by Stephan himself, obtained by the FBI, Stephan can be heard proclaiming: "The concern is that if I'm subpoenaed, then, you know, I'm in a real box. There are an awful lot of people that know a lot more about this. Everytime I turn around, it seems like I'm talking to somebody that got a little snatch of this or a little snatch of that." [Laughter]

This tape, which was made public by Cantwell during Stephan's 1990 campaign, raised questions about his sworn testimony that he had been ignorant of the terms of the settlement agreement in 1985.

These public revelations did not disturb Dole, who continued to support Stephan throughout his 1990 reelection campaign, which Stephan began with a commanding thirty-point lead in the polls over Cantwell.

Dole's support provided the margin of victory that enabled Stephan to eke out a narrow victory. But in 1991, increasingly damaging revelations led inexorably toward a federal indictment for perjury. The indictment of January 19, 1992, charged that in 1988 Stephan and Storey conspired to concoct false testimony for Stephan to give at his trial. If convicted on all three counts, he would have faced fifteen years in prison and a $750,000 fine. The indictment was the first time in Kansas history that a state official was charged with a felony. Stephan pleaded not guilty to the perjury-related charges.

Meanwhile, Federal Judge Bruce Jenkins of Utah, assigned to the Stephan case, postponed the trial repeatedly. When Stephan finally went to trial on two counts of perjury in March 1995, he was acquitted, and effusively burst into tears upon hearing the verdict. The prosecutors then dismissed related perjury charges against his former lawyer, Bob Storey.

By the time the case was tried, however, Stephan was no longer attorney general.

On July 29, 1992, Governor Finney of Kansas publicly demanded that Bob Stephan resign his office. Finney blasted him for "the disgrace he's brought on that office and the state. If anybody knows about wrongdoing, it's the Attorney General," said Finney. "It's a great abuse of his power," she added. In August 1993, the Kansas State Senate Minority Leader, Jerry Karr, called on Stephan to resign, and he was echoed by House Minority Leader Tom Sawyer.

Stephan was also lambasted for failing to properly investigate a scandal over missing state public employee pensions, involving the Kansas Bureau of Investigation (KBI), which he controlled.

Stephan announced his retirement in 1994, after Bob Dole finally saw him as a liability and urged him to get out when polls showed him plummeting in support. Interestingly, the Republican candidate for attorney general, elected in November 1994 to succeed Stephan, was a woman.

VII

THE GREAT OBSTRUCTIONIST GURU OF WASHINGTON GRIDLOCK

Gridlock is good. Gridlock was planned by our Founding Fathers in the Constitution.

—Bob Dole

The Duty of an opposition is very simple—to oppose everything and propose nothing.

—Edward Stanley, 15th Earl of Derby

29

THE DARK PRINCE OF
WASHINGTON GRIDLOCK

By the time Bill Clinton began his term as president in 1993, Senator Dole was already running for the 1996 Republican presidential nomination, a race which for once in his life he has begun as the front-runner. Vastly outgunning his likely primary Republican opponents in terms of name recognition, national respect, and the all-important "mother's milk of politics," money, Dole's every move has been made with an eye toward embarrassing Clinton and making himself look good for 1996.

"Gridlock is good," he told the media. "Gridlock was planned by our Founding Fathers in the Constitution." So what if the American people had just elected a new president who had expressly promised to "end gridlock in Washington"?

Unlike previous Senate Minority Leaders who had played a low-key role in opposing a new president of the opposing party, Dole set a precedent with a unique form of obstructionism. His tool was the filibuster, a parliamentary device unique to the U.S. Senate, which enables any senator to talk any bill to death unless at least sixty Senators vote for cloture to shut off debate.

Surveying the 103rd Congress, Dole counted forty-two Republican senators and fifty-eight Democrats.* He thus

*By mid-1994, the Republicans increased their Senate presence

realized that if he could keep his troops together, he
could always filibuster successfully because the Democrats had fewer than sixty senators, and thus would need
at least two Republicans to obtain cloture. The record for
a Senate filibuster was set in 1957 by Dole's colleague,
Senator Strom Thurmond, who spoke for twenty-four
hours. The filibuster is an anti-majoritarian device that
can, in effect, bring legislation to a standstill if used to the
hilt by minority leaders like Dole. Many constitutional
lawyers have condemned the filibuster, which creates
"Tyranny by a minority," and have urged its abolition.
As used by Dole, the filibuster amounts to a de facto
constitutional amendment requiring sixty votes to pass
any bill in the Senate. Dole has made history by his
routine use of the filibuster.

On election night, November 3, 1992, Dole was interviewed on television and mentioned Ross Perot's 19
percent of the vote. "You add that to the Bush voters, it
is a pretty clear majority of 57 percent," said Dole. "And
it seems to me that they [the voters] didn't want Clinton
to be president, so he doesn't have any mandate." At
a post-election news conference, Dole proclaimed that
"Senate Republicans will represent the 57 percent anti-
Clinton majority in the country. I intend to represent that
majority on the floor of the Senate. If Clinton has a
mandate, then so do I."

On the "Larry King Live" television program the
night after the election, three of the program's twelve
callers complained about Dole's critical and arrogant
post-election comments: "Very negative and divisive . . .
Sour grapes . . . Bitterness." Larry King asked Dole,
"Do you think you were a little harsh last night?" Dole
responded, "I think they are probably Clinton supporters, but, I don't think so."

A week after his defeat in the November 1992 election,
George Bush, sixty-eight years old, symbolically handed

---

to forty-five, and the Democrats went down to fifty-five, thanks
to special elections in several states, heavily influenced by Dole.

over the mantle of Republican leadership to Dole, sixty-nine, prompting some members of the audience to quip about "the passing of the torch to the same generation." (President-elect Clinton, then forty-six, and Vice-President-elect Gore, then forty-four, are young enough to be Dole's sons.)

This advanced Dole one step closer to his dream of the presidency. For the first time in his life, there was no major Republican national figure above him in the hierarchy of elected officeholders. He had free rein.

Privately, Dole mocked Clinton as a "Fraternity Boy" who "gets his hair dyed gray so he can look older." Just as soon as Clinton began his administration in January 1993, Dole emerged as a battering ram for the "disloyal opposition." He opposed Clinton on almost all proposals, claiming they would "increase the deficit and lead to higher taxes." He opposed Clinton's budget and tax hike bills, the idea of a national youth corps, the crime bill, and other far-reaching proposals.

Yet it was Dole himself who supported Republican President George Bush's increase of $137 billion in taxes in 1990, in spite of Bush's broken campaign promise of "read my lips, no new taxes."

In addition, in 1982, Dole was the chief architect of TEFRA, the tax act that increased taxes by a record $98 billion. Dole's record of mindlessly supporting Republican presidents' tax increases while mechanically opposing any Democratic presidents' tax increases must be seen for what it is: a double standard and a shrill intolerance for the opposition.

Dole aggressively used the filibuster as a strategy to defeat virtually all of Clinton's major proposals in the Senate, including campaign finance reform, health-care reform, the economic job stimulus package, gun control, and numerous other bills. Senate majority leader George Mitchell (D-ME) was not pleased, noting that "The Republican leader has come up to use the filibuster as never before, and this is now a regular party tactic in the Senate." Mitchell pointed out that for more than fifty years, the number of filibusters had averaged fewer than one per year, but beginning in the first session of Congress in 1993, Dole led forty-eight filibusters against Clinton's proposals. Dole responded by saying, "We are not a monarchy. We have a president, not a king."

Early in the new presidency, Dole lashed out at Clinton's call for admitting gays into the U.S. military, immediately threatening a filibuster and other obstructionist tactics. Congressman Barney Frank, one of only two openly gay members of the Congress, attacked Dole as being anti-gay. "Dole is the Dana Carvey of gay bashers," said Frank. "He does the best imitation of one." Dole claimed that the gay ban was really a "question of behavior and morale, not of status," which is exactly the same argument that was used to segregate blacks in the military until 1948. Up until that time, bigots claimed that blacks could not behave like whites and whites would fight with blacks if the two were forced together in the military. President Truman, bucking popular prejudice, issued an executive order that ended the ban against blacks in the military, but Clinton, by contrast, backed down and yielded to Dole and the military brass, most of whom shared Dole's fear and hatred of gays.

But Dole scored points with the public and military brass. When Clinton backed down on the gay issue, Dole was encouraged to try for more, convinced that Clinton was spineless.

A week into his new administration, Clinton broke his campaign promise to cut taxes for the middle class, and instead proposed raising taxes to cut the deficit. Dole seized on this and pilloried Clinton as "another tax-and-spend liberal."

When Clinton fired his White House travel staff and replaced it with Arkansas cronies and his cousin in early 1993, Dole was in front of the television cameras denouncing the move as "Travelgate" and calling for a congressional investigation, claiming that Clinton had used both the FBI and IRS in the process. "The most terrifying letters in the English language," said Dole, "are IRS and

FBI." Again Clinton backed down. Former Senator Alan Cranston of California, who had served twenty-four years in the Senate with Dole, described him as the "Republican Prince of Legislative Darkness, the Senator Gridlock of Parliamentary maneuvering, able to take a proposal by the new president and—despite Democratic majorities in the Senate and House—drop it into the black hole of procedural defeat."

Cranston, who found Dole "fascinating" to work with, said that "Dole's partisanship is extreme. His mood can shift suddenly." Cranston explained that Dole possesses "extraordinary complexity" and that "he is gifted with incredibly sensitive political antennae. But he also has both a dark side and a light side, and those who do business with him don't know which Dole they are dealing with. They've got what Ross Perot might call a 'world-class problem.'"

In an interview, Cranston said that Dole is very unpredictable and that it is impossible to predict whether he will appear on a particular day as the "Good Bob" or the "Bad Bob." "Dole's acerbic wit never leaves him," said Cranston, "but the stilettolike effect of his words is often camouflaged by the broad smile and outward appearance of geniality he projects." Cranston called Dole a "Nightmare on Capitol Hill" and a "Freddie Krueger" figure.

Senator Cranston pointed out that "In early 1981, Dole gave a speech in the Senate and urged all of us to 'give this new president a chance' by supporting Reagan's new supply-side economics programs, including massive tax cuts and social spending cuts." Cranston, a liberal Democrat, went along to his subsequent regret, because "I felt that Reagan deserved a chance since he had just won a large mandate from the country." Dole, by contrast, took the opposite position vis-à-vis Clinton. He "pursues gridlock deliberately as a strategy," said Cranston.

"The Senate used to be a much more congenial place in 1969," noted Cranston. "Filibusters were used rarely then and only on great national issues." By contrast, Dole in 1993 turned the filibuster into a frequently used partisan weapon aimed at obstructing for the sake of obstruction per se. He had a filibuster ready to meet nearly every bill proposed by Clinton.

The only check on Dole's obstructionism seems to have been the negative public and press reaction. In the summer of 1993, a lawyer from California, Douglas Page, filed a lawsuit against Dole and the other Senate obstructionists in which he accused them of violating the Constitution by denying "equal protection" to citizens in the country. "If one senator can obstruct the whole country's legislative proposals," noted Page, "then there is no equal protection of the laws."* This was the first such lawsuit ever filed by a private taxpayer, Page told me.

More significantly, numerous media bigwigs and political cartoonists began blasting and ridiculing Dole for his obstructionism. One of the most significant political cartoons was produced by cartoonist Pat Oliphant in April 1993, shortly after the Waco, Texas, conflagration of David Koresh and his Branch Davidians. Depicting Dole as a sinister, Koreshlike "cult leader of the Branch Bobbians," Oliphant showed Dole surrounded by bug-eyed Republican senators, reading to his sect from "The Seven Seals of Bobbism." The cartoon is entitled, "Armageddon, His Way."

As 1993 drew to a close, Dole started to tone down his strident obstructionism in the Senate and even had a much publicly ballyhooed dinner with Clinton in a Washington, D.C., restaurant. But his words still dripped with venom, and his obstructionism reignited with fury in 1994.

Meanwhile, CBS broadcast an unusually flattering portrait of Dole on "60 Minutes" on October 24, 1993. Cameras followed him around the country, and to his

---

*Page's lawsuit, filed in the U.S. District Court for the District of Columbia, finally came to a hearing in June 1994 and was dismissed on the technical grounds of legislative immunity and privilege. The court said that under the Constitution senators cannot be sued for anything they do in the Senate.

hometown in Russell, Kansas, where they interviewed him on the porch of his boyhood home on Maple Street. A particularly moving part of the broadcast showed Dole recounting how his father, Doran Dole, would take the train to visit him in the hospital where Bob was recovering from his grievous war injury in 1945. "His ankles were all swollen when he finally got to the hospital, from standing in the crowded train," said Dole, breaking down into tears.

Because he was entertaining and unique, Dole became a media darling. The media loved this paradoxical, "sensitive man" of the '90s who also had steel in his bones. In 1993, Dole appeared on thirty-one weekend television talk shows, including "This Week with David Brinkley," "Meet the Press," and "Face the Nation." He was featured on CNN's "Newsmaker—Late Edition" nine times, appeared on nineteen morning talk shows, and was on the "Larry King Live" show six times, much more frequently than in 1992. In 1994, he appeared on television even more often. In February 1995, Dole chose David Letterman's *Late Night* show to announce "unofficially" that he would run for president in 1996—two months before his official announcement in Topeka on April 10.

Dole compared himself to a company CEO: "If you are the head of the company, you have got to go out and keep the company going. The company in this case happens to be the party and the party's governors, congressmen, senators."

Now that he was the nation's top Republican, his Campaign America PAC swooped up much of the Republican campaign money that had been going to Bush and Reagan. Dole used it to finance favorite candidates in special elections across the country. One such candidate was Kay Bailey Hutchison, who won a special election to the Senate in Texas in May 1993. Hutchison was later indicted for using her state staff to perform illegal campaigning, but before the trial was completed the charges were dropped. Dole stood by her and added her to his gallery of loyal acolytes who have been accused of improper conduct.*

Dole also sought to consolidate his power among Senate Republicans by trying to neutralize two pesky rivals, Senators Phil Gramm and Trent Lott. Gramm had been using his position as head of the influential National Republican Senatorial Committee to further his own presidential ambitions, and Dole put up Kentucky Senator Mitch McConnell to run against him. Gramm won, but by only one vote. Dole also tried to discourage his Republican colleagues from electing Senator Lott to the position of Secretary of the Senate Republican Conference. Again, Dole lost, but in a close race.

During a typical whirlwind fund-raising tour during the week of December 3, 1993, Dole went to Michigan, Missouri, five cities in South Dakota, Montana, six cities in California, two cities in Arizona, and two in Texas, flying mainly on corporate jets. In 1993, Dole most frequently visited New York and Virginia (eight times each), New Hampshire (three times), Florida and Texas (six times), and Missouri (five times). His goal was to get a Republican majority in the Senate in the 1994 elections, thus providing him a tremendous springboard for the presidency in 1996. He succeeded, for the November 1994 election produced a 53–47 GOP Senate Majority.

A Dole fund-raiser easily generated more than $100,000 in one night, big crowds, plenty of contacts, and heavy local press coverage virtually everywhere in the country ("except in Hope, Arkansas," joked Dole). Doing across the country what he had done in Kansas, for so well and so long, Dole established a major network of loyal politicians and cash cows. He also mailed out millions of letters to Republicans, soliciting donations to the Republican National Committee, identifying himself as "Republican Leader."

---

*Hutchison was Texas State Treasurer in 1993, and was indicted for using her state-paid office staff to campaign for the Senate. The District Attorney of Travis County dropped criminal charges against her in February 1994.

Back in Washington, Dole excoriated Clinton for "tax-and-spend liberal policies" and called for congressional investigations into Clinton for the latter's role in the Whitewater scandal.

A bizarre episode occurred in late 1993, when President Clinton nominated Bobby Inman, a former CIA director and career navy man, to be Defense Secretary. Dole criticized Inman for failure to pay Social Security taxes for a housekeeper, a history of business problems, and plans for cutting the Defense budget. Then Dole found himself being accused of being part of a "conspiracy with [*New York Times* columnist] William Safire" to destroy Inman's character and nomination. Inman, who withdrew his name from consideration, claimed that Dole had cut a deal with columnist William Safire to "turn up the heat" on his nomination in exchange for Safire's attacking Clinton for the Whitewater land development scandal in scathing op-ed hit pieces. "I have been around a while, but I cannot figure out this man's behavior," Dole said in response. Inman withdrew his nomination soon thereafter.

In the spring of 1993, when Dole blasted the Clinton administration for using "devious accounting methods" to "cook the numbers" when making its projections on the deficit reduction plan, the *Washington Post* printed a nasty editorial showing Dole also had "cooked the numbers" in 1990, while promoting Bush's deficit reduction plan that raised taxes by a record $137 billion. "Mr. Dole knows better," said the editorial.

The Republican policies of corporate tax giveaway and corporate welfare have all but bankrupted the country, yet Dole blames "liberal Democrats" for his own party's actions.

But no one seems to notice the inconsistency in Dole's position, least of all his own party.

Dole has displayed considerable skill in uniting his disparate Republican troops to oppose Clinton proposals. Larry Sabato, professor of political science at the University of Virginia, said, "He's got one of the most impressive high-wire acts in American politics today." Noting that Dole wears "seven faces" and plays many roles, Sabato was amazed Dole has not "bobbled" the ball.

One of the few areas where Dole agreed with Clinton was NAFTA, the "free trade" agreement that would eliminate tariffs among the United States, Mexico, and Canada. Supported by Dole's core constituents, NAFTA was bitterly opposed by labor unions and consumer and environmental groups that formed the base of the Democratic Party. Sensing that Clinton was a "wannabe Republican" desperate to get anything passed, Dole shrewdly sided with the president. NAFTA passed Congress in November 1993.

Throughout 1993, 1994, and 1995, Bob Dole made repeated trips to Iowa and New Hampshire, the sites of the first two caucus and primary states in 1996. "I am still the President of Iowa," he reminded people, referring to his upset win over Bush in the Iowa February 1988 primary campaign. But in Washington, he rules as the Prince of Gridlock with the exception of co-opting Clinton on NAFTA and GATT. His strategy of obstructionism worked brilliantly in discrediting Clinton and the Democrats. On November 8, 1994, Republicans gained eight seats in the Senate and fifty-two in the House, to take over both houses of Congress for the first time in forty years. The Democratic defeat was so devastating that thirty-seven Democratic incumbents lost their seats, including House Speaker Tom Foley, the first sitting Speaker to be defeated for reelection since 1860. No Republican incumbents lost their seats in 1994. On the day after the election, Senator Richard Shelby of Alabama switched from Democrat to Republican, giving Dole a 53–47 Senate GOP majority.

In November 1994, Bob Dole became Senate majority leader for the second time in his career.

30

THE BULWARK AGAINST
HEALTH-CARE REFORM

By skillfully portraying the 1,100-page Clinton Health Care Reform Bill as "another tax-and-spend liberal nightmare," by insisting that "there is no health-care crisis in America," and by threatening more filibusters, Senator Dole has torpedoed Clinton's plan to provide universal health-care coverage, the flagship of Clinton's armada of legislation.

As many as 20 percent of the American public do not have health insurance and cannot afford it, and the vast majority of Americans in 1993 supported the concept of universal health care. The question was, who was going to pay for it?

When Clinton took over the presidency in January 1993, he appointed his ambitious but unpopular wife, Hillary, to head a secret commission that would craft a proposal on health-care reform. Its progress was dogged by delay, mistakes, and inexperience on the part of Clinton and his team. Dole's opposition to health-care reform was unrelenting; it's based on his strong ties to big business and the health insurance industry, which have strongly opposed the Clinton plan. Dole has nonetheless presented Republican proposals that purport to bring about limited health-care reform more cheaply than Clinton's, while in fact they essentially preserve the system's status quo. In September 1993, Dole and a group of other Republican senators unveiled their own plan, which was supposed to be an alternative to earlier proposals and to the forthcoming Clinton plan.

Dole upstaged Clinton and revealed the details of his health-care plan about two weeks before Clinton proposed his. While under the Clinton plan all employers would have to contribute to health insurance for their workers, Dole's proposal placed the burden on individuals, who would be required to obtain health coverage, much like states that require car owners to buy auto insurance. Both proposals would define a uniform benefits package that would be guaranteed to every legal resident and U.S. citizen. For those individuals who could not afford to buy a health policy, Dole's plan would provide government "vouchers" to people with incomes as much as 240 percent above the poverty level.

Both plans were similar in setting up regional insurance buying pools in each state, banding business and consumers together to spread the risk over the largest number of people. Whereas the Clinton plan would require all but the largest employers to join one of the pools ("health alliances"), Dole's proposal makes enrollment in such pools voluntary. The buying pools differ in another major way. Whereas Clinton's plan would establish only one alliance per region, Dole's plan would allow competing pools called "purchasing cooperatives" to be set up in an area. The insurance industry, which supports Dole, has protested Clinton's idea of single, mandatory purchasing pools.

On October 30, 1993, Dole appeared in Garden City, Kansas, to participate in a forum on health-care reform attended by farmers, doctors, and hospital administrators. Talking to a group of about 450 Kansans in a high school auditorium he indicated a willingness to "compromise" on the Clinton plan and said, "Give us time in Congress to do it right." Dole claimed that the Clinton plan would cause job losses, higher taxes, and more federal bureaucracy. Republican Congressman Pat Roberts, an ally of Dole's, got many cheers by saying, "I don't believe the American dream is for everyone to be leveled with everyone else."

In Washington, Dole met conspicuously with Hillary Clinton and said he was willing to work with her on health-care reform, while at the same time undercutting the Clinton proposal. Dole's top Senate aide, Sheila Burke, took a "no quarter" attitude in negotiating with Clinton.

Dole told audiences that he had "genuine concerns" about Clinton's proposal, especially the one that required employers to provide health insurance for their workers. So-called employer mandates requiring employers to buy insurance for their workers would "damage the economy and hurt those who need help the most—new hires, small businesses, and low income workers," said Dole. He vowed to mount his "filibuster" horse again and drive the Clinton plan off the map.

By mid-1994, it was clear that the Clinton health-care proposal was going nowhere on Capitol Hill. In June, even Senator Daniel Patrick Moynihan, chairman of the Senate Finance Committee, which has jurisdiction over the health-care issue, said that Clinton's plan would not pass that year. Dole and his allies, the insurance companies, ran television ads that scared the American people into believing that Clinton's plan would raise their taxes, deprive them of their choice of doctors, and produce substandard health care. Dole capitalized on the inscrutable, complicated nature of Clinton's plan, a turgid 1,100-page treatise that nobody seemed to understand or appreciate.

By June 1994, there were more than seventy-five separate health-care reform bills pending in Congress, and on June 29, Dole came up with yet another, which he got thirty-eight other Republican Senators to cosponsor. At a news conference, Dole unveiled his plan, which provided for token insurance reforms, "voluntary" insurance pools, subsidies for poor folks to buy insurance, and some limits on denying coverage for preexisting illnesses and injuries. But it did *not* provide for universal coverage nor mandates forcing employers to buy coverage for their employees. By late September 1994, the Clinton plan was officially pronounced dead, and no health reform bill of any kind passed Congress—a failure that helped defeat the Democrats in the November election.

Interestingly, while Dole denigrates the need for universal health coverage, he and his wife are enrolled in precisely that type of "universal" health insurance plan through the U.S. Senate. Dole and his wife are members of the Federal Employees Health Benefits Program, through Blue Cross and Blue Shield, in which he pays a measly $101 monthly premium, with an annual deductible of only $200. His insurance policy covers all preexisting conditions, and pays for all hospital stays and injuries and 75 to 95 percent of all surgical and testing costs. In addition, he is eligible for treatment at a military hospital. Thus, Dole himself enjoys what he denies to the American people.

In the end, Clinton's Health Plan was killed not because Dole had a better plan of his own, but because Dole succeeded in convincing his colleagues and the public that the Clinton plan was too costly, too bureaucratic, and too complicated. "It's like having the post office deliver your health insurance," he noted scornfully.

31

THE RAMPART AGAINST
CAMPAIGN FINANCE REFORM

Senator Dole has put a stranglehold on any meaningful campaign finance reform bills, even *after* both houses of Congress passed their own versions of such bills in 1993. He frequently utters public comments that make him appear to be a "champion of reform," and then belies his own position by leading the opposition to any Senate effort whatsoever to bring about reform. His statements in public are fully in tune with the fact that most Americans feel that the political campaign system is institutionally corrupt and needs a thorough housecleaning, and yet Dole knows that his own position and career are totally dependent upon this very institution.

A famous political cartoon by *Washington Post* cartoonist Herblock in 1987 shows Dole as a rifleman holding a submachine gun behind a barrage of money bags and dollar signs, holding up a sign proclaiming: "They shall not pass." In front of him is the bullet-ridden body of a man holding a poster reading "Campaign Spending Reforms," by the threshold of a door marked "U.S. Senate."

The Washington Post has called the congressional campaign finance system "fundamentally corrupt" and claimed that "so does every citizen and so does every legislator." But not Bob Dole.

In 1985, Dole said, "The system cries for reform. I think it is incumbent upon all of us to try to achieve that." But on August 12, 1986, Dole was one of only thirty senators who opposed the Boren-Goldwater Senate bill to limit PAC contributions to Congressional and Senate candidates. In the Senate on January 6, 1987, in a debate regarding reform bill S.2, Dole said "I do not believe there will be any effort to stop any such legislation." But then he led an obstructionist filibuster, and voted seven times to stall and kill S.2. In a letter dated May 14, 1987, Dole said that he was "opposed to the public financing provisions of S.2, which would result in the American taxpayer subsidizing the Senate election contests and deny him the opportunity to support candidates of own personal choosing." But as of November 9, 1987, Dole himself had requested $2.3 million in public matching funds for his 1988 presidential campaign and accepted far more than that, which is surely "subsidized by the American taxpayer."

On September 15, 1987, S.2 was pulled off the Senate agenda because there were not enough votes to support cloture. As a result, after seven cloture votes failed, the filibuster succeeded and the bill was killed.

Dole has argued that any such campaign finance reform bills would necessarily freeze out challengers to incumbents by limiting the amount of money required for strong campaigns against entrenched, long-term incumbents. But in fact, the status quo system of unlimited PAC money and spending inherently *favors* entrenched incumbents like Dole himself. According to a 1987 study in *The New York Times*, Dole received more PAC money over the previous fifteen years than any other member of the Senate, an astounding $3.3 million.

Several genuine campaign finance reform bills actually were passed by the Senate in 1990, 1991 and 1992. These would have established spending limits and provided public campaign resources for Congressional and Senate races. In addition, they would have limited the influence of special interest PAC money and ended "soft money" abuses. (Soft money—untraceable aggregate contributions often raised at the state level and used to support an entire party ticket and party-building activities—is outside the purview of the Federal Election Law.)

·However, President Bush vetoed these bills, and Dole supported the vetoes. Common Cause President Fred Wertheimer, condemning Dole's similar tactics in 1993, said that, "If Dole's obstructionist tactics are successful, real campaign finance reform will be killed and the corrupt system in Washington will continue to thrive. If Dole is successful, he will preserve the extraordinary undue influence that special interest money has in Congress, the enormous campaign finance advantages that incumbents have over their challengers, and the tens of millions of dollars in corrupting soft money contributions that national political parties have been raising." As Wertheimer puts it, "The current campaign finance system is the ultimate incumbents' protection system. It is Senate Republican incumbents who benefit." They can always raise more than the challengers.

Since the presidential public financing system began in 1976, every Republican presidential candidate (except John Connally) has requested and received public matching funds, including Presidents Ford, Reagan, and Bush. Republican presidential candidates have requested and received a total of more than $278 million in public financing. Former Republican Senator Paul Laxalt of Nevada, who chaired Reagan's presidential campaigns in 1976, 1980, and 1984, has publicly stated that "There is far too much emphasis on money and far too much time spent collecting it. It is the most corrupting thing I have seen on the congressional scene. The problem is so bad we ought to start thinking about federal financing of congressional campaigns."

On "Meet the Press" on April 8, 1993, even Bob Dole told a national television audience, "You know, I have told my Republican friends in the House that if they were smart, they would accept the public financing provision and sunset it after four years. That would give us enough time to take over the House of Representatives."* Then he filibustered against S.3.

President Clinton's Reform Bill of 1993, S.3, would have established spending limits for each Senate race depending on the state's size and would also have provided for public financing of campaigns. It would also have eliminated the tax deduction for lobbying expenses, a tax break now enjoyed by corporate and other lobbyists. Instead of subsidizing lobbying, public funds would have been used to help clean up the political system. Public campaign resources freed in S.3 would then have been available for direct public communication with voters, such as to buy broadcast time and newspaper ads and postage.

To wage a successful filibuster in 1993, Dole pressured Republican senators who previously had voted for campaign finance reform to abandon their previous position and to join him in another filibuster. Three senators, David Durenburger of Minnesota, James Jeffords of Vermont, and John McCain of Arizona, all Republicans, had voted for campaign finance reform legislation in 1990, 1991, and 1992, and each of them had voted to override Bush's veto of these bills. Other Republican senators who have supported such campaign finance bills were Senators John Chaffee of Rhode Island, William Cohen of Maine, and Larry Pressler of South Dakota. Dole pressured all of them to kill "Clinton's bill" in 1993, and to filibuster a Conference Committee Compromise in 1994.

If the spending limits embodied in bill S.3 had been in effect for the 1992 elections, the Republican and Democratic incumbents seeking election would have had their campaign spending cut by $44.9 million (down from $117 million to $72.1 million). Republican and Democratic challengers, by contrast, would have had their spending

---

*"Sunsetting" means that the bill would automatically expire by its own terms after four years. The Republicans did take over the House and Senate in 1994, sans any public financing system.

cut by only $843,000 overall, and would have received nearly $12 million in additional campaign matching funds from public financing, thus "leveling the playing field," and making the elections a more fair game than the "David vs. Goliath" races that now characterize U.S. elections.

In 1992, Republican Senate incumbents outraised their Democratic challengers by more than two to one. The twelve Republican incumbents raised an average of $5,553,000 while their twelve Democratic challengers raised only $2,553,000 under the present system. Similarly, the sixteen Democratic incumbents raised $3,487,000 while their fifteen Republican challengers raised only $1,158,000.

Interestingly enough, in 1993 Dole offered his own bill, S.7, which is supposed to be an alternative to S.3 for campaign finance reform. But the Dole bill does not establish any campaign spending limits, does not provide any public resources for campaigns, and does not close down the soft money loophole.

S.7 would do virtually nothing to shut down soft money abuse. Soft money is a gigantic loophole that enables many different individuals of an entity in a particular state to pool together their untraceable money and contribute as one on party candidate slates, thus clearly circumventing contribution limits in the current law. Under the soft money loophole to the current system, both political parties have raised huge amounts of otherwise illegal political contributions from corporations, unions, and wealthy individuals.

During the 1991–92 election cycle, according to FEC records, the Republican national party committees raised $46.9 million in soft money, including $4.7 million raised by the National Republican Senatorial Committee. The Democratic National Committee has raised $35.3 million in soft money, including $153,000 raised by the Democratic Senatorial Campaign Committee's building fund. Dole's bill, S.7, would perpetuate this abuse by renaming it as an "allocation system."

Interestingly, S.7 bans PAC contributions. But this appears to be a hoax because Dole must know the courts are likely to declare such a provision unconstitutional, for such a ban would probably violate the First Amendment's right to freedom of speech.

In late September 1994, Dole dealt a death blow to the Campaign Reform Bill, preventing it from coming to a full Senate vote from a conference committee, by means of the filibuster. The bill was dead, even though it had passed both houses of Congress eighteen months earlier, thanks to Dole's ruthlessness and Clinton's ineptitude and inability to confront Dole.

The facts also show that Senator Dole broke the campaign laws and accepted public taxpayer money on his 1988 presidential campaign and also has used taxpayer money to pay for mass mailings under the "franking" privilege of his Senate office, which is a system of public financing for incumbents only. In addition, the Republican Party requested and received more than $32 million of the taxpayers' money in public financing to pay for its presidential nominating conventions in 1988 and 1992.

As the most powerful, entrenched Senate incumbent in modern history, Dole has much to thank the current system for. But to really appreciate the full extent of why he opposes campaign finance reform, we must examine his record as a major recipient and distributor of PAC money, as well as a violator of existing campaign laws. Dole is basically a major broker for special interests. Like Pac-Man of video game fame, he gobbles up PAC money, transforms legislation into made-to-order laws benefiting campaign contributors, and winds up with a big smile on his face.

For those who say that campaign contributions to a politician amount to a de facto gift, Dole replies that such money cannot be converted to "personal use."

But the loopholes in the law are so broad that an elephant could easily jump through them.

EPILOGUE

FROM THE GARDEN OF EDEN TO THE ROSE GARDEN: DOLE AS PRESIDENT

The Child is Father to the Man

—William Wordsworth

Ad Astra per Aspera (To the Stars Through Difficulties)

—Kansas State Motto

B ob Dole has come a long way from Russell, Kansas, giving new meaning to the state motto, *Ad Astra per Aspera*. Unless he again self-destructs, he may finally wind up at 1600 Pennsylvania Avenue in 1997.

Dole, who was born in 1923, originally wanted to be a doctor. Tall, dark, handsome, energetic, and an impeccable dresser, he appears robust and healthy. He has a low cholesterol level and seems fit and tanned. But his troubled medical history makes Dole the most seriously handicapped national political figure since Franklin D. Roosevelt, who was so severely crippled by polio that he was unable to walk on his own during his presidency.

In 1976, Bob Dole would not reveal his medical records. In 1988, he went ballistic when *The New York Times* demanded copies of all his medical records when he campaigned for president. And lately he has been very sensitive about having prostate cancer in 1991.

Dole's most obvious handicap is his right arm, which is partly disabled, and his right hand, which is unable to grasp anything heavier than a light pencil, booklet, or coat, and that cannot even be raised to shake hands, clap or drive a car. Dole also occasionally suffers numbness in his fingers.

Dole has only one kidney, having lost his other to a war-related infection in 1945. This one remaining kidney occasionally flares up, as it did in 1981, when he required surgery. "One kidney is better than no heart," Dole often jokes, but the status of his heart is another issue in dispute. During the 1980 presidential campaign some of his medical charts were released to a reporter and turned over to a "neutral" doctor, who concluded that Dole had suffered a "silent heart attack" years earlier. Dole disputed this assertion, which appeared in the February 18, 1980, issue of *Medical World News*.

But the most serious threat to Dole's health came in December 1991, when at the age of sixty-eight, he was diagnosed as suffering from prostate cancer. The senator underwent three hours of cancer surgery at Walter Reed Army Medical Center on December 18, 1991. Since that time, he has insisted he has been "cured" of the cancer. He has become a personal crusader urging men to have tests for prostate cancer. During the Republican National Convention in 1992, Dole sounded like a carnival barker as he shouted to men passing a booth in an exhibition hall adjacent to the Houston Astrodome, "Better get your tests. It's a lifesaver. When you get to be forty, stop here. It might save your life."

In the booth, a giant picture of a smiling Dole dominated a display advertising the booth's purpose, which was to persuade men to take the so-called PSA or Prostate Specific Antigen blood test, an early blood test for prostate cancer. The booth was sponsored by the *Saturday Evening Post*, and its poster boy was Dole. Dole pointed out that "We spend $2.1 billion on AIDS research and $27 million on prostate cancer research, and about the same number of men die each year in the country from both diseases, about 35,000 each.''

In October 1992, Dole sponsored a health fair at the University of Kansas Medical Center and enlisted former Kansas City Chiefs quarterback Lenny Dawson, another victim of prostate cancer, to help promote it. Dole beamed as he encountered men who told him, "You saved my life." "We have got to spread the word that it is nothing to fear if you catch it in time," Bob insisted.

However, while Dole has not suffered any relapse, the statistics about this disease are far less optimistic than he might hope. Prostate cancer strikes 110,000 American men every year, and is the second leading cause of death in men, killing 35,000 per year. According to one standard work in the field, *Cancer: Principles and Practices of Oncology* by Samuel Hellman and Steven Rosenberg, more than half of its sufferers die within ten years of being diagnosed and more than two-thirds suffer local or systemic progression of the disease, despite therapy. Hellman and Rosenberg also cite a study published in the *International Journal of Radiation Oncology* in 1991 showing that the five-year recurrence rate ranges from between 10 percent and 41 percent.

While Senator Dole is certainly to be commended for his high-profile role in promoting the PSA test as an early warning for prostate cancer, it seems that he is being overly optimistic in advising men that prostate cancer is a fairly mild disease that can be totally cured easily if detected early. Cancer of any kind is deceptive, tends to recur years after a patient has supposedly been "cured," and may spread quickly and suddenly.

Dole would be seventy-three if elected President in 1996. Whether he would be limited as president by having only one good arm and a history of kidney disease and cancer is anyone's guess.

What would Dole be like as president? Given Bob Dole's well-documented fanatical support for Nixon and their psychological similarities (see chapter 3), it is possible that President Dole would resemble President Nixon.

But Dole is much more complicated than Nixon, has a great sense of humor, and seems to possess more sensitive political antennae than Nixon. More troubling is the self-destructive streak Dole has displayed in all three of his campaigns for national office. As a president he may sabotage himself by pursuing unpopular, losing policies, as Nixon did.

Comparing a prospective president to past officeholders is a useful exercise, provided the task is approached systematically and according to certain well-established criteria. Professor James David Barber of Duke University, in his book *The Presidential Character,* has identified three key factors affecting a man's performance as president: his character, his worldview, and his leadership style. The most important is character, particularly in a crisis. "Does he give off negative vibes, or does he try to solve the problem?" asks Barber.

"The best way to measure a candidate's character," Barber told the author, "is by looking at the signals he gives off in private—how he talks and acts around the people closest to him, like his staff, in unguarded moments—when the press isn't watching."

Barber has put each president into one of four character categories: active positive (for example, John Kennedy, Franklin D. Roosevelt, George Bush, Harry Truman), active negative (Lyndon Johnson, Richard Nixon, Woodrow Wilson, Herbert Hoover), passive positive (Ronald Reagan, William Howard Taft, and Warren Harding), and passive negative (Dwight Eisenhower and Calvin Coolidge). This four-pronged topology is based on an assessment of each president's predominant personality traits from childhood.

According to Barber's theory, active presidents are those who expend a great deal of energy in their work, while passive presidents tend to be laid-back or lazy.

"I don't think there's any doubt that Dole would be an active President," Barber told the author. "The real question in Dole's case is whether he would be active positive or active negative."

Positive presidents tend to enjoy their work, reveling in the battles of politics, joking about the criticism they receive, and generally giving off very positive cues and nuances in their unguarded moments with staff. Franklin D. Roosevelt, for example, reacted to media criticism by "sitting on the White House lawn and joking about it with reporters." By contrast, says Barber, Richard Nixon "was always expressing bitterness or anger or unhappiness with his work and with media criticism." Into which category should Dole be placed? "I find it very interesting that Dole took a course in Speech Dynamics [from Dorothy Sarnoff, following his 1976 election defeat] and that he married an outgoing, positive woman [Elizabeth] as a sort of compensatory exchange," Barber told the author. By engaging in such compensatory activities, Barber feels, Dole is implicitly acknowledging a lack of these qualities in himself. In other words, he is really an "active-negative" personality. Various traits—Dole's pessimism, cynicism, strident partisan attacks, hair-trigger temper, belligerence, and workaholism—support this conclusion.

But Dole's dual personality, a Dr. Jekyll-Mr. Hyde persona, complicates matters. This duality has manifested itself not only in Dole's personal relations, where he varies from humorous barb to vicious gunslinger, but also in his political opportunism. This makes Dole something of a hybrid between "active negative" and "active positive" in Barber's scheme. The problem for a President Dole is that the public would never know which Bob was running the country from day to day. Perhaps Bob wouldn't know either. "If a president has no beliefs, that is bad," says Barber, "because the country can't predict what he will do."

In the course of my research, I encountered a striking dichotomy of responses from those who have come in contact with Senator Dole. Many respect and like him, but there are those who literally hate his guts. Similarly, many people regard him as highly intelligent, while others consider him a dolt. Many find him ethical and honorable, while some view him as a dangerous demagogue.

Joseph Rauh, the dean of the Washington civil rights lobbyists, referred to Dole as "almost Jekyll-Hyde," and right-wing guru Paul Weyrich described the change in Dole's voting pattern after 1985 as "overwhelming . . . almost impossible to describe." Though these two men were referring to his behavior in Congress, their comments shed light on Dole's character. (See chapter 4, "Senator Flip-Flop.") What sort of man would be able to elicit such extreme comments from men at opposite ends of the political spectrum?

Dole may, like Nixon, fall victim to flaws that have destroyed other active negative presidents. "These guys tend to compulsive rigidification in support of a losing public policy," Barber said, discussing active negatives in general. "They often cling to a doomed policy long after its futility has been revealed." Examples would include Lyndon Johnson's clinging to his fatally flawed Vietnam War Policy, Nixon's stubborn stonewalling on Watergate, Herbert Hoover's adamant policy against relief programs and his fiscal restraint during the Great Depression, and Woodrow Wilson's equally stubborn intent of forcing the League of Nations on America. "The critical question for a presidential candidate," Barber explained, "is whether he has demonstrated such a pattern of behavior in his career." Dole certainly has. In 1980, for example, he clung to his presidential campaign long after its futility was clear to everyone around him, nearly wrecking his Senate career and weakening his power base in Kansas. And in the 1988 presidential primary, he retained ineffective campaign staffers and refused to declare whether he would support tax hikes.

We need to consider what kind of foreign and domestic policy Dole would pursue as president.

On foreign policy, Dole might well pursue a bellicose, aggressive policy because of the reservoir of pent-up anger inside him. This might be a good thing, because, unlike Clinton and other "positive" presidents, Dole would not hesitate to send in the Marines to accomplish his ends, when a calmer president might back down. If President Dole felt *personally* challenged or humiliated by a foreign foe, he might order a military strike, since that is his pattern in personal relations when challenged or frustrated.

On the other hand, because Dole tends to vacillate, he could pursue a very contradictory foreign policy with friend or foe alike, belligerent one day and benign the next. Would they be dealing with Good Bob or Bad Bob?

Dole is not likely to be a solid friend of Israel. Whether he would go so far as to "dump Israel" completely, is another question. He is more likely to clamp down on the Israeli government and to press it to make concessions to the Palestinians, and to return more of the territory Israel annexed in the Six-Day War in June 1967.

On the Eastern European front, Dole is likely to pursue a Nixonian geopolitical policy of opening America's veins to shower Russia and its satellite "democracies" with money and aid. His public comments on the Bosnian civil war have called for U.S. air strikes to pound the Bosnian Serbs and for lifting the arms embargo. Such policies might well lead the United States down the inexorable road toward war in the Balkans.

Dole's former support of Saddam Hussein, the "Butcher of Baghdad," is ample evidence that he is likely to look the other way regarding human rights abuses in China and other totalitarian countries.

Dole has spoken approvingly of Reagan's invasion of Grenada in 1983 and of Bush's invasion of Panama in 1989. He may offer more of the same in Latin America. Yet he opposed Clinton's plans to intervene in Haiti and Somalia in 1994, so one can never be sure.

When planning his military and foreign policy moves around the world, President Dole is likely to pursue a very "secretive" policy, acting very much like a loner and keeping Congress shut out of his plans. Because he is so distrustful of people in general, and so contemptuous of his opponents, he is likely to bypass Congress and act alone in ordering troops to combat, much as Nixon did in Vietnam, Cambodia, and elsewhere.

How about domestic policy? Dole is likely to pursue pro-business, anti-consumer domestic policies as president. Government regulatory rules are likely to loosen up, corporate taxes to decline, and special-interest laws benefiting business to flourish. As president, Dole's main domestic theme is likely to be "deficit reduction," but the deficit would probably skyrocket, as under Reagan and Bush, because he would raid the treasury to benefit his corporate clientele.

Dole is likely to cut back drastically on social welfare policies. If he gets his way, Social Security and Medicare COLA's are likely to be frozen and the number of homeless could increase.

President Dole would probably support a constitutional amendment and/or federal statute to ban all abortions, and he is likely to appoint only conservative, pro-life judges to the federal bench. Getting elected president would require the support of the religious right, symbolized by Oliver North, and he is likely to pursue its conservative social agenda. This would further exacerbate tensions between Dole and American Jews, who fear the Christian Right as a vanguard of anti-Semitism.

Given Dole's professed admiration for Nixon, he might be inclined to adopt Nixon's tactic of ordering the IRS to audit and harass political opponents. With his Campaign America PAC and the Dole financial octopus, President Dole would use hardball tactics to influence elections and Congress. He would try to generate a climate of fear, much like Nixon.

Dole's attempts to control the country are likely to be hampered, however, by his personality. If his previous presidential campaigns are any indication, a Dole Administration would probably be highly disorganized. He is likely to have difficulty in delegating authority and producing a coherent policy in the huge executive branch of the government. He would never trust his own cabinet secretaries, and could try to run every department on his own. A vituperative and punitive leader provokes resistance and dissent, which could lead to a siege mentality in the White House, similar to Nixon's imposed more than twenty years ago.

If Dr. Jekyll surfaces more often than Mr. Hyde, Bob Dole might do very well.

Although Barry Goldwater was quoted in the *Arizona Republic* of October 21, 1993, as saying that Dole "isn't presidential timber," he later told the author that he had been misquoted. He also said Dole would make an outstanding president, and would "compare favorably" with Reagan, Carter, and Bush.

Bob Dole's ruthlessness, lust for power, and intolerance for opposition can also be very useful presidential traits. An Oval Office occupied by political weaklings floundering around benefits few, a tough President Dole would at least be a "hands-on" President with a very personal agenda. Perhaps that is what the country needs. Perhaps that is what it really wants.

And is Senator Dole's tendency to cater to private interests necessarily a bad thing? His realism accurately reflects the fact that the American electoral system is indeed "for sale," because elections are so expensive that virtually all candidates have been reduced to professional fund-raisers. Dole is a master of our "One Dollar, One Vote" system. He truly believes that corporate welfare ultimately benefits the economy by creating jobs. Whether one agrees with him or not, one cannot help but admire the man's chutzpah.

Dole's ceaseless activity, his dogged perseverance, and his obsession with the presidency all derive from his perpetual quest for the love and praise he rarely received as a child and from his struggle to overcome his war injuries that left him asking the existential question, "Why me?" His view of the world as an unfair and dangerous place has made him eternally vigilant. Like Sisyphus in Greek legend, he is a man who must struggle perpetually to roll uphill the huge stone of achievement, yet is destined never to be satisfied. For Dole, each triumph calls forth only greater challenge. As president, he would try to consistently provoke challenges to test himself.

How would a view of life as unfair affect his performance in the White House? Bob Dole would never be satisfied with results under any circumstances. He is not likely to underestimate dangers or to discount the strength of an adversary. A Dole administration would be ceaselessly in motion, for Dole feels uncomfortable "wasting time." Like his father, who never took time off from work, Bob is a human perpetual-motion machine.

Part of Dole's problem is his difficulty communicating and articulating coherent views and policies. He likes to communicate with staffers in short, superficial, impersonal one-page memos that always have "Approve/Disapprove" boxes at the bottom, for his checkmark. He does not like to discuss issues in detail, and relies on instinct rather than reason to make his decisions. Indeed, he has been called "the Aya-Dole-Ah" by his staff.

As Theodore Roosevelt once said, the presidency is largely "a bully pulpit," a rostrum from which the president can speak out to the American people and inspire and uplift them. All successful presidents have been great speakers, able to inspire trust and confidence through the spoken word.

Dole's poor speaking style—his delivery is usually banal and uninspiring, and his voice has a disturbing Kansas twang—is due in part to his lack of interest in anything other than politics. He has no interest in music, literature, movies, or pop culture, making it difficult to relate to the public. Nor does he like to read or write much. Also, as said by Elliot Kaplan, "Dole doesn't believe in America or the American Dream. He just believes in government, when it serves his interests." He is too cynical.

Professor David McClelland of Harvard has studied the inaugural addresses of all of America's presidents and has scored them under criteria related to the Thematic Apperception Test ("TAT"), a psychological test. He has also learned that charismatic presidents, like John Kennedy, convey a sense of "self-confidence" to their audiences, which helps account for their success as orators and presidents. By this standard, a President Dole simply cannot measure up. He can't communicate a sense of self-confidence because he is not a self-confident person.

The real danger of a Dole administration would be the absence of any ideological center.

Like Lyndon Johnson, Dole is the type of politician who, in the words of his old Kansas rival Norbert Dreiling, "always accurately reflects the views of the constituency he happens to represent." If Dole "still doesn't know if he's a liberal or a conservative, as he didn't know in 1950," as John Woelk, the Russell Republican who recruited him to run for his first legislative office in 1950, has said, and if he always waits to see "which way the political wind is blowing," as Kansas Senator Nancy Kassebaum remarked, he could find himself pursuing presidential policies that he does not really believe in, just to win support.

On the one hand, such a president might embody the democratic principle that leaders should reflect the opinions of their constituents. On the other, Dole's zigzagging could get out of hand unless it is checked by a sound set of values, deep-seated beliefs that would give his seemingly rudderless boat a sense of ballast and direction.

Finally, there is the matter of press relations. Ultimately, Presidents Johnson and Nixon failed because they came to see the press as an enemy. No president today can manage the news—much as he might like to—but the ability to handle sharp questions with skill and a touch of humor is an enormous advantage. Though often highly quotable for his acerbic wit, Bob Dole has never enjoyed an easy relationship with reporters and regards the press with hostility and suspicion. A man with an insatiable appetite for publicity, Dole resents the press for ignoring him and is made furious by unfavorable stories about him. He definitely has favored certain reporters and bears a lasting grudge against any journalist he regards as unfriendly. Many of his present and former aides declined to be interviewed for this book or would talk only on condition of anonymity. Dole himself declined to be interviewed.

In the final analysis, Bob Dole is a man who revels in a good fight, who is always thinking of all the angles and who is a very sore loser. Because he always plays to win and always plays for keeps, he has the potential to become one of the truly great presidents. On the other hand, he also has the potential to wrap himself stubbornly around a truly flawed policy and to become a very unpopular president. His ultimate fate would depend on the extent to which he permits his brighter side to prevail over his darker nature. And that, ultimately, would depend on the kinds of challenges and crises he confronts as president.

In a nationally televised eulogy for Richard Nixon on April 27, 1994, Dole described what he regarded as President Nixon's best qualities: "The American People love a fighter," Dole told the nation. "And in Dick Nixon, they found a gallant one," one who woke up each day "to confound his enemies." A President Dole would do the same. The question is: What would he be fighting—and for whom?

INDEX